UNIVERSITY OF NORTH CAROLINA
STUDIES IN THE ROMANCE LANGUAGES AND LITERATURES
Number 108

A CRITICAL EDITION OF THE OLD PROVENÇAL EPIC *DAUREL ET BETON*

A CRITICAL EDITION OF THE OLD PROVENÇAL EPIC

DAUREL ET BETON

WITH NOTES AND PROLEGOMENA

BY

ARTHUR S. KIMMEL

CHAPEL HILL

THE UNIVERSITY OF NORTH CAROLINA PRESS

ACKNOWLEDGEMENTS

I would like to express my thanks to Ronald N. Walpole of the University of California at Berkeley and John L. Grigsby of Washington University for the care and erudition they contributed to every page of this edition, to the late E. B. Ham of the University of Michigan who first introduced me to textual criticism, to my wife, Irene, who typed and edited many successive drafts of manuscript, and to the Bureau for Faculty Research and the Department of Foreign Languages and Literature of Western Washington State College for making possible the publication of *Daurel et Beton*.

Bellingham, Washington
July 14, 1971

PRINTED IN SPAIN

DEPÓSITO LEGAL: V. 4.617 - 1971

ARTES GRÁFICAS SOLER, S. A. - JÁVEA, 28 - VALENCIA (8) - 1971

TABLE OF CONTENTS

INTRODUCTION

The twelfth-century Provençal epic *Daurel et Beton* lay undiscovered until the 1870's, when a manuscript acquired by the publisher Firmin Didot was presented for edition to the Société des Anciens Textes. Paul Meyer undertook the task of editing the manuscript and in 1880 published the first edition of this unusual work, [1] which, along with the Franco-Provençal *Girart de Roussillon* and the fragmentary *Aigar et Maurin*, makes up all we know about the original southern epic. Meyer's edition, which contains much illuminating information on the problems of language and versification, has been of inestimable value in the preparation of the present edition, which is intended to reach a new generation of scholars.

Submerged in the flood of epics being discovered and edited towards the end of the nineteenth century, *Daurel* elicited little interest in the years following its publication. Most critics and literary historians were content to accept Léon Gautier's opinion that the poem was little more than a poor translation or adaptation of a northern epic. [2] In the years following the appearance of Meyer's edition, only two review articles appeared. Camille Chabaneau offered a detailed criticism of the text, challenging many of Meyer's readings and emendations, [3] while Gaston Paris concentrated on the problems posed by

---

[1] Paul Meyer, ed., *Daurel et Beton: Chanson de geste provençale*, SATF Vol. 14 (Paris, 1880).

[2] *Les Epopées françaises*, 2nd ed. (Paris, 1878), I, 133-134. As early as 1876, Gautier had examined the MS and had published a short analysis of the poem, which he called the *Roman de Betonet*, in *Le Monde*, April 4, 1876.

[3] In *Revue des Langues Romanes*, XX (1881), 246-260. In a rebuttal in *Romania*, XI (1882), Meyer defends his glossary against Chabaneau's charge that it was insufficient.

the existence of a Provençal epic tradition and pointed out the originality and uniqueness of *Daurel* from a literary point of view. [4]

Although no major article has been dedicated to the poem since
that time, it is often mentioned in works dealing with the *chanson
de geste,* medieval history and civilization, and in editions of various
poems. Most Provençal linguistic studies, notably Joseph Anglade's
Grammaire de l'ancien provençal [5] and the Emil Levy and Karl Appel
Provenzalisches Supplement-Wörterbuch, [6] cite examples from *Daurel.* [7]

In recent years, however, the whole question of the originality of
the Provençal epic and its role in the evolution of the northern *chanson
de geste* has been re-opened, notably by Rita Lejeune and Ferdinand
Lot. Since *Daurel* is one of the only three original Provençal epics
which have survived, it must be studied with this problem in mind.
Thus we have stressed the typically southern quality of *Daurel* in
our literary study, while not neglecting to point out the very close
relationship existing between this poem and the northern feudal epic.
We have tried to present the evidence, however fragmentary, concerning the genesis of *Daurel,* in the hope that it will cast some light
on the rôle of the Midi in the evolution of the French *chanson
de geste.*

---

[4] *Mélanges de littérature française du moyen âge,* ed. by Mario Roques
(Paris, 1912), pp. 138-150. See also D'Arco Silvio Avalle (*La Letteratura
medievale in lingua d'oc nella sua tradizione manoscritta: Problemi di critica
testuale* [Torino, 1961], pp. 77-78) who, while praising Meyer's linguistic
analysis, points out «ma necessiterebbe forse una nuova edizione per le nu-
merose sviste in cui il Meyer è incorso tanto per quel che riguarda la lettura
del manoscritto quanto nell'applicazione dei criterî da lui adotati in sede di
restitutio.»

[5] Paris, 1921.

[6] Leipzig, 1894-1924.

[7] R. Nelli and R. Lavaud give a brief literary analysis of *Daurel* followed
by extracts of the text with translations in French in *Les Troubadours,* II
([Bruges]: Desclée de Brouwer, 1966), 392-420.

CHAPTER I

THE MANUSCRIPT

Paul Meyer gave a detailed description of the Didot MS in his introduction to *Daurel et Beton*;[1] some years later, H. Omont and A. Jeanroy examined the MS for William P. Shepard's edition of the *Passion Provençale*[2] and were able to confirm Meyer's findings. Since my contact with the MS has been limited to the examination of photocopies of the folios containing *Daurel*, I have based the description that follows upon Meyer and Shepard.

The Didot MS, now catalogued in the Bibliothèque Nationale as *Nouv. Acq. Franc.* 4232, is composed of 112 folios in-quarto, bound in book form, measuring 205 × 140 mm. With the exception of folios 14 to 17 in parchment, the leaves are paper. In its present state it is missing folios at both beginning and end and has lost several in the inside section. An old pagination in red ink informs the reader that the book has lost its first seventy-two leaves. The last folio numbered in this fashion is the next-to-last of the *Passion*, which ends on folio 76^r, except for its final verse, which is repeated on the verso side, where *Daurel* begins.

The MS is written by different hands, all of which belong to the mid-fourteenth century, except for several lines in *Daurel*, which appear to have been added by a later hand.[3] Meyer distinguishes ten or twelve hands, but considers it hardly probable that so many different individuals would have collaborated on the manuscript and

---

[1] Cf. the appendix, pp. lix-cxx.
[2] *La Passion provençale du Manuscrit Didot: Mystère du XIVe siècle,* SATF (Paris, 1928), pp. ix-xv.
[3] 1321-22, and, possibly 2038-43.

goes so far as to assert that some of the handwritings which appear at variance with the rest might actually be attributed to a single person. [4] The fact, moreover, that some of these hands are poorly executed would support Meyer's theory. The MS appears to be the work of amateur copyists. Shepard accepts Meyer's conclusions and reduces the number of copyists to five. An examination of errors in the MS leads Shepard to suggest that

> Beaucoup de ces fautes ne peuvent s'expliquer que si le scribe copiait à la hâte un texte qu'il avait devant lui. L'abondance et le caractère des fautes, ainsi que les écritures, montrent que le MS. Didot a été fait par des copistes amateurs qui n'étaient pas des scribes de profession. [5]

With the exception of the conclusion of the *Passion* and all of *Daurel,* the MS appears to have been copied by Gascons.

The Didot MS contains several marginal notes, notably on the folios containing the *Passion,* three of which are of some importance in dating and placing at least that part of it. On fol. 5^r (LXXVII in the old pagination), at the bottom of the page, we read the following:

> Finito libro sit laus, et Xto Ament Anno Domino MCCXLV Ar^{dus}; [fol. 5^v] iste liber e Arnadi Glibi de Togete et de la Portas et de Anye [or Anxe]

and on fol. 45 (fol. 45 (CXXIIII)), we find:

> l'an miel catre cccc e caranta e dos lo permier gont [= jorn] d'abriel que foro Pascas cumenyeron xxvi preconas a S. Peire d'Aryfat.

Since it appears that the Didot MS was formed by successive additions, the date 1345 and the words *finito libro* are meaningful for only the first five folios of the book (and the missing seventy-two indicated by the old pagination). The fact that *Arnadi Glibi* calls himself *de Togete* (probably Touget in the *arrondissement* of Lombez) is no certain proof that this part of the MS was executed there, as he may have been called *de Togete* because he or his an-

---

[4] Meyer, *Daurel,* pp. lxxi-ii.
[5] Shepard, *Passion,* p. xi.

cestors originally came from there to settle in Aryfat,[6] where the MS was located a century later, according to the note found on fol. 45. This note places the MS in the hands of a priest of Saint Pierre d'Aryfat in 1442. Aryfat (Tarn) is in the *arrondissement* of Castres.

However, since one can often accept at face value an ordinary forename and surname followed by a place of origin, we cannot altogether eliminate the possibility that the MS was located in the Lombez region in 1345.[7] Note that Arnaud's surname *Glibi* (=Gilbert?) is followed by Touget, the name of a town, and by *de la Portas et de Anye*, possibly the names of his properties in or around Touget.

Whether Arnaud came from Touget or lived in Touget is of no consequence to *Daurel*, which had probably not wandered very far from its place of composition when it was appended to the *Passion* in Aryfat. There are no marginal indications in *Daurel* to cast any light on its date or place of composition, but we have shown that the MS, up to and including the *Passion*, was in the church library at Aryfat in 1442. *Daurel* does not share either the ecclesiastical character or the Gascon linguistic traits that distinguish the rest of the MS.[8] Thus we can assume that our poem's presence at the end of a series of religious texts compiled by Gascon scribes is purely a matter of accident, and, we might add, good luck, since this chance juxtaposition is probably the sole reason for *Daurel's* survival through centuries hostile to anything written in *langue d'oc* and especially to non-religious works in that tongue.

---

[6] Robert Sabatino Lopez, «Concerning Surnames and Places of Origin,» in *Medievalia et Humanistica*, VIII (1954), 6-16, states that a toponymic surname is often strong *prima facie* evidence of its bearer's origin or ancestry for two or three generations, after which it becomes a fixed, hereditary family name. Therefore, the interest of a toponymic surname is greatest when it originates with the person who bears it, decreasing with each generation.

[7] Cf. Richard W. Emery, «The Use of the Surname in the Study of Medieval Economic History,» in *Medievalia et Humanistica*, VII (1952), 43-50, who demonstrates that surnames had become hereditary by the late twelfth century and generally cast no light on place or origin or birth. He adds, however, that one can often accept as evidence a name such as Johannes de Dodo de Placentia, meaning that Johannes lived in Placentia. R. S. Lopez (cf. *supra*) strongly disagrees with Emery.

[8] Meyer, p. lxxii.

The sole redaction of *Daurel et Beton* occupies folios 76^v to 112^v of the Didot MS, which ends at this point, having lost an unknown number of pages at the end. We cannot evaluate the extent of the MS in its intact state. However, since most epics contain at least 4000 verses, usually more, we may assume that about half the poem is missing. The fact that an entirely new episode concerning the mature Beton's vengeance against Charlemagne begins on fol. 111, the next-to-last of the extant MS, supports this hypothesis.

The text of *Daurel* is written in one hand, belonging to the mid-fourteenth century, with the exception of the following verses:

314-329: a very formal hand found nowhere else in the MS.

1321-1322: Added by a more recent (fifteenth-century?) hand.

2038-2043: a style distinctive from the main hand but possibly attributable to the same scribe.

With the exception of the indentations at the beginning of each laisse, every line begins with a capital letter, usually enclosed in the pair of crudely-drawn guidelines running down the left margin of each page. The beginning of a laisse is indicated by a capital or an indented space left blank for one, but these capitals and *alinéas* do not always coincide with a change of rhyme.

The several illustrations to be found in the text on folios 93, 94, 97^v, 101, 105, 108 are described in the notes. They are crudely executed line drawings, certainly not the work of an accomplished illuminator of manuscripts, which make use of stick figures whose attitudes indicate quite clearly their rôle in the story and which relate closely to the text. Except for the drawing of a ship with sail set and pennant flying found on fol. 108, they are done with little graphic skill. Perhaps the scribe drew them to provide suggestions for an illuminator, but it seems more likely that he did them for his own amusement. It is also possible that they were added later by an interested reader, but we must make a closer examination of the inks used in the text and in the drawings before setting down any firm conclusion.

The fourteenth-century character of the MS, the large number of erasures, scribal errors and defective verses demonstrates clearly that this is not an author's MS, nor even a direct copy of one. Nor, in spite of its unprepossessing appearance, can it be called a «MS de jongleur» [9] given its late date of composition. *Daurel* is somewhat

---

[9] Martín de Riquer, «Épopée jongleresque à écouter et épopée romanesque à lire,» in *La Technique littéraire des chansons de geste,* Université de Liège:

larger than the pocket format usually associated with the *jongleur* MS
(205 × 140 mm. as compared to 160 × 110 mm.) but smaller than
the library MS (the Venice 4 MS of the *Roland* measures 340 × 240
mm.). The *jongleur* MS was fast disappearing by the end of the
twelfth century, not having the artistic value of the deluxe, illuminated
MS and no longer being prized for its literary contents. [10] Since *Daurel*
has neither the antiquity of the typical *jongleur* MS nor the artistic
beauty of the library MS, it probably represents the work of an amateur
or apprentice scribe.

Biblio. de la Faculté de Philosophie et Lettres fasc. Cl (Paris; «Les Belles
Lettres,» 1959), pp. 77-79. The collection is hereafter cited as *Technique*.

[10] Maurice Delbouille, «Les Chansons de geste et le livre,» in *Technique*, p. 324.

Chapter II

VERSIFICATION

The 2199 verses of *Daurel et Beton* are divided into fifty-two rhymed laisses, of which the first five (138 verses) are in alexandrines, the rest in decasyllables, except for a number of hypermetric verses scattered throughout the poem.[1] Most of the decasyllabic verses are of the 4 + 6 type common in Provençal narrative poetry, with the notable exception of *Girart de Roussillon*.[2]

The elision of the unaccented vowel ending a hemistich is usually required by the meter, but the author, as is generally the case in the Provençal narrative, follows no clear-cut rule in this matter, as exemplified by *Flamenca*,[3] *Girart*,[4] *Roland à Saragosse*,[5] and the *Chanson de la Croisade albigeoise*.[6]

The appearance of alexandrines in a poem written in the epic decasyllable occurs frequently in Provençal. For example, alexandrines are found grouped together at the end of the *Vie de Saint Trophime*, in certain sections of the *Saint Porchaire* or the *Saint Honorat* of Raimon Feraud, and scattered throughout the *Roman d'Arles*. The author of the fourteenth-century epic *Roland à Saragosse* uses scattered

---

[1] 155, 437, 675, 742, 968, 1295, 1318, 1493, 1543, 1608, 1636, 1655, 1656, 1686, 1687, 1698, 1872, 1877, 2012.

[2] *Girart de Roussillon*, ed. by W. Mary Hackett, SATF (Paris, 1955), III, 501.

[3] *Le Roman de Flamenca*, ed. by Paul Meyer, 2nd ed., V. I [V. II, announced by Meyer, was never published] (Paris, 1901), pp. xxxvi-viii.

[4] *Girart*, III, 502.

[5] *Roland à Saragosse: Poème épique méridional du XVI*e *siècle*, ed. by Mario Roques, CFMA (Paris, 1956), pp. xx-xxi.

[6] *La Chanson de la Croisade contre les Albigeois commencée par Guillaume de Tudèle et continuée par un poète anonyme* (Paris, 1875), I, xcvii, cx.

alexandrines as a rhetorical device to focus attention on a noble attitude, a trait or an exploit. [7]

In *Daurel*, however, many of the alexandrines are little more than hypermetric decasyllables which apparently serve no esthetic function and can be explained in large measure by the scribe's tendency to add grammatically superfluous words to an otherwise correct verse, as for example *e* in 401 and 412, *vos* in 120 and 148, and by his writing out in full those words whose syllable counts should be reduced by elision or use of proclitic or enclitic forms. One has only to read *ve · us* for *vec vos* in 1301 and 1319, *se · l* for *se lo* in 117, *qu'ieu* for *que ieu* in 243 to correct the scansion of the verse. Of the alexandrines scattered throughout the 2061 verses of the decasyllabic section of *Daurel*, only twenty (cited *supra*) can be accepted without great reservation as being attributable to the author and even these cannot be accepted without question.

The first 138 verses pose a different problem. Were these verses written in decasyllables or alexandrines in earlier versions of the poem? A cursory glance at these lines shows them to be far below the caliber of the rest of the *Daurel* from both a metrical and grammatical point of view. The awkwardness of the style shows us that the author (or copyist) is not at home in this meter, and one feels a sense of relief when he turns to the facile, but fast-moving, decasyllable after the ragged, uneven and plodding alexandrines of the first part of the poem. In these 138 verses, we find eight that are hypermetric, two with less than nine syllables (9, 87) and several that could be scanned as either decasyllables or dodecasyllables (e.g., 3, 68). The very first verse of the poem is a perfect decasyllable, and many of the alexandrines in this section of *Daurel* can be made into perfect decasyllables by the elimination of syntactically superfluous words. Meyer, who considered it «tout à fait invraisemblable qu'on ait mis en vers de dix syllabes un poeme en alexandrins,» [8] points to this facility as partial evidence that the poem must have been originally composed in decasyllables.

On the other hand, many of the 138 verses cannot easily be reduced to decasyllables, and this fact caused Gaston Paris to question Meyer's

---

[7] *Roland à Saragosse,* pp. xviii-xix.

[8] Meyer, *Daurel,* p. xxxiii, rewrites the first ten verses of *Daurel* in perfect decasyllables as proof of this facility.

hypothesis that the alexandrines in *Daurel* are the work of a copyist who set out to rewrite the poem in this meter, but soon tired of the task. It was these verses that led Paris to accept the hypothesis of a first redaction in alexandrines. [9]

The question is an important one. If an earlier or the earliest version of *Daurel* existed in alexandrines, it could not have dated before 1170, the approximate date of the first known version of the *Roman d'Alexandre* in dodecasyllabic verse, and would have been an anomaly among other *chansons de geste* similar in form and subject to *Daurel* and composed about the same time. Thus, if we accept Paris' hypothesis, the author of the hypothetical dodecasyllabic *Daurel* would have been a pioneer in the use of this meter, since we know that the poem existed before 1170.

It is possible, but hardly likely, that an author would have started a poem in one meter, changing after only 138 verses, without either rectifying the early verses or repeating the original meter in sections elsewhere in the other 2000 verses. The probability of such an occurrence is greatly enhanced if we place the responsibility for it on a copyist. Thus, we conclude that if a version of *Daurel* in alexandrines ever existed, it was (1) posterior to the original version upon which our text is based; (2) due to a redactor rather than to the author; (3) without influence on our version in decasyllables, with the possible exception of the first 138 verses. Nor can we attribute these verses to the fourteenth-century scribe, who, if we are to judge by his frequent errors in meter and orthography, was unskilled in versification and unschooled in Latin.

Indeed, many of the defects in versification found in *Daurel* are directly traceable to the scribe, since they involve obvious errors. Metrically deficient verses (e.g. 9, 68, 87, 736) appear to be the result of his inability to understand the text he was copying or his attempt to fill an obvious gap in the MS. In addition to supplying superfluous words, the scribe is often guilty of omitting words or syllables required by meter and syntax. Meyer emends sixteen of the first thirty lines of the poem to correct these defects.

---

[9] Paris, *Mélanges*, p. 143.

Since the rhymes are generally quite exact, except for two examples of assonance, *els* 687 (*-es* rhyme) and *corredor* 346 (*-os* rhyme), [10] the assumption can be made that the author wrote perfect verse and that the obvious errors in rhyme can be attributed to the scribe. [11] The scarcity of assonance and the nature of the examples found in the poem indicate that *Daurel* was originally composed in rhyme, and, most probably, in rhymed decasyllabic laisses.

The use of the rhymed laisse in Provençal is attested in the earliest texts: the eleventh century Limousin *Boecis* [12] is composed in decasyllables arranged in laisses of unequal length. Its lack of feminine rhyme (like *Daurel* which has only one feminine laisse, XIX) probably indicates a relatively early date of composition, since this feature places the *Boecis* in «una fase di tecnica più primitiva (che non vuol dire più grossolana, anzi) non solo delle *chansons de geste,* ma persino delle altre Vite de santi.» [13]

Like *Daurel, Boecis* is composed in rhyme with a mixture of assonance. The preponderance of rhyme in a poem as early as the *Boecis* is not surprising, given the advanced stage of poetic sophistication achieved in the South by the end of the eleventh century, which caused assonance to be looked upon with scorn. [14]

---

[10] In the same laisse, *corredors* 340 is not, properly, an assonance, since *r* often falls in this position. In the first laisse of the poem, *valor* 9 and *Aspremont* 10 can be attributed to the scribe.

[11] We consider the following verses scribal errors: 9, 111, 123, 227, 318, 340, 638, 701, 817, 861, 1093, 1152, 2123. Verses 89, 172, 1381 are not considered in error, since the use of *-er* in an *-ier* laisse is common usage in the Provençal epic.

[12] Clovis Brunel, *Bibliographie des manuscrits littéraires en ancien provençal* (Paris, 1935), p. 40, No. 130.

[13] Cesare Segre, «Il *Boeci,* i poemetti agiografici e le origini della forma epica,» *Atti della Accademia delle Scienze di Torino,* LXXXIX, t. ii (1954-55), 260 (note 3). Segre suggests (p. 288) that the *Boecis* is older than the epics with which it shares form.

[14] Cf. Segre, «Il *Boeci,*» 287-288. The question of whether the *Boecis* was rhymed or assonanced (more of form than of substance, according to Segre (287, note 2) is discussed by: Rene Lavaud and George Machicot, eds., *Boècis* (Toulouse, 1950), pp. 76-77. Maurice Wilmotte, *L'Épopée française: origine et élaboration* (Paris, n. d.), p. 203, points to the variety of elements in the *Boecis,* astonishing in one of the earliest manifestations of the decasyllable.

The *Chanson de Sainte Foy* was composed towards the end of the eleventh century, [15] like the early-twelfth-century *Alexandre* fragment and *Gormont,* in octosyllables arranged in laisses of unequal length. Of these poems, which represent the debris of an epic poetry in octosyllables, the *Sainte Foy* is by far the superior in its poetic perfection and finesse. In its use of rhyme at a time when French versification was still using assonance, it typifies a phenomenon which distinguishes the early poetry of the Midi from that of the North. [16]

Girart de Roussillon, in its oldest extant form of rhymed decasyllables, could have been written as early as 1136, according to Miss Hackett. [17] Since the rhymed octosyllable and decasyllable are found in the very earliest narrative poems of southern provenance, as well as in all known Provençal epics, it is reasonable to assume that *Daurel,* composed in rhymed decasyllabic laisses, could well have existed as early as 1130 or 1140. However, the version known to our fourteenth-century scribe must have been written after 1170, the probable date of the introduction of the alexandrine in epic. Our version could not represent a reworking later than the mid-thirteenth century, since a *remanieur* would probably have done the poem into prose rather than into dodecasyllables after that date. Our text, then, is the work of a copyist who lived at a time when the alexandrine was in vogue, from the late twelfth to the mid-thirteenth centuries.

The earlier version of *Daurel* which he copied was composed in decasyllables between 1130 and 1170. The poem may have existed in a still earlier form, given its archaic and primitive qualities, but we see no convincing or concrete evidence to support this hypothesis.

---

[15] Brunel, *Bibliographie,* p. 82, No. 282. H. Gavel (*Annales du Midi,* 56-60 [1944-48], 210-230) puts the composition at 1098-1100. Antoine Thomas (ed., *La Chanson de Sainte Foi d'Agen,* CFMA [Paris, 1925], p. xviii) suggests the second third of the eleventh century.

[16] Ernest Hoepffner, ed., *La Chanson de Sainte Foy* (Paris, 1926), I, 226-230. Cf. Thomas, *Sainte Foi,* p. xxx. Both editors discuss the significance of the «lei francesca» mentioned in verse 20.

[17] *Girart,* III, 478-480.

Chapter III

LANGUAGE OF THE AUTHOR

A brief examination of rhymes in *Daurel* demonstrates that the author, a *jongleur* well-versed in northern epic, was from the Midi and composed his poem originally in a South-French language. Although he used French rhyme-words frequently, he did so in unsystematic fashion, as was often admissible in medieval verse. And although some laisses rhyme equally well in northern and southern French, others, notably those in *-os* (XI) and *-es* (XX, XLIV), rhyme only in meridional areas. In the case of *-an*: *-en*, and the *-ar*: *-ier* rhymes, the author felt free to distinguish between them when he wished to do so, and to follow northern usage with equal casualness.

In laisses IX and LI, the author readily combines the *-an* rhyme with the easier *-en*. The six laisses in pure *-en* and *-ens* (II, VII, XXVIII, XLI, XLVI; XXXVI) confirm that the author, while distinguishing phonetically between the two sounds, was also willing to follow the example of numerous French *chansons de geste* which permit the mixture of *-an* and *-en,* acceptable in northern French.

There are eight laisses in *-ar* which rhyme only in meridional spelling. In addition to these (XII, XVI, XXIII, XXV, XXVII, XXXIII, XXXVII, XLII, XLVII), the *-ier* rhymes found in laisses III and VIII can be uniformly transposed to *-ar* in Provençal (e.g., *estier = estar, menier = menar*). The same is true of the predominantly *-ier* laisse XV, where in South French the infinitives are commonly of the *-ar* variety.

Laisses XXIX and XXXIX (except for *chiers* 1571) rhyme equally well in South or North; but III, VI, XXXV and LI contain rhymes, notably those with first conjugation infinitives, which should be *-ar* in the South, side by side with words ending in *-ier* in any French region. These can be divided into three classes:

(1) North and South French *-ier* from the Latin suffix *-arium* (e.g., *trotier* 56, *volontier* 59, 68, *olivier* 60).

(2) Northern *-er*, southern *-ar* from Latin tonic *a* not preceded by a palatal (e.g., *retornier* 55, *parlier* 57).

(3) Northern *-ier*, southern *-ar* from Latin tonic *a* preceded by a palatal (e.g., *tarzier* 57, *cortegier* 73).

We have seen that the *-ier* rhymes in laisses III, VIII and XV can easily be transposed to southern *-ar*. But the fact that the *-ar* rhymes in these laisses cannot be *-ier* in the South, and that the reverse is true in laisse XXIX where the *-ier* rhymes cannot be *-ar* in southern French, demonstrates that the author came from a region where the general usage of these endings was observed, but that he permitted himself the license of following a freer usage in the mixed *-ar*: *-ier* laisses. Even the troubadours occasionally took this license, which is commonplace in Provençal narrative: *Aigar* follows the same pattern as *Daurel* in the use of these rhymes, and numerous examples are found in other works. [1]

In his introduction to *Roland à Saragosse,* which offers the same mixture of *-ier* and *-ar* endings, Mario Roques points out the elements of false analogy and imitation which influenced leading authors to adopt the *-ier* rhyme:

> elle s'explique par l'idée inexacte qu'à l'*-a* provençal correspond un *-ie* de la langue littéraire française sans conditions, que *cabalcar* ayant pour correspondant *chevalchier, par* ou *bar* ont naturellement pour correspondants *bier* (126, 1097) et *pier* (107) [cf. *Daurel* 507 *pier*]; cela aboutit à créer une forme aussi manifestement impossible en français que *dier* (1102) pour fournir un équivalent en style de chanson de geste au provençal *dar*. [2]

---

[1] C. Th. Gossen, «Die Einheit der französischen Schriftsprache im 15. und 16. Jahrundert,» *ZRPh* LXXIII (1957), 454, notes that the earliest troubadour, Guillaume IX, used infinitives in *-ier*; also that *-er* (beside *-ier*) from Latin *-ariu* is a trait typical of the southwest, especially Poitou and Saintonge. See Meyer, *Daurel*, pp. xli-xlv, for exs. from Peirol, *Chan. Crois. Alb., Guerre de Navarre, Fierabras.*

[2] *Roland à Saragosse,* pp. xxiii-iv.

In the medieval tradition, northern French was the epic language *par excellence*; it is, then, not surprising that the *Daurel* author freely exploited this license in an attempt to ornament his southern poem with northern epic elements such as the future forms in *-om* (e.g., *farom* 26, *casarom* 318, *conquero* 321) and the nasals (e.g., *Aspremont* 10, *hom* 12) in an *-o* laisse. Just as the northern *trouvère* decorated his poems with provençalisms to give his language a Provençal coloration, but limited his borrowings to endings and words,[3] the *Daurel* author makes use of certain rhymes to give his poem an epic ring. Outside of the rhyme, he limits his imitative ornamentation to a handful of northern words, all commonplace in epic (e.g., *causea* 314, *espeia* 1325, *daimas* 496, *ruas* 1996, *sire, sira, cira* 262, 12, 292).

I have not felt it neccessary to repeat Meyer's extensive study of the problem posed by the *-ier* rhymes which was designed to answer Gautier's charge that

> le *roman de Betonet* est exactement dans le cas du *Fierabras* provençal. C'est une oeuvre calquée, évidemment calquée sur un roman français.... Ces rimes en *ier* sont vraiment terribles: elles sont toujours là pour dénoncer ces sortes de fraudes. [4]

Indeed, Meyer and, more recently, René Louis and C. Th. Gossen, have shown that the lack of distinction between infinitives in *-ier* and *-er* is a linguistic trait typical of the border region between northern and southwestern dialects: Poitou, Angoumois and Saintonge.[5] Meyer cites a poem by Richard Coeur-de-Lion, who wrote in the Poitevin dialect, in which *demander* and *lever* rhyme with *deresnier, querrier* and *aidier*.[6] However, this trait alone does not prove that the *Daurel* author was a Poitevin, in spite of his obvious familiarity with the region, since we find it also in a text such as *Roland à Saragosse*.

---

[3] Paul Zumthor, *Langue et techniques poétiques à l'époque romane (XIe-XIIIe siècles)*, Biblio. Française et Romane, Faculté des Lettres de Strasbourg, Série C, no. 4 (Paris, 1962), p. 80.

[4] *Les Épopées françaises*, I, 133-34. Cf. Meyer's refutation of Gautier, *Daurel*, pp. xxxviii-lxvii.

[5] René Louis, *De l'Histoire à la légende: Girart, Comte de Vienne dans les chansons de geste: Girart de Vienne, Girart de Fraite, Girart de Roussillon* (Auxerre, 1947), II, 277-278.

[6] Meyer, *Daurel*, p. xlvii, *Dalfin ieus voill deresnier*.

Actually, the evidence thus far presented neither confirms nor denies the possibility that our author was a Poitevin; however, this remains our strongest hypothesis and leads to the conclusion that, whatever the origin of its author, *Daurel* was composed in a semi-artificial language created for the epic, designed to be understood by a southern audience, but liberally sprinkled with the northern French forms and clichés that such an audience associated with the epic genre. It is noteworthy that the author of *Girart* chose to create a southern epic in the dialect of the Limousin border region, since it was there that the earliest troubadours fixed the language of the Provençal lyric, «car le poète de *Girart de Roussillon* semble bien avoir fait école, et si nous ne pouvons plus citer maintenant que deux de ses imitateurs [*Daurel* and *Aigar*], dont les poèmes nous sont parvenus dans des copies plus ou moins incomplètes, nous avons lieu de croire qu'il en a suscité beaucoup d'autres.» [7]

In his study of the traits common to *Girart, Daurel* and *Aigar,* Louis demonstrates the close relationship that exists among them phonetically, morphologically, and to a lesser degree, lexically:

I. *Phonetic traits:*

(1) Tendency to substitute *ei* for *ai.*

(2) Substitution of *au, eu* for *ai, ei* (apparently a trait of the Poitou and Saintonge regions).

(3) Reduction of *ie* to *i* (this trait, banal in Picard and Lorrain, is also found in certain western dialects).

(4) Substitution of *ai* for *a* (so-called parasitic *i*): possibly a graphical confusion due to the fact that *ai* was so often reduced to *a.*

(5) Hesitation between protonic *e* and *a,* especially before *r* + consonant (the passage of protonic *e* to *a* before *r, l* and even other consonants is current in modern Poitevin and Limousin, but the trait is commonplace).

All of these traits are common to *Daurel, Aigar* and *Girart.* Several points not applicable to *Daurel* have been omitted.

---

[7] Louis, *De l'Histoire,* II, 276.

II. *Morphological traits*:

(1) Second person plurals ending in *-et* or *-eit* (instead of *-etz*) and in *-at* (instead of *-atz*); plurals in *-et* and *-at* are often found in earliest Old Limousin texts. E.g., *Daurel*: *et* 12, *podet* 211, *donat* 1225, *desconortat* 996. *Girart*: *volet* 463, *avet* 2006, none in *-at*. *Aigar*: none.

(2) Forms derived from Latin pluperfect indicative: Numerous in *Girart* and *Aigar* as preterits and conditionals, but only banal forms such as *fora* 410 and *pogra* 386 are found in *Daurel*.[8]

Gossen's study of southwestern written language shows the following traits, found in *Daurel*, to be typical of the Poitou and Saintonge dialects:

(1) Poitou *louc, leouc* from Latin *locu* (*Daurel luoc* 1836 *fuoc* 609).

(2) The *-gui* perfect is quite characteristic of thirteenth century Poitevin (*Daurel prengui* 18).[9]

In conclusion, *Girart*, *Daurel* and *Aigar*, which represent almost the totality of the twelfth-century southern epic known to us through texts, belong linguistically to the Poitou, Saintonge and Limousin regions. «La brillante floraison littéraire que ces provinces ont connue au XIIe siècle ne s'est donc pas bornée à la poésie lyrique des troubadours, elle s'est étendue aussi à l'épopée, pour laquelle s'est constitué un idiome hybride.[10]

In the case of *Daurel*, the linguistic evidence is supplemented by the geography of the poem, in which Poitiers plays an important rôle. The author's frequent mention of St.-Hilaire of Poitiers would seem to indicate a certain attachment on his part to this particular church, which would be difficult to explain if he were not a Poitevin.

---

[8] Louis, *De l'Histoire*, II, 279-283.

[9] Gossen, «Die Einheit,» 454-455.

[10] Louis, *De l'Histoire*, II, 285. Cf. Hans-Georg Koll («Pour une étude des rapports entre langue et pensée dans la poésie des troubadours occitans,» *RLiR*, XXVIII [1964], 29-30) who suggests that, while the language of the troubadours was the first great *koiné* in Romania, contemporary southern epic texts still show all the symptoms of an adolescent language without fixed norms. See also, W. Mary Hackett, *La Langue de Girart de Roussillon*, Pub. Romanes et Françaises CXI (Genève, 1970); Jakob Wüest, «Sprachgrenzen im Poitou,» *Vox Romanica*, XXVIII (Bern, 1969), 14-58; Carl Th. Gossen, «Zum Thema 'Sprachgrenzen im Poitou,'» *Vox Romanica*, XXVIII, 59-71.

Chapter IV

LANGUAGE OF THE SCRIBE

We have noted the following traits which appear to characterize the spelling habits of the scribe. However, since we know *Daurel* through a single MS, many of these traits may also pertain to the language of the author.

Vowels

Alternance and substitution

1) *i* and *y*: *mayzo* 16 *maio* 20, *faray* 53 *farai* 245.
2) *u* and *ue*: *vulh* 136 *vuelh* 148, *puscas*, 237 *puesca* 244.
3) *o* and *uo*: *loc* 617 *luoc* 1836, *fuoc* 609.
4) *a* and *au*: *sap* 334 *saup* 264.
5) *ai* and *au*: *au* (= *ai* < *habeo*) 165, *alaita* 706 *alautatz* 1242 (cf. *aleutatz* 1017), *cautieu* 990, *messauge* 59.
6) *ei* and *eu*: *Peutieus* 135 *Peitieus* 1673, *veuret* 1331 *veires* 1322.
7) *ei* and *ai*: *lei* 45 *lai* 213, *gueiamen* 79, *diriei* 1001 *diray* 181.
8) *ie* and *i*: *vinetz* 1940, *vinet* 847 (imperfect).
9) *ai* and *a*: *daimas* (= *damas*) 496, *aicel* 1009 *acels* 1964.
10) *a* and *e* (especially before *r* + consonant): *sarcar* 1294 *sercas* 237, *garizo* 1160 *guerizo* 1835, *darier* 358, *sazia* 6 *sezia* 289, *dalfis* 1423.
11) *i* and *e*: *venc* 287 *vinc* 60, *aminas* 135 *amena* 141, *arsebes* 129 *arcivesques* 151.
12) *ei* and *oi*: *pueis* 188 *puois* 626.
13) Aphaeresis of initial *a*: *dobero* 68.

14) Effacement of intertonic *a*: *mendray* 75 (cf. *menaray* 299).

15) Effacement of intertonic *e*: *sostrar* 530 (cf. *sosteratz* 749).

CONSONANTS

16) Presence of *h*: *hum* 10 *hom* 25, *ho* 120 (cf. *o* 124), *pahor* 480 (cf. *paor* 653), *auh* 565 (cf. *au* 555).

17) Use of *h* in notation of palatal *l* and *n*: *cosseh* 683 (cf. *cosselh* 824), *compaho* 29 (cf. *companh* 21), *seher* 14 (cf. *senher* 52).

18) Replacement of *i* by *g*: *vegatz* 961 (cf. *veiatz* 1039), *espeiga* 1710 (cf. *espeia* 1325), *baga* 1191 (cf. *baia* 326).

19) Alternance between *g* and *j*: *mangar* 664 *manjar* 1939.

20) Use of *g* in notation of *n* + palatal: *seger* 16, *compagier* 71 (cf. no. 17 *supra*).

21) Effacement of *n*: *evia* 64, *a[n]c* 885, *esenhar* 925, *so* (= *son* poss. adj. 1045) 1065, *viro* 32 *mesclero* 35 (third person plur. verbs *passim*).

22) Effacement of *r*: *alagar* 363, *venados* 364 (cf. *venadors* 369), *aute* 30 (cf. *altre* 367), *paube* 12, *Ebratz* 780.

23) Introduction of *n* or *r* in consonant group: *junbentut* 5, *arculhir* 116, *sostreratz* 534.

24) Dissimulation of *n* and *r* to *l*: *colsel* 673, *molra* 138.

25) Reduction of *iers* to *ies*: *saumies* 567 *somies* 539, *volonties* 53.

26) Metathesis involving
r: *cramba* 323 (cf. *cambra* 344), *pre* (= *per*) 117, *prejurs* 1398.
rd: *tradier* 166 (cf. *tardier* 246).
ldr: *flodres* 641 (= *foldres* 'foudre').
s: *trasiho* 30.

27) Replacement of *t* by *d*: *audre* 33, *mardiers* 914.

28) Replacement of *l* by *r*: *arma* 532, *artre* 1754, *brizaut* 1426 (cf. *blizaudo* 1815).

29) Replacement of *s* by *r*: *irla* 715, *raro* (= *razo*) 317, MS *Aremyer* (= *Azemar*) 93.

30) Replacement of *r* by *y*: *vayley* 93.

31) Introduction of final unetymological *z*: *cortz* 75, *Esmenjartz* 173, *ostz* 1735, *tostz* 1603.

32) Use of prosthetic *z*: *az anier* 108, *daz els* 816.

33) Effacement of *z* in plural object forms: *det* 325, *fairit* 1299, *escut* 1317, *triat* 1387, *mart* 1465. In second person plural verb forms: *fares* 712, *veires* 1795 (in rhyme), *amas* 164, *anas* 50; *passim* in pres. ind, imperative, imperfect, future cond., pres. subjunctive.

34) Hesitation between *s* and *c*: *cieu* 709, *cira* 302, *merses* 711, *sist* 209, *silh* 212.

35) Effacement of *s* + consonant: *aqueta* 398, *seta* 89, *depolhar* 1431.

36) Reinforcement of intervocalic *s* by *z*: *deszirat* 2032, *mezsisses* 1482 *nosz, vosz* (before words beginning with vowel) 1098, 1549, 1768.

37) Hesitation between intervocalic *b* and *v*: *Boves* 26, *Bobes* 70, *eparbiers* 1135, *cavelhs* (=*cabelhs*) 762.

Origin of the Scribe

The carelessness with which the MS was executed does not facilitate the task of determining the scribe's origin. Moreover, the majority of the traits cited above are widely distributed throughout Languedoc and Provence and can be attributed to author as well as to scribe in many cases. Recent language studies have shown many of these traits to be common to the dialects of the Southwest, notably those of Toulouse, Albi and Quercy. Åke Grafström, whose study of Languedocian dialect is based on charts from this region,[1] points out a number of linguistic features that coincide with those of the *Daurel* MS:

9) *ai* and *a*: Albi, Toulouse (p. 36:5).[2]

7) *ai* and *ei*: Albi, Toulouse (p. 38:6).[3]

4) *a* and *au*: Agen, Toulouse, Quercy, but characteristic of North and East Provençal as well (p. 46:7).

---

[1] *Étude sur la graphie des plus anciennes chartes languedociennes avec un essai d'interprétation phonétique* (Uppsala, 1958). Refs. are to page and paragraph.

[2] Cf. Jules Ronjat, *Grammaire istorique des parlers provençaux modernes* (Montpellier, 1930-41), II, para. 282.

[3] Cf. Ronjat, *Grammaire*, III, para. 588 (shift in Mod. Prov. of *ai* to *ei* (Foix, Toulouse, Albi, Narbonne).

10) *a* and *e* (esp. in presence of *r* + consonant): Toulouse, Foix, Quercy (pp. 46-52:8).

11) *e* and *i*: Widespread, but common in Toulouse, Albi, Quercy (pp. 52-64:9).

1) *i* and *y*: *y* rarely replaces *i*; only a few examples are found: in Toulouse and Quercy (p. 36:4).

Of these traits, numbers 7, 9 and 10 are common in Poitou and Saintonge as well and have been so noted under the language of the author, but could just as well be attributed to the scribe. Our list is far from exhaustive, since many more traits can be cited which point to the same general area. For example:

cumergas 428: *u* often replaces *o* before a nasal in Toulouse, Albi, Quercy (p. 89:23).

sor (from *soror*) 623: Toulouse, Albi, Quercy (p. 89:23).

senes 421: predominant form in Toulouse, Albi; only form in Quercy.

ses 13: rare, only examples found in Agen, Albi, Rouergue, Lodevois.

speia (after vowel) 1365, 1951 (elsewhere *espeia*: cf. Quercy, Albi *la strada,* Toulouse *la estrada* (p. 86:21).

Looking at the consonants, we find much the same pattern:

21) Effacement of *n*: occurs regularly in Albi (pp. 159-60:53).

29) *s* replaced by *r*: Nîmois *irla* (p. 164:54).

17) Notation of *l* or *n* + palatal: *ng* and *gn* in Quercy, Toulouse, Albi; *nh* in Quercy, Toulouse; *lh* in Quercy (pp. 209-212:74, 75).

19) *j* and *g* alternate before *e* or *i*: *baia* 326 *baga* 1191 (*baisar*); Nîmois *Ermenjard*; Toulouse, Albi, Quercy *aia, aga* (from *habeat*); Toulouse *poia, poga* (p. 178:65). [4]

s = *ss*: Toulouse, Quercy, Albi *aisi, aissi, maiso, cosell.* Alternance *maio* — *maiso* found in Quercy, Albi, Toulouse (pp. 167-70:56). [5]

---

[4] Grafström (*Étude*, p. 178:65) cites Toulouse *aujo* as an ex. of long *i* = *j*. However, *aujo* 15 (in *Daurel*) is a doubtful reading, probably related to *audio*, rather than *avio*.

[5] Cf. S. Dobelmann, *La Langue de Cahors des origines à la fin du XVI*e *siècle,* Bibliothèque Méridionale, 1e série, 24 (Toulouse / Paris, 1944), p. 58, 60.

Treatment of (*aticu, -ĭcu, -acu*: *mesage* 55, *messauge* 59, *messagier* 62 (in rhyme), *mesagier* 52: Quercy, Toulouse, Albi *-atgue, -atge, -age, -aige* (pp. 188-89:70).

The evidence thus far presented points repeatedly to the area which can be defined as follows: [6]

Quercy = Lot, Tarn-et-Garonne (North of Toulouse);

Albigeois = Tarn (East of Toulouse);

Toulousain = Haute-Garonne, Tarn-et-Garonne, Tarn, Ariège.

However, the fact that the *Daurel* scribe used the *scripta* of this area does not necessarily prove that he was born in or around Toulouse. As we shall see, it would not be inconceivable for a Gascon to have written flawlessly in this *scripta*, betraying his origin, if, at all, by the slightest of slips. With this possibility in mind, we cannot state with certainty that the scribe was a native of the Toulouse region; we can, however, characterize his choice of written language as being that of Toulouse, Albi and Quercy.

It is interesting to return to Paul Meyer's conclusions, which, although based on somewhat different evidence, indicate the same general area. According to Meyer, the scribe was a native of the area included in the regions of Lot, Tarn-et-Garonne, the northern part of Haute-Garonne, Aude, Tarn, and the western part of Hérault. [7]

Unlike Poitou, where French gained hegemony as the official language from 1250 on, Toulouse, although a seat of government, retained its local dialect until the fifteenth century, allowing French only an official position overshadowed by Latin. [8] The vitality of the Toulousain *scripta* is almost certainly responsible for the transmission of *Daurel,* since elsewhere during the fourteenth century, a MS in southern dialect would either have been ignored or translated into northern French.

WAS THE *Daurel* SCRIBE A GASCON?

The similarity between the scribe's initial *b*'s and *v*'s led Meyer (who reads *bay* and *benga* in v. 1093 — a verse so much in error

---

[6] Cf. Grafström, *Étude*, pp. 16-24.

[7] Meyer, *Daurel*, p. lxv.

[8] A. Brun, *Recherches historiques sur l'introduction du Français dans les provinces du midi* (Paris, 1923), pp. 194-195. Cf. Ch.-Th. Gossen, «De l'histoire des langues écrites du domaine d'oïl,» *RLiR,* XXVI (1962), 272.

that it is obviously due to the scribe — and *ban* 1608) to conclude that the scribe, although not a Gascon, could not have come from a region north of Agde or east of Aveyron.[9] The absence of third person plural verb endings in *-en* and the hesitation between *ai* and *ei* or *iei* allowed him to further limit this region to the northern section of Haute-Garonne and the Tarn. This localization is further supported by the use of preterits in *-ec* used concurrently with forms in *-et* (e.g., *trobec* 61 *trobet* 226), which, if attributable to the scribe, points to Albi, Toulouse and Foix, since the *-ec* preterit appears to have been limited to this area in the thirteenth and fourteenth centuries.[10]

Chabaneau disagrees with Meyer's dismissal of the possibility that the scribe was a Gascon and lists many traits which, while not limited to the region between the Garonne and the Pyrenees, are not found as a group except in the texts of this area:[11]

arculimen 54, *arculhir* 116;[12] *Dauretz* 651;[13] *Sen Alari* 749;[14] *fort* (= *fors*) MS 646; *romper* (= *rompre*) 1318; *ceze* (= *sezer*) 1640, *traje* (= *tracher*) or *trade* [the reading is not certain] 2039; the effacement of final *r* in such cases is found only in Gascon territory at this date; *ente* 438 *aute* 30, *voste* 52: Chabaneau finds these forms in thirteenth and fourteenth century documents which are all of Gascon

---

[9] Meyer, *Daurel*, pp. lxiii-lxv.

[10] Meyer, *Daurel*, p. lxiii, cites numerous texts in support of this hypothesis. Cf. Jean Boutière, «Les 3ᵉ personnes du singulier en *a* des parfaits de 1ᵉ conjugaison dans les 'Biographies' des troubadours,» *RLiR*, XXVIII (1964), 1-11. Boutière discusses the presence — besides the usual 3rd person sing. in *-et* — of a certain number of forms in *-a*. According to B., «normales en français, usuelles dans une partie du domaine gascon (surtout Béarn du Centre et de l'Ouest), en catalan et dans quelques dialectes de l'Italie du Nord, les formes en *-a* apparaissent notamment, en pays d'Oc, dans *G. de la Barre, Daurel et Beton, Girart de Roussillon*, la *Vie de sainte Enimie* et la *Nobla Leiçon*, et aussi dans les "Biographies" des Troubadours» (1). B. concludes that these forms are due to scribes (10). Unfortunately, it is impossible to distinguish the *-a* forms in *Daurel* as preterits, since they can just as well be presents.

[11] Chabaneau, *RLR*, XX, 248-249.

[12] Grafström, *Étude*, p. 88, cites the syncope of *re-* (as in Toul. *derlinquiro* [from *derelinquere*]) as a Toulousain trait.

[13] T. Scharten, «La Posizione linguistica de 'Poitou'», *Studj Romanzi*, XXIX (1942), 77, lists *-et* from *-ellus* as a Gascon trait, distinct from the characteristic *-el* found in Languedoc. In Poitou, however, *-eau* alternates with the southern form.

[14] Grafström, *Étude*, p. 206 finds the forms *sent, sen* (alternating with *sainz*) very common in Toulousain and present in Agenais.

origin; *remado* 1292; *de questa* (= *d'aquesta*) 1189; *lu* (= *lui*) 500; [15]
los (plural dative pronoun) 1392 1576; *ba* (= *o*) MS 1437; *daries*
(= *dariatz*) 183; *pagaram* 775, *trobaram* 1295, *vieuratz* 214, *auziratz*
1918 (= *-rem, -retz*); [16] *fon* (from *fuerunt*) 76; *-ec* preterits: found,
in addition to the territory mentioned by Meyer, in the Gascon part
of the Haute-Garonne; *e* (= *ai*) 1185, *trobe* (= *trobei*) 748; *peuis*
(= *pois*) 47: early examples of this trait are found in texts which are
purely and frankly Gascon, according to Chabaneau; *lains* 1394,
1403 (in an *-ens* laisse); [17] *aprot* 728; hesitation between *b* and *v*;
use of *h* for *n* + palatal, and contrasting use of *nh* for *n*; *tz* reduced
to *t* in second person plural verbs.

Is the evidence presented by Chabaneau convincing enough to
support his assertion that «l'unique copie de *Beton* que l'on connaisse
est l'ouvrage d'un homme qui parlait gascon, ou qu'elle dérive d'un
exemplaire transcrit par un Gascon.»? [18] We have seen that many
of the traits listed by Chabaneau are, in his own words, not limited
to Gascony; indeed, many of them point to Toulouse and lend
credence to the already-drawn assumption that the scribe used the
written language of that area.

However, as Kurt Baldinger has shown in his study of Old Gascon
documents, the written language of a scribe does not necessarily
reflect his spoken language, especially in the case of the Gascon scribe,
who used standard Old Provençal as his model. [19] Thus, the rarity
of Gascon traits in Gascon charts is explained by the fact that there
is no *scripta* which could be called Gascon. The Gascon notary avoided
using his mother tongue while writing, by modelling his written language after Old Provençal, Latin, and later on, French. These models
provoked hypercorrect forms, which are of great interest in determining
the relationship between dialect and model, and among the models
themselves. For example, one finds, dating from the twelfth century,

---

[15] Grafström, *Étude*, p. 85, cites this form in Toulousain. Cf. the *le*
(Toul.) *lu* (Alb.) frontier in Mod. Alb. dialect in E. Nègre, «Traits caractéristiques de l'Albigeois,» *RLiR*, XXVIII (1964), 91-92.

[16] Grafström, *Étude*, pp. 46-52, indicates that the alternance of *a* and *e* is
common in Foix and Toulouse.

[17] Grafström, *Étude*, pp. 52-64. The alternance of *e* and *i* is widespread,
and especially common in Toulouse, Albi and Quercy.

[18] Chabaneau, *RLR*, XX, 249.

[19] Kurt Baldinger, «La langue des documents en ancien gascon,» *RLiR*,
XXVI (1962), 332-335.

the graphy -*au* for -*o*-: *austage* 'otage', *aunor* 'honneur'; in *Daurel*, *Augier* 146 'Ogier'. The notaries knew that French -*o*- often corresponded with Old Provençal -*au*-; being mistrustful of the -*o*-, which they thought to be French, they transcribed it as -*au*-, following the Provençal model. [20] However, *Augier* represents the normal Provençal form of *Autcharius* (cf. *Girart, Auchier*) rather than a hypercorrection due to a Gascon scribe; thus, this form proves nothing about the *Daurel* scribe.

Although the Gascon traits in *Daurel* are few, they are supported by the history of the Didot MS and the evidence presented by Baldinger. The location of the Didot MS, which is far more Gascon in character in its earlier accretions, at Arifat (Castres), seventy-two km. to the east of Toulouse in 1442, and possibly in Touget (Lombez), fifty km. to the west of Toulouse a century earlier, in other words, in proximity to the Gascon domaine, as well as the fact that most of the traits noted as Gascon can be attributed to the scribe, lead to the conclusion that *Daurel* was copied by a man of Gascon origin, living and working in the Toulouse region. Perhaps Arnadi Glibi of Touget, who possessed the first five sections of the Didot MS in 1345, added *Daurel* himself (or had it copied by one of his students); however, since his name is nowhere present in the *Daurel* folios, this must remain pure hypothesis.

Lacking the final verses of the poem, which ordinarily would be followed by the name of the scribe and the date of execution, one can only speculate that *Daurel* was added to the MS in the mid-fourteenth century at Touget, or, as seems more likely given the Gascon character of the Didot MS (with the exception of *Daurel*), that the MS was carried from Gascony to Arifat (Castres), where *Daurel* was copied by a mid-fourteenth-century scribe who wrote the written language of the Toulouse region, but who was either of Gascon stock or acquainted with Gascon dialect.

---

[20] Baldinger, *RLiR*, XXVI, 346.

CHAPTER V

DATE AND PLACE OF COMPOSITION

In the notes on versification, I have tentatively established a *ter-minus a quo* of 1130, which appears to be the earliest conceivable date for the composition of *Daurel* in rhymed laisses. The *terminus ad quem* is more easily fixed by the clear reference to *Daurel et Beton* found in the *Ensenhamen* of Guiraut de Cabrera:

> Ja de Mauran
> on no·t deman
> ni de Daurel ni de Beton. [1]

According to Riquer, this poem, which enumerates the literary works in Cabrera's repertory supposedly unknown to his *jongleur* Cabra, was composed as early as 1150, but not later than 1168. Guiraut refers to four troubadours in verses 25-30 of his *Ensenhamen*: Jaufré Rudel, Marcabru, Eble II de Ventadour and a certain Anfos, whose identification remains doubtful. The production of both Rudel and Marcabru ceased around 1150, yet Guiraut speaks of *vers novel Bon d'En Rudell* and apparently knew Marcabru personally. The work of Eble de Ventadour is attested between 1096 and 1147. [2] On the other hand, nowhere does he mention Raimbaut d'Orange, Bernart de Ventadorn, Giraut de Bornelh or Bertran de Born. If Cabrera had written his poem around 1170, he would hardly have omitted them from his cat-

---

[1] Martín de Riquer, *Les Chansons de geste françaises*, 2nd ed. (Paris, 1957), pp. 332-351. The reference is found in verse 120 of the *Ensenhamen*.
[2] A. Jeanroy, *La poésie lyrique des troubadours* (Toulouse/Paris, 1934), I, 156.

alogue. Nor does he mention a fellow Catalan, Guilhem de Berguedan, who wrote between 1172 and 1192.[3]

The *Ensenhamen* must have been written after 1130-1140, the date of the *Canso d'Antiocha,* mentioned in verse 124. The allusions to the *Estoire de Troie* (c. 1155) and to the pre-1150 troubadours are solid arguments in favor of the 1150 date proposed by Irénée Cluzel.[4] Riquer, however, chooses to be more prudent and sets the *terminus a quo* at 1155, the *terminus ad quem* at 1168 (or 1170), the probable date of Guiraut's death.[5]

In his *Ensenhamen,* Cabrera alludes to a large number of epics, most of which have been satisfactorily identified: *Aigar et Maurin, Aiol et Mirabel, Amis et Amile, Anseis de Cartage, Aye d'Avignon, Beuve de Hantone* [see *infra*], *Daurel et Beton, Elie de Saint-Gilles, Girart de Rossilho, Gormont et Isembart, Mainet, Ogier, Raoul de Cambrai, Roncevaux, Saisnes.*[6] It appears that the feudal epics, among which I shall attempt to situate *Daurel,* were in vogue as early as 1150, but that sequels such as *Jourdain de Blaye* and *Gui de Nanteuil* did not yet exist. These latter may not have been written until after 1168, since they are not mentioned in the *Ensenhamen.* Guiraut's evident familiarity with the southern epic should be noted: all three that have come down to us are mentioned.

Riquer's identification of *Beuve de Hantone* is not beyond question, since it is based on verse 138:

> ni de Bernart
> ni de Girart.
> De Viviana ni de Bovon,

Instead of Viviana, according to Riquer, the poet intended to say Josiane, heroine of *Beuve.*[7] It should, however, be recalled that *Aiol*

---

[3] Riquer, *Chansons de geste,* pp. 335-339. Guilhem de Berguedan was a friend of Ponç de Cabrera, who was thought by Milá y Fontanals to have composed the *Ensenhamen.* According to Riquer, the father of Ponç, Guerau III Ponç de Cabrera, is most likely the author of the *Ensenhamen,* since he is the only Cabrera who could have known Marcabru before 1150 and who presumably died in 1168 or 1170.

[4] «A propos de l'*Ensenhamen* du troubadour catalan G. de C.,» in *Boletín de la Real Ac. de Buenas Letras de Barcelona,* XXVI (1954-56), 87-93.

[5] Riquer, *Chansons de geste,* p. 338.

[6] Riquer, *Chansons de geste,* p. 340.

[7] Riquer, *Chansons de geste,* p. 347 (note 138).

includes a Bevon de Viane. Moreover, *Amis, Saisnes, Aymeri de Narbonne, Aye,* and many other poems, including *Daurel,* have characters named Beuve.[8] Still, while the *Ensenhamen* contains other, more conclusive references to the epics mentioned above, it has none alluding to *Beuve de Hantone,* while three of the names immediately preceding Bovon and Viviana refer to characters found in *Aigar* and *Girart.* Thus, there is sufficient reason to doubt Riquer's attribution, and to postulate that Cabrera, when he wrote the name Bovon, had in mind Boves d'Antona, father of Beton. Viviana poses a problem, since the feminine form of the name is rare in epic, but several examples of Viviane or Niniane are found in later Arthurian romances.[9]

The dating of epics is a hazardous task, since, with the notable exception of the Digby 23 MS of the *Roland,* extant MSS are posterior to 1200. André Burger, debating Bédier's hypothesis that epic production was concentrated between 1050 and 1150, suggests that the majority of the poems, except for *Roland, Guillaume* and *Gormont,* were composed after 1150 in their present forms.[10] Since it would be useful to determine which of these epics may have influenced *Daurel,* I propose the following chronology, based on Cabrera's testimony, historical tradition (*Ogier, Raoul* and *Girart* legends), and the datings generally accepted by modern scholarship:[11]

---

[8] Ernest Langlois, *Table des noms propres de toute nature compris dans les chansons de geste imprimées* (Paris, 1904), pp. 120-122.

[9] L.-F. Flutre, *Table des noms propres avec toutes leurs variantes figurant dans les romans du moyen âge écrits en français ou en provençal et actuellement publiés ou analysés* (Poitiers, 1962), p. 146. See discussion of MS Viviane, the source of the enigma, by Michel Rousse, «Niniane en Petite-Bretagne,» *Bulletin Bibliographique de la Société Internationale Arthurienne,* No. 16 (1964), 107-120.

[10] Andre Burger, «La Question rolandienne: faits et hypothèses,» *CCM,* (1961), 270.

[11] Raphael Levy, «Chronologie approximative de la littérature française du moyen âge,» Beiheft 98 zur *ZRPh* (1957); Paul Zumthor, *Histoire littéraire de la France médiévale: VI*e*-XIV*e *siècles* (Paris, 1954), pp. 209-211; Urban T. Holmes, Jr., *A History of Old French Literature From the Origins to 1300,* new ed. (New York, 1962), pp. 90-122. Levy's work, which takes into account the findings and opinions of Gröber, Voretzsch, Bossuat, Holmes, Zumthor and others, remains the most useful study of its kind now available, although it has been criticized, notably by H. Tiemann, «Die Datierungen der altfranzösischen Literatur,» in *Romanistisches Jahrbuch,* VIII (1957), 110-131. Cf. L.'s rebuttal and T.'s counter-rebuttal in *Romanistisches Jahrbuch,* X (1959), 39-58.

Before 1130: *Roland, Gormont.*

Before 1160 (earlier versions may have existed before 1130) and mentioned by Cabrera: *Girart, Aye, Ogier, Amis, Raoul.* [12]

Before 1168 (possibly before 1150) based on the *Ensenhamen*: *Aigar, Daurel, Aiol, Mainet,* and possibly *Orson* and *Aymeri.* [13]

After 1190: *Beuve de Hantone, Jourdain de Blaye, Gui de Nanteuil, Doon de la Roche.* [14]

It is obvious that these dates reflect cautious interpretation of manuscript filiations and literary allusions. Nevertheless, the *terminus ad quem* of 1168 proposed for *Daurel* is indeed earlier than the dates assigned to *Amis, Aye,* and *Raoul* by Zumthor and Levy, who ignore the testimony of the *Ensenhamen,* although these poems were almost certainly anterior or contemporary to *Daurel.* On the other hand, *Beuve* and *Jourdain,* in their extant forms dated no earlier than 1200, and not convincingly attested before that date, could hardly have influenced *Daurel.*

Leaving aside for the moment the question of filiation, which has for so long clouded its reputation, *Daurel* could have existed as early as 1130 and was manifestly known to Cabrera between 1150 and 1168. One would accordingly expect *Daurel* to share names, places, and events with other epics of that period and to have certain links with the earlier traditions represented by *Roland* and *Gormont.* As a feudal epic, *Daurel* would be expected to resemble *Girart, Ogier* and *Raoul* in at least some respects. If Daurel belongs to and depends on this earlier tradition, one could reasonably propose a date of composition as early as 1150.

i. Onomastics and Toponymy

The *Daurel* author linked his poem, which has no known historical basis, with early epic tradition, represented by *Roland* and *Gormont,*

---

[12] In her edition of *Girart* (III, 478-480), Miss Hackett proposes the dates 1136-1180. The extant versions of *Ogier, Aye* and *Amis* probably did not exist before 1200, although Levy accepts Holmes «after 1160» for a primitive version of *Aye.* Levy and Zumthor propose 1180 for *Raoul.*

[13] *Daurel* is dated 1180-1200 by Zumthor; «possibly as early as 1170» by Holmes, accepting Meyer's conclusion. Levy, who does not date *Daurel,* proposes 1180 for the *Mort Aymeri,* 1210 for *Orson.*

[14] Neither *Beuve* nor *Jourdain* is dated before 1200 by Levy, Holmes or Zumthor.

and with southern-oriented legends of respectable historical tradition, typified by *Girart* and *Ogier,* by making use of many of the names found in these works. But, unlike the authors of epics such as *Doon de Mayence,* written around 1200, he made no attempt to set up a complicated genealogy linking his characters to a particular cycle or family of epics. Nor did he need to draw his subject matter directly from history, since the *Roland, Guillaume, Ogier, Raoul,* and *Girart* legends offered ample quasi-historical situations for a hundred epics. Research into these legends has re-opened the old debate on the origin of the *chanson de geste* and has led to a re-evaluation of the rôle of the South in its creation and evolution. [15]

The toponyms fall into three categories:

(1) those commonplace in the epic: one finds numerous examples in Langlois, including in most cases, *Roland, Girart, Ogier:* [16]

> Antona (*Girart, Roland*)
> Ardena (*Girart, Roland*)
> Aspremont (*Aye, Roland, Girart* Montaspel)
> Brunas Vals (*Renaut, Aye* Valbrun)
> Fransa (*Roland, Ogier, Girart*)
> Monclar (*Ogier, Girart* Beuclar)
> Paris [as capital] (*Ogier, Girart*)

---

[15] Since the link between *Daurel* and history is at most a tenuous and second-hand one and is of no aid in dating the poem, this subject is beyond the scope of the present work. See R. Lejeune, *Recherches sur le thème: les Chansons de geste et l'histoire,* Bibliothèque de la Faculté de Philosophie et Lettres de l'Université de Liège, fasc. CVIII (Liège, 1948), esp. p. 156 concerning the Provençal epic and the possibility that it predates the northern one; p. 154 dealing with Boson, king of Provence in 876; chap. IV, i, «Ogier et la Provence,» in which she presents proof linking Ogier with the South of France. See also: F. Lot, *Etudes sur les légendes épiques françaises* (Paris, 1958). A collection of Lot's articles on *Raoul, Girart, Gormont, Guillaume, Ogier,* and *Roland* in history and legend.

René Louis, *De l'Histoire,* on the *Girart* legend.

Pauline Matarasso (*Recherches historiques et littéraires sur «Raoul de Cambrai»* [Paris, 1962]) takes up the question of the origins and evolution of the legend, passing in review the theses of Longnon, Paris, Bédier, Acher, Lot, in an attempt to arrive at «le juste milieu.»

Reto R. Bezzola, *Les Origines et la formation de la littérature courtoise en occident* (Paris, 1958-60), II, 485 ff., «De l'Epopée féodale au début du roman courtois.»

[16] Langlois, *Table.* See also Willy Schober, *Die Geographie der altfranzösischen Chansons de Geste* (Diss. Marburg, 1902), I, under *Agen, Agenois, Ardenne, Aspremont.*

(2) exotic place names:

> Babilonia (*Roland, Ogier, Girart*)
> Tir (*Roland, Ogier, Girart*)

(3) southern place names: these are much less common in the epic than are the first two categories:

> Agen (*Girart, Ogier, Aigar*)
> Bordels (*Girart*)
> Peitieus (*Girart, Ogier*)
> Sant-Alari (mentioned only in *Daurel*)

Since the first two categories represent the conventionalized geography of the *chanson de geste,* they are of little value in determining the origin of *Daurel.* The third one, however, is more helpful. Most of the action in *Daurel,* with the exception of the voyages to Paris and to the Orient, takes place in the area between Poitiers, Bordeaux and Agen, the area given to Beuve as a dowry by Charlemagne. It is at Saint-Hilaire de Poitiers, for example, that Beuve and Daurelet are buried, Beton and Erimena married (vv. 135-136, 200-201, 531, 749, 2083). It is significant that Saint-Hilaire is mentioned in no other epic, and is thus the only place-name that the *Daurel* author could not have borrowed from epic tradition, and, more specifically, from the *Girart, Ogier,* and *Roland* legends.

The author composed his poem in the language of this region of France, presumably for an audience which would understand it; therefore, it would be reasonable to expect him to have been geographically accurate when dealing with places familiar to his listeners. Unfortunately, his descriptions are too vague to permit anything but the most tenuous of identifications once we leave Poitiers and Saint-Hilaire in order to seek out a Monclar or Aspremont in this area that would fit the poem. We assume that, having associated *Daurel* with Poitiers, he was content to borrow conventional place-names from works such as *Girart,* for example, or from the general toponymy of the Midi. *Girart* contains, in some form at least, all but one of the place-names found in *Daurel* and in addition provides one of the few credible explanations for the unusual personal name Beton, which appears both as the name of a character (Beton is the father of Isembart d'Aunon) and as the site of an important battle (Valbeton or Vaubeton).

Even the more stylized geographical names, so common in the epic, can be related to the South of France. The Ardennes, traditionally the deep forest, the repair of outlaws, the site most suitable for murder and treachery, can be located anywhere in France. [17] And in at least one poem, *Renaut de Montauban*, Ardene represents a forest near Bordeaux. [18] Nor need one look to Hampton in England to find the model for Antona, Bove's castle. Antoine is a common family name in the epic and Antonniat is found as a place-name in the Dordogne. [19]

Actually, Hamtone or Hantone appears in the epic only in the early thirteenth-century *Beuve de Hantone* and *Doon de Mayence*. The Anglo-Norman version of *Beuve* may have been responsible for the deformation of Antone into Haumtone, although it is also reasonable to asssume that the change was made under the influence of the courtly romance. In *Cligés* and *Perceval*, for example, Hanthone (= Southampton) is found as a castle in Great Britain. [20] There is no evidence to link the Antona of Duke Bove in *Daurel* with the Hantone in *Beuve*.

Aspremont, Guy's castle, is a name commonly given to the home of a traitor (e.g., in *Gaidon, Galien, Mort Garin*) as well as to a battleground where the French fought the Saracens in the South of Italy (*Roland* Paris MS, *Saisnes, Ogier*). [21] In modern France, there are two Aspremonts, both in the South, one near Gap and the other near Nice. Monclar, the name of Daurel's castle, is a common place-name in the epic and in the Midi. There are Monclars in the Basses-Alpes, Aude, and, more pertinently, Aveyron. [22]

The name Daurel, found nowhere else in the epic, is listed by Dauzat as meaning «originaire d'Aurel (Drôme, Vaucluse);» similarly,

---

[17] William C. Calin, *The Old French Epic of Revolt: Raoul de Cambrai, Renaud de Montauban, Gormond et Isembard* (Geneva/Paris, 1962), p. 188.

[18] Langlois, *Table*, p. 46.

[19] A. Dauzat, *Dictionnaire étymologique des noms de famille et prénoms en France* (Paris, 1951), p. 10, cites «la localité Antony (région parisienne: ancien *Antoniacum* gallo-romain, 'domaine d'Antonius').»

Auguste Longnon, *Les Noms de lieu de la France* (Paris, 1920), p. 211, lists under *Antoniacus*: Antony (Seine), Antogny (Indre-et-Loire), Antoigny (Orne), Antoigné (Maine-et-Loire), Antonniat (Dordogne).

[20] Langlois, *Table*, p. 324; Flutre, *Table*, p. 250.

[21] Langlois, *Table*, p. 50.

[22] *Dictionnaire national des Communes de France* (Paris, 1959).

Daurelle refers to the town of Aurelle (Aveyron).[23] In addition, the troubadour Bertran d'Aurel is a possible source for the name Daurel, although it is probably a coincidence that the former is a troubadour and the latter a fictional *jongleur*.[24]

The identifications of Aurelle and Monclar, although tenuous (since in our poem Daurel is used only as a proper name and Monclar is described as being on the sea), point towards the Southwest, and, more specifically, the Aveyron. The existence of a Monclar-d'Agenais in Lot-et-Garonne and an Antonniat in the Dordogne indicates the area between Agen and Bordeaux. In view of the author's manifest familiarity with Poitiers, these facts take on some significance. Was it by coincidence that the *Daurel* author used geographical names found in southwestern France, wrote a dialect of that area, and is the only epic *jongleur* to mention Saint-Hilaire de Poitiers? There is no irrefutable proof that he was a Poitevin, but the evidence supports this hypothesis.

Although the poem has strong linguistic and geographic roots in the area between Poitiers, Bordeaux and Agen (the extent of Beuve's fief in *Daurel*), the author drew freely on personal and place names common in epic literature. A brief onomastic analysis supports the thesis that the *Daurel* author borrowed primarily from the earlier epic tradition represented by *Roland, Gormont, Ogier,* and *Girart*. The personal names, like the toponyms, fall into three categories:

(1) those commonplace in epic and (with the exception of Biatris, found in *Girart* and *Ogier*) associated with the *Roland* tradition: Augier, Biatris, Boves, Carles, Guis, Olivier, Requier, Rolan.

(2) exotic names:

Erimena (cf. *Roland* Ermines 'Armenians.' Historically, Ermina was one of King Dagobert's daughters).[25]

---

[23] Dauzat, *Dictionnaire des noms,* p. 178. Cf. Werner Kalbow, *Die germanischen Personennamen des altfranzösischen Heldenepos* (Halle, 1913), who etymologizes *Diurilo + ellus* for Daurel.

[24] Meyer, *Daurel,* p. xxx; see also Clovis Brunel, *Les plus anciennes chartes en langue provençal: Supplément* (Paris, 1952), p. 182.

[25] Ernst Förstemann, *Altdeutsches Namenbuch* (Bonn, 1900), I, cols. 470-485, Erma, Ermin, etc. Cf. Franz Settegast, «Armenisches im *Daurel et Beton*,» *ZRPh,* XXIX (1905), 413-414, who suggests, on basis of name Erimena (= 'Armenia'), *Hermen* as reading for *amic* or *danne* (*Daurel,* v. 146), in an attempt to link Beton (from Bagrat, the name of an Armenian king, according to Settegast) to Armenia. However, there are a good number of examples of the name Ermin and its derivatives, usually in masculine form,

Gormons (*Gormont et Isembart*). [26]

(3) Names of southern origin or form:

Abram or Ebrartz (*Ogier, Roland* Abirun). [27]

Aicelina (*Girart, Roland, Orson, Raoul* Acelin). [28]

Azemars (*Girart* Aïmar, *Ogier* Aymer)

Bertran (*Girart, Ogier, Roland* Paris MS)

Beton: Although the name Begon is common in the epic and in history, it would be difficult to accept the substitution of *t* for *g* in such a widely-known name. *Girart*, which contains the only other example of the name, appears to be the sole logical source of Beton. [29]

Daurel, Daurelet (found only in *Daurel*; see pp. 40-41).

Esmenjartz: a common name in epic and history (usually as Hermant or Hermenjart). It is perhaps significant that Hermingarde, the wife of Louis le Debonaire, is attested as a patron of Saint-Hilaire de Poitiers in 808. [30]

Gauserans (*Ogier, Girart, Roland*): common only in OFr. Joserant.

Jaufré (*Ogier, Girart, Roland*): common only in OFr. Joffroi and Godefroi.

The majority of personal names are common and lead to no significant conclusion about relationships between *Daurel* and other epics. However, as in the case of the place-names, almost all can be found in some form or another in *Roland, Girart*, and *Ogier*. The use of the

---

in Langlois, *Table*, p. 193, and Flutre, *Table*, p. 69 (n.b. Ermin, a king in the *Roman d'Arles*).

[26] Langlois, *Table*, p. 295, also lists *Aymeri, Hugues Capet*, and *Enfances Vivien* for this name, which is not common in the epic.

[27] Langlois, *Table*, pp. 2-3, lists several exs. of Abraham, none of Ebrartz. For Abirun (= a biblical character who revolted against Moses) cf. J. Bédier, *La Chanson de Roland commentée* (Paris, 1927), p. 505.

Paul Lévy, *Les Noms des Israélites en France* (Paris, 1960), p. 99, notes that the name Abram is attested in Marseille as early as 1486, but that Abraham dates from 777; Abramon is found in Carpentras in 1276.

[28] Aicelina in the feminine appears nowhere else in the epic except as the wife of *Orson de Beauvais* (Aceline). Kalbow, *Die germanischen Personennamen*, p. 57, explains the form Aisilineta as a double diminutive similar to Amelinette, *Azza + ila + ina + itta* or *eta*. Cf. Dauzat, *Dictionnaire des noms*, p. 19, «*Aza* (Calvados) anc. n. de bapt.: du norrois *Asa*, nom de divinité.»

[29] Langlois, *Table*, pp. 81-82; R. LeJeune, *Recherches*, p. 154. Förstemann, *Altdeutsches Namenbuch*, I, cols. 224-226, lists *Beto* under stems *Bado* and *Badu*, < OHG *beadu*, ON *Bôdh* (= 'hampf').

[30] Alfred Richard, *Histoire des Comtes de Poitou* (Paris, 1903), I, 8 (note).

name Gormons for a Saracen king may indicate that the author was
familiar in some way with the oldest feudal epic, attested as early as
1125. The use of southern forms of personal names such as Jaufré,
Gauserans, Azemar, and Requier would be difficult to explain if the
author were copying or imitating a northern text, since he did not
hesitate to use northern forms, such as those taken from the *Roland,*
and was not averse to flavoring his poem with rhymes and words of
northern character. It is worth noting that he chose for his main
characters very uncommon names: Daurel and Beton, and that these
names can be attached only to the South. Thus, an important number
of the personal and place-names in *Daurel* are linked to the author's
meridional environment; the remainder are part of the mid-twelfth-
century epic tradition, with which he was obviously familiar. The
dating of *Daurel* does not depend on supposed or suspected ties with
epics written after 1170, judging from the evidence presented by the
personal and place-names.

ii. Two Epics: Daurel and Beuve

There is no doubt that *Daurel* is linked to epic tradition, but the
mere fact that it shares basic themes and situations with other *chansons
de geste* is hardly sufficient proof either that *Daurel* is an imitation
of them or that the reverse is true. The regional character in itself of
Daurel serves to set it apart from the others, as does the author's
originality in his treatment of certain themes (see Chapter VIII, vi).
Daurel can be termed an epic of primitive feudalism, but this alone
is no guarantee of antiquity. The Scandinavian epics, for example,
which reflect a very primitive society, are not necessarily at the origin
of those written in Germany.[31] Episodes such as the murder of Bove
by his sworn companion, the disinheriting and ensuing exile of Beton,
the injustice of Charlemagne could have occurred in the context of the
twelfth century as well as in the ninth and would have been considered
acts of tyranny in either period.[32]

---

[31] W. T. H. Jackson, *The Literature of the Middle Ages* (New York,
1960), p. 176.

[32] Calin (*Epic of Revolt,* p. 124) discussing similar episodes, adds that
«such 'primitive realism' is, as often as not, just another form of epic
stylization.»

The feudal epic generally reflects the period of political and social anarchy extending into the second half of the eleventh century and following on the decline of the Carolingians. *Girart, Raoul, Ogier* and *Gormont,* though products of the twelfth century, are based upon historical events which took place in the period between 750 and 950. One might add that the glorification of the rebel baron in the epic is more or less contemporary with the corresponding decline in importance, grandeur, and power of the feudal lord, since the twelfth century marks the beginning of a gradual extension of royal influence and sovereignty destined to destroy feudalism. Just as the *Roland* glorified Charlemagne and nationalism in an age when royal power was at a low ebb, the twelfth-century *jongleur* wrote epics in praise of barons who had rebelled against the abuses and injustices of this sovereignty precisely at a time when the feudal lord was being stripped of his ability to resist them.

Since the provinces in general and the South of France in particular were the last strongholds of the older forms of feudalism, it is not surprising that the feudal epic prospered there. It is precisely in the South, more specifically, in Aquitaine, that we find the brand of feudalism, the regional patriotism, the fight against central authority, the devotion to *seigneur* rather than to *suzerain* that characterize the feudal cycle. Epics such as *Girart,* perhaps the finest of the feudal *chansons,* and *Daurel,* to a lesser degree, prove the existence of a meridional epic tradition based on the very lack of political unity, of a rallying point for growing nationalistic feelings, of a hero such as Roland or Charlemagne, which caused H. J. Chaytor to declare the epic genre «not native to the genius of southern France.» [33] This charge, echoed by several generations of scholars, can be traced back to L. Gautier's incomplete and one-sided analysis of epic literature in Provençal entitled: «Il n'y a point d'épopée provençale.» [34] Nyrop, writing a few years later, also questioned the existence of the southern epic, considering *Daurel* as a northern-influenced poem which does not support the arguments for the existence of a great Provençal epic

---

[33] *The Provençal Chanson de Geste* (London, 1946), p. 17; *From Script to Print: An Introduction to Medieval Literature* (Cambridge, Eng., 1945), pp. 37-38.

[34] *Épopées,* I, chap. 18. Gautier's romantic view of the Middle Ages and his religious interpretation of the epic have been largely discredited by modern scholarship.

tradition.[35] Since the late nineteenth century, manuals on medieval literature have usually been content to accept Gautier's assertion that *Daurel* is little more than a poor imitation of *Beuve de Hantone*. Riquer, for example, describes *Daurel* as a Provençal imitation of an earlier *Beuve* now lost.[36] In a later chapter we intend to show that the resemblances between *Daurel* and *Beuve* are superficial. Both are feudal epics and share many of the commonplace features of the genre, but there is no real evidence indicating any close relationship between them.

I cite Riquer to demonstrate how the existence of the name Boves d'Antona in *Daurel* has prejudiced the dating of both epics:

> De cette chanson [*Beuve de Hantone*], on conserve une version fragmentaire anglonormande du XIIe siècle et deux versions du siècle suivant. Tant C. Boje que Becker considèrent que la rédaction continentale est postérieure à 1200, opinion à quoi s'opposent de sérieux arguments, parmi lesquels: l'existence d'une imitation provençale intitulée *Daurel et Beton*, qu'on regarde comme écrite entre 1170 et 1200; une claire référence à *Buf d'Antona* faite par le troubadour catalan Guilhem de Berguedan dans une poésie écrite entre 1187 et 1190; et le sirventés du troubadour Guiraut de Luc, en strophes de décasyllabes qui devaient être chantés *el son de Boves d'Antona*, et qui a été composé entre 1191 et 1194. Tout cela est corroboré par deux autres références de l'*ensenhamen* de Guiraut de Cabrera.[37]

It is true that *Beuve*, a *roman d'aventures* with a complicated episodic plot more to the taste of the thirteenth century, enjoyed a tremendous popularity throughout Europe, while *Daurel* remained localized in southwestern France. This is not at all surprising when one considers

---

[35] Cristoforo Nyrop, *Storia dell'epopea francese nel medio evo*, trans. by Egidio Gorra (Torino, 1888), pp. 150-151; Appendice I.

[36] *Chansons de geste*, pp. 273-275.

[37] *Chansons de geste*, pp. 274-275. Riquer's references are to: C. Boje, *Die Uberlieferung des... Beuve de Hamtone* (Kiel, 1908); Ph. Aug. Becker, «*Beuve de Hantone*,» *Berichte über die Verhandlungen der Sächsischen Akademie* (1941). Cf. Erich von Richthofen, *Estudios épicos medievales*, trans. by José Pérez Riesco, «Biblioteca Románica Hispánica» (Madrid, 1954), p. 80, who agrees with Becker that *Beuve* was written between 1215 and 1225, and certainly no earlier than 1200. Richthofen, who refers to *Daurel* as the «verdadero doblete del *Beuve*,» dates the former before 1240.

that *Girart,* firmly based in historical tradition, of authentic literary excellence, and written in a border dialect, nevertheless had to be translated into Burgundian before it could achieve popularity. It was unlikely that a northern audience would have listened with much interest or understanding to an epic in southern dialect. Thus, neither *Beuve*'s relative success nor *Daurel*'s lack of success is any proof of antiquity. Yet Riquer concludes from his study of Cabrera's *Ensenhamen* that, since *Daurel* may have existed by 1150 and certainly before 1168, at least one lost version of *Beuve* must have been written still earlier; in other words, that the popular *Beuve,* not attested convincingly by anyone before 1200, must have pre-dated the unsuccessful *Daurel.* It is interesting to note that all three pre-1200 references (to Bovon, Buf d'Antona and Boves d'Antona) are found in the works of Provençal and Catalan troubadours. Cabrera, who wrote at least twenty years earlier than Berguedan or Guiraut de Luc, knew *Daurel et Beton*: his reference is explicit. On the other hand, did he know *Beuve de Hantone*? Cabrera speaks of Bovon, a name which can, as we have already seen, refer to several epics, including *Daurel.* Guilhem de Berguedan, whose poem was an imitation of Cabrera's *Ensenhamen,* is more specific in referring to Buf d'Antona, which name could be interpreted as a reference to only two epics: *Daurel* or *Beuve.* It is noteworthy that both Berguedan and Guiraut de Luc wrote Antona, the form found in *Daurel,* not Hanstone or Haumtone; we have already seen that the *Daurel* author did not have to look to England for this place-name.

Was Guiraut de Luc alluding to *Daurel* when he noted that his decasyllabic strophes were to be sung to the tune of *Boves d'Antona*? Is it possible that a lost version of our poem, in which Bove would have played a greater rôle, was known to Berguedan and Luc under the title of *Boves d'Antona*? It is not uncommon for an epic to be named after one character, although most of the action revolves around another; such is the case with *Orson de Beauvais,* where the son Milon is a more important character than his father, Orson.

If *Beuve de Hantone* did not, indeed, exist before 1200, is it not logical to assume that two meridional poets, writing around 1190, were alluding to an epic composed in a southern dialect in the Southwest of France, a work manifestly known to their mentor Cabrera twenty years earlier, when they set down the name Boves d'Antona.

iii. Conclusion

Daurel et Beton was composed in the mid-twelfth century in or near Poitiers. It may have been in existence by 1150 or earlier and could not have been written later than 1168, depending on the date of Cabrera's *Ensenhamen,* the single valuable piece of evidence we possess in this regard. None of the elements studied so far in *Daurel* casts doubt on the mid-twelfth-century character of the poem.

The poet's desire to center his story in Poitiers and to associate it with the church of Saint-Hilaire is a strong indication of the poem's provenance, supported by the linguistic evidence reported in the chapter on language of the author. Like *Girart, Aigar,* and the *Croisade Albigeoise, Daurel* was written in a southwestern border-dialect, in the southern epic *koiné* which appears to be the product of the area between Poitiers and Bordeaux. [38]

The description of feudal society in the poem is consistent with what we know of twelfth-century Poitou. The Count of Poitou was hereditary abbot of Saint-Hilaire, and «held extensive lands, both allods and benefices.» [39] The history of this province is one long struggle

---

[38] Chaytor, *Provençal Chanson de geste,* p. 14; Louis, *De l'Histoire,* II, p. 276, p. 285; Scharten, *Studj Romanzi,* XXIX (1942), 118; Brun, *Recherches historiques,* p. 50. Alfred Brossmer (ed., «*Aigar et Maurin,* Bruchstücke einer Chanson de Geste,» *Romanische Forschungen,* XIV [1903], 44) situates *Daurel* «im Westen der 'Grenzdialekte,' vielleicht etwa in Poitou oder nördlichen Gascogne,» and links it linguistically to *Aigar,* esp. in the liberties taken with rhyme. Zumthor, *Histoire,* p. 210, describes *Daurel* as a poem «en langue mixte franco-occitane, sorte de roman d'aventure utilisant les prestiges orientaux, d'origine poitevine ou limousine...» Elsewhere, Zumthor (*Langue et techniques,* p. 79) remarks on the curious medieval concept that French was the narrative language 'par excellence,' while «l'occitan... est la langue par excellence de la poésie lyrique. C'est pourquoi, sans doute, il arriva souvent que l'on introduisit, comme pour les rehausser par cet ornement, dans des chansons françaises quelques éléments linguistiques provençaux. Mais ceux-ci n'atteignent jamais l'étendue d'une membre de phrase.» We have also seen the reverse in the epic, where the meridional poet chose a border-dialect *koiné,* easily understood by his southern audience, but with a distinctly northern flavor.

[39] Sidney Painter, «Castellans of the Plain of Poitou in the Eleventh and Twelfth Centuries,» *Speculum,* XXXI (1956), 244.

to retain feudal rights in the face of increasing centralization. [40] There is, unfortunately, no specific historical source that appears to have inspired the composition of *Daurel* and no mention of a particular event that would aid in dating the poem more accurately.

---

[40] Richard, *Comtes de Poitou*, I, covers rulers from 778 to 1126. See also Joseph Calmette, *Le Monde féodale* (Paris, 1951), p. 109; Marc Bloch, *La Société féodale* (Paris, 1949), II, 239-240.

CHAPTER VI

SUMMARY

(1-5) *Introduction*

The narrator invites the audience to listen to «a noble song» about a worthy duke of France, Count Guy, Daurel the *jongleur,* and Beton, who in his youth endured such suffering.

(6-30) *The Pact*

The wealthy Duke Bove of Antona, and Guy, an impoverished count whose sole possession is the castle of Aspremont, swear brotherhood in the presence of Bove's barons. In exchange for Guy's companionship and aid in managing his vast fief, Bove wills all his property, including his wife if the duke should marry and remain childless, to the traitorous Guy.

(31-109) *The Summons from Charlemagne*

For ten years Bove and Guy live together in harmony when one day, during court, a messenger arrives from Charlemagne requesting Bove's presence in Paris. Rewarding the messenger with the gift of a horse, Bove sends for Guy, who soon arrives from Aspremont, and the two companions prepare to depart.

Daurel, a poor *jongleur,* demonstrates his talent so skillfully that Bove asks him to accompany the party to Paris. Bove again displays his generosity by ordering his valet, Azemar, to provide for Daurel's wife and two sons during his absence, and to the *jongleur* himself gives a palfrey.

(110-173) *Bove's Marriage to Ermenjart*

Early Sunday morning, Bove, Guy and Daurel go to the court of the emperor who escorts Bove to the seat of honor, next to the throne. With his arm around Bove's neck, he explains why he has sent for him [and in return for his loyal service, offers him great wealth, an extensive fief, and his sister Ermenjart in marriage]. Guy mutters to himself ominously, «Companion, you will die because of that woman.»

In the presence of Roland and Oliver, the twelve peers and the «flower of nobility,» Charlemagne performs the marriage ceremony for Ermenjart and Bove. He makes Bove lord of Poitiers and Bordeaux; bearer of his battle flag (*gonfanier*) in the royal armies. As Bove accepts the hand of Ermenjart in marriage, Guy, the traitor, reiterates his threat under his breath.

Duke Bove and his company remain at court one month; he then takes leave of the emperor, who, at the duke's request, appoints Guy one of his counselors. Daurel entertains the court so well that the king of France rewards him with the gift of a stallion.

(174-201) *The Journey to Poitiers*

As Bove and his entourage return home, Guy, ostensibly in jest, says to the duke: «Companion, I'll tell you what is on my mind: My lady is lovely and has a fine figure, will you share her with me as agreed?» Bove suggests laughingly that Guy pray for his death, for then he will have her, since he desires her so greatly.

They enter Poitiers and are well received by their subjects. Bove grants Guy the command (and the income) of all of the land between Bordeaux and Agen.

(202-223) *Daurel's Reward*

Daurel receives an exemplary gift in exchange for his services; Bove grants the castle of Monclar to the *jongleur*, as a hereditary fief.

In the years that follow, Guy thinks only of amassing a large fortune, while Bove, whenever called upon, serves the emperor faithfully.

(224-274) *Guy Declares his Passion for Ermenjart*

One day, while Bove is out hunting, Guy visits Ermenjart, who receives him cordially. But, when he bluntly declares his passion for her and his intent to possess her immediately, she rejects him with horror. Furious, Guy swears to kill Bove within two months.

The duke returns home at dinnertime ; seeing his wife downcast, he thinks she is homesick for Paris. After dinner, she tells what has happened, but, because Bove cannot believe his sworn companion capable of such villainy, he seeks to interpret the episode as a trial of Ermenjart's virtue. His faith in Guy cannot be shaken.

(275-359) *Beton and Daurelet are Born*

Ermenjart gives birth to Beton, who is sent to Roland to be baptized. The infant's life is soon disturbed when his father, the duke, goes hunting in Ardena-La-Gran. A great boar has been reported in the vicinity; Bove sends for Guy and prepares to hunt the animal. In spite of repeated warnings from Ermenjart of Guy's treacherous intentions, Bove insists on going, and is on the point of leaving when Daurel appears, announces the birth of his third son, and asks Duke Bove to be the child's godfather. The duke baptises the boy Daurelet of Monclar.

Bove mounts his steed and Ermenjart kisses him farewell, «the last kiss she was ever to give him.»

(360-393) *The Boar Hunt*

The dogs finally raise the boar, who scatters them easily and heads for the deep forest. Leaving their hunters behind, Bove and Guy give chase on horseback, and Bove mortally wounds the boar just as Guy rides up. Instead of helping Bove kill the animal, Guy drives his pike into the duke's shoulder. The duke tries to rise but cannot; the pike is implanted in his body. He regrets not having heeded Ermenjart's warnings, but still does not fully realize the extent of Guy's treachery.

(394-475) *The Death of Bove*

In his agony, Bove attempts to forgive his perfidious companion, even suggesting that, had he known Guy's desire, he would have given

up Ermenjart and become a pilgrim. He accepts his fate with resig-
nation, and such is his generosity that he even suggests to Guy a way
to avoid being suspected of murder. Reminding his assassin of their
oath, he begs Guy to care for Beton and to ask Charlemagne for
Ermenjart's hand.

His pleas fall on deaf ears; Bove's saintly demeanor further enrages
Guy, who swears to kill Beton, even refusing to give Bove the battlefield absolution with leaves (practiced by knights in the absence of
clergy). Bove, realizing at long last the full extent of Guy's villainy,
prays to the Virgin and to Christ for forgiveness of his sins and for
the protection of his son from the traitor. As Guy withdraws the pike
from the duke's body, Bove dies.

Following Bove's suggestion, the traitor fixes the boar's teeth in
the duke's side and his own pike in the boar. The hunters arrive but
are not fooled by this attempt at deception or by Guy's explanations.
The traitor weeps, but out of joy rather than sorrow.

(476-533)   *Ermenjart Accuses Guy of Murder*

Guy rushes back to Poitiers to tell Ermenjart that her husband
has been killed by the boar. She accuses him of having carried out
his threat to murder the duke; she is overwhelmed by sorrow, anger
and despair. The nobles and townspeople lament over the body of
their beloved lord, tearing their clothing, scratching their faces, and
fainting. «Never has such sorrow been seen.» Ermenjart attempts to
kill Guy but is held back. She addresses the crowd, tells of Guy's
threats and of her own heartbreak. Lifting up the shroud, she points
to the wound in Bove's side and declares: «Never was such a wound
inflicted by a boar.»

More than ten thousand people mourn the loss of the good duke.
Upon hearing the news, Daurel falls to the ground unable to speak.
His sorrow is beyond description. Three days later, Bove is buried in
Saint-Hilaire, next to the altar.

(534-643)   *Guy bribes Charlemagne and marries Ermenjart*

No sooner is the duke buried than Guy hurries to Aspremont, has
his treasure loaded on pack-animals, and sets out for Paris, where
Charlemagne and his court show deep grief upon hearing the news
of Bove's death.

The emperor quickly forgets his sorrow, however, when Guy offers him the treasure of silver and gold, since the royal coffers are almost empty. In return, Guy requests that Charles grant him the heritage bequeathed by Bove, as well as the hand of the widowed Ermenjart. Charlemagne thanks Guy for the treasure and prepares to set out for Poitiers after dinner.

The emperor and Guy arrive in Poitiers, where Charles, refusing to listen to his sister's pleas for vengeance, accepts Guy's word that he could never have been guilty of killing a sworn companion. Ermenjart offers to undergo a trial by fire in order to prove her accusations, but Charlemagne, remarking that such an act will not bring the duke back to life, marries her to Guy without further argument. Throwing Guy's ring into the fire, she curses her brother for having given her over to the traitor by force.

(644-734) *Ermenjart conceals Beton from Guy*

The assembled nobles and townspeople are touched by Ermenjart's plight, but no one dares challenge the authority of the emperor. Daurel, realizing the imminent danger to Beton, offers to care for the boy, but Ermenjart tells him that she has already sent him away to one of her sisters. She then asks advice of her ladies-in-waiting, who counsel her to hide the boy until he is old enough to avenge her. Charlemagne takes leave, accompanied by Guy. Ermenjart sends for a rich townsman who had served Bove faithfully in the past. He offers his help, suggesting that his daughter Aisilineta, who, because of the loss of her own infant would be able to nurse Beton, take care of the boy in an island hiding place. His son will take supplies to them by boat. The infant is brought to the island, where Aisilineta takes care of him for two months.

(736-768) *Guy's Brutality to Ermenjart*

Ermenjart is not deceived by Guy's professed love for Beton. She lies to him, telling him that the boy has died during his absence and has already been buried. He reproves her for lying; she, in turn, reproaches him for his greater lie and treachery in murdering the duke. Seizing her by the hair, he strikes her with his golden spurs, causing the blood to flow from her sides. She begs him to kill her; distraught, she confesses that Beton is, indeed, alive and will avenge her.

(769-899) *Ebrart's Treachery Exposes Beton*

Guy offers a reward for the capture of Beton. One day Ebrart, a
fisherman, comes upon Aisilineta in her island hiding place. Swearing him to secrecy, the girl tells Ebrart that she is caring for Beton, his rightful lord. Ebrart claims to love Beton, but says «with
clenched teeth: 'I've found a thousand silver marks in the sea today.'»
He rushes off to claim the reward from Guy, who is delighted and
orders Daurel to pay Ebrart if he can reveal where Beton is being
hidden.

Learning of the boy's whereabouts, Daurel dashes off to save him.
He is halted by water, but Aisilineta's brother arrives with his boat.
Together they cross over to the island, tear Beton away from the
tearful girl, and depart. Daurel takes the infant to Monclar, where
his wife, Beatrix, welcomes Beton with joy. All forget the nurse, who
has been left behind to face Guy's anger.

(900-941) *Guy's Cruelty to Aisilineta*

The next morning, Guy, accompanied by three hundred men, sets
out to trap the infant Beton. They find the boat and reach the island.
Guy asks for the boy, but Aisilineta, who has cried herself to sleep
the night before, relates how the boy had been kidnapped by hunters
[or sailors] and carried away to sea. Refusing to believe this story,
Guy orders Ebrart to torture her by beating her on the breasts with
nettles, causing her to cry out the truth. Guy plans to take his revenge
on both Daurel and Beton, but, since it is past dinnertime and they
have not yet eaten, they decide to wait until the next day to attack
Monclar.

(942-1089) *Daurel's Sacrifice*

Guy, with his men, reaches the walls of Monclar. In spite of the
formidable fortifications of the castle, Daurel is not prepared to
resist an assault; therefore, when Guy threatens to set fire to Monclar
unless the child is delivered to him. Daurel is faced with a painful
dilemma. He accepts Guy's ultimatum, re-enters the castle and laments
his fate. His wife, Beatrix, suggests a cruel solution: sacrifice their
own son to the traitor in order to save their lord.

Daurel delivers his son, wrapped in the cloth in which he had been baptized by the late duke, to Guy, who promises not to harm the boy. Guy looks at the child and says: «Beton, you'll be well taken care of in a short time.»

The traitor turns to Daurel and accuses him of disloyalty by hiding an enemy of a superior. Daurel responds that he did it out of loyalty to his lord. The traitor answers: «Look what I am going to do with your lord.» He takes Daurelet by the feet and smashes his head against a pillar. The onlookers are horrified and lament bitterly. Guy, thinking he has disposed of Beton, leaves Monclar. Daurel, angered beyond description, wraps his son's remains in a silk cloth, goes to Poitiers to tell Ermenjart that Beton is safe. He asks her to see to the defense of Monclar during his absence, for he must take Beton across the sea into exile, not to return until the boy is old enough to bear arms.

Fittingly, Daurelet is buried with great honor next to Duke Bove, whose lineage he died to preserve. Returning to Monclar, Daurel quickly fits out his ship for a long voyage, stocking it with ample food and drink, taking his arms, horses, harp and vielle. Accompanied by his squire and a nurse for Beton, he sets sail from Monclar. As the ship disappears over the horizon, a heartbroken Beatrix jumps from the tower and dies.

(1092-1139) *Monclar Prepared for Siege*

Ermenjart puts Azemar in charge of Monclar, giving him enough money to buy provisions and equipment sufficient to withstand a siege of twelve years or more, after which time Daurel and Beton will return to kill the traitor.

Azemar provides for a company of sixty knights and their ladies, three thousand archers and twenty arbalesters. While the traitor wages war against them, they engage in the noble pastimes of gaming and falconry.

(1140-1172) *Guy's First Attack on Monclar*

Upon hearing of Beton's escape, Guy flies into a rage and puts Ermenjart in prison for a year. He attacks Monclar with a small force, but is easily repulsed after an exchange of threats and insults between his men and the garrison. The poet returns us to the heroes, saying: «Let's leave Monclar and the traitor Guy, and let's speak of Daurel and the infant Beton.»

(1173-1280) *Daurel and Beton Arrive in Babylonia*

During the long sea voyage, Daurel keeps the infant amused by singing to him. He composes a lay about the duke's murder and their exile. They arrive in Babylonia (the seaport of Cairo), go to the Emir's palace, and are well received by him. Daurel entertains the court, explains that he has come to Babylonia because of the Emir's reputation for liberality. Daurel refuses the Emir's offer of a fief and great riches, asking only that he agree to raise Beton in his court. The child, who has already charmed the Emir with his smile, is given into the care of the queen.

Until the age of three, he remains in the ladies' chambers; when he comes out, everyone admires his beauty. The Emir, struck by the boy's noble mien, declares that Beton could not possibly be the son of a poor *jongleur*. Daurel chides the Emir for doubting the boy's paternity.

Beton, at the age of four, is very precocious. He steals the Emir's gold-embroidered gloves to give to the queen. The Emir remarks that he would give thirteen cities to have a son like him.

At the age of five, he is courageous and intelligent; he knows how to tame horses, speak and reason well, play backgammon, chess and dice. The poet returns us to Monclar saying: «Let's leave Daurel and little Beton in peace.»

(1281-1405) *Guy Lays Siege to Monclar*

Count Guy is caught sight of hunting with a hundred companions, and Azemar decides to ambush his party. Battle is joined, but Guy defends himself courageously and rallies his men. He is finally unhorsed by Azemar, Bertran and a third knight, but is saved by Jaufré, one of his men. His small force is routed and many are taken prisoner.

The count, furious, raises a large army of thirteen hundred knights and a thousand servants in order to lay siege to Monclar, but the besieged are supplied with food for twelve years and sufficient running water. They lead a merry life both day and night.

(1406-1563) *Beton's Nobility is Tested and Proved*

At the age of six, Beton is handsome and courteous. The king
and queen love him, as does their daughter Erimena, a lovely girl.
Daurel tells the boy to learn the harp and vielle, a skill which will
bring him much joy.

At seven, he was an accomplished musician, and even knew how
to *trobar* by himself. One day, while Daurel is out fishing for dolphins,
little Beton sees some noble children gambling. He joins the game and
wins their tunics as soon as he throws the dice. When the Emir learns
that the boy gave away his winnings, he is certain of Beton's noble
birth.

The queen proposes to test him by having him entertain the
princess Erimena, who will then offer him a large sum of money.
If he accepts, he is beyond doubt the son of a minstrel, if not, he is
certain to be of noble birth. With the king and courtiers secretly
watching, Beton plays and sings for the girl, refuses the money in
spite of her entreaties, accepting only a set of finely-worked dice as
a token from her.

The Emir remarks to his barons: «It is not possible that such
a child was ever born of Daurel.» After his test that day, Beton was
loved a thousand times more.

(1564-1640) *Beton's Knightly Education*

At the age of nine, Beton engages in all the noble diversions.
Everyone loves him, especially the princess Erimena. He serves the
king at table and willingly entertains the nobles. Daurel is very proud
of his charge.

When he reaches eleven, he can fence and serve as a knight's
squire. Daurel buys him a horse and furnishes him with arms small
enough for him to bear; then hires a Saracen master-at-arms to teach
him how to use them in a tourney.

By the age of twelve, he has developed good judgement, and
Daurel decides that the time has come to put Beton's manhood to
test. He orders the boy to joust with him — Beton refuses at first,
but Daurel insists — and they lower their lances and strike hard at
each other. Beton unhorses Daurel and makes his turn gracefully. The
minstrel laughs at the boy's tears and congratulates him, giving thanks

to God, for he is now confident that the boy will be *pros*. They lay
down their arms and sit together on the grass.

(1641-1685)   *Recapitulation of Story*

Daurel tells Beton the truth about his birth, the story of Guy's
treachery, their flight into exile, etc., and counsels him to keep the
secret until it is time to leave Babylon and seek revenge.

(1686-1809)   *Beton's First Feat of Arms*

At the age of thirteen, Beton proves his valor. King Gormon, who
had been warring with the Emir for the past twenty years, suddenly
attacks Babylon with a powerful force. The Emir, considering it
foolhardy to engage such a large army, orders Beton, who has made
ready his armor and charger, to put the armor away and take the
stallion back to the stables.

Beton puts on the king's armor, mounts the stallion, rides out of
the gate to challenge two knights from Gormon's army. With everyone
watching, including the king and queen who fear for his safety, he
defeats his opponents one by one, and calmly returns to the city when
three thousand Saracens start advancing toward him. After giving
away the stallions he has taken as booty, Beton disarms in the square,
where he is admired by all.

The crowd attempts to dissuade Daurel from punishing Beton for
having gone out without his permission. The Emir threatens to put
Daurel in jail unless he tells the truth about the boy's origin. The
jongleur needs no further coaxing and asks the Emir to convene his
court.

(1810-1898)   *Beton Accepts Erimena's Hand*

After a brief recapitulation of the story, Daurel tells the assembled
barons that the time has come to seek revenge; therefore, they must
leave Babylonia. The king and queen embrace Beton, and willingly
accede to the barons' demand that they give him their daughter in
marriage. Beton is quite in accord, but dutifully asks Daurel's
permission, which is granted on condition that the girl be baptized.
Erimena modestly acquiesces to this demand.

The Emir grants Daurel's request for three thousand armed men to aid them in their revenge. After taking solemn oaths, they prepare the ships and set sail for Monclar, arriving there after three months of travel through storms.

(1899-1970) *Daurel and Beton Enter Guy's Camp*

Daurel, seeing Monclar besieged by Guy's army, realizes that vengeance is close at hand and plots his strategy. He and Beton will enter the enemy camp disguised as minstrels, will provoke him to anger, and, at a given signal, the forces inside Monclar will join those from the ships in an attack. Guy, failing to recognize Daurel, who has not cut his beard in seven years, invites them to entertain the company. Accompanied by Beton, Daurel sings a *chanson* about the treachery of Guy, who raises his knife to strike the *jongleur*. Beton throws down his vielle, draws his sword and cuts off the traitor's right arm. They shout their battle cry, «Antona!», and the others rush in and kill most of Guy's knights, sparing the foot soldiers who had been forced into service by Guy.

(1971-2066) *Execution of the Traitors*

Daurel faints upon hearing of his wife's death, but is consoled by Beton and by the reunion with his sons. Beton is greeted by his mother, Ermenjart; the people praise God for the return of their rightful lord.

Guy confesses his crime and is put to death by being dragged around Poitiers tied to a horse's tail. His body is tossed into a ditch. At the request of Aisilineta, Ebrart is flayed alive.

(2067-2086) *Beton Rewards his Faithful Vassals*

The barons are overjoyed to have recovered their rightful lord. In a plenary court, Beton rewards his faithful subjects: Aspremont is granted to Azemar; Bertran is knighted and receives two castles; his younger brother is made a squire. Beton marries Erimena in Saint-Hilaire, and they live happily ever after.

(2087-end) *Beton Seeks Redress From Charlemagne*

Some time has passed. One fine spring day, Beton decides to seek either vengeance or redress from Charles for his rôle in dishonoring

Ermenjart. Ermenjart advises her son to avoid warring with the emperor, since he is a close relative and powerful, on condition that he right the wrong. Should he refuse to do so, they can count on a hundred thousand men to march with them against her brother, and they can expect substantial aid from the Emir.

Beton sends Bertran, Azemar and Gauseran as ambassadors to Paris. The emissaries salute Roland, Oliver and the twelve peers, but refuse to salute Charlemagne. They recount briefly the story of Guy's treachery and deliver Beton's ultimatum. The Emperor laughs and praises their courage in challenging him in such a manner before his court.

At this point, the manuscript breaks off.

CHAPTER VII

STYLE AND STRUCTURE

In our study of the *Daurel* author's technique we shall look at
his use of traditional elements of epic composition, beginning with the
formulaic epithet and hemistitch, proceeding to a discussion of laisse
and episode, to arrive at an over-all view of the narrative structure
of the poem. It is impossible in the course of our discussion to
ignore the current important controversy between traditionalists and
individualists over the genesis of the epic: whether, as M. Delbouille
holds, the *chanson de geste* was written by an individual poet to be
sung, or, whether, as J. Rychner believes, the epic was created orally
and written down only when the genre had already declined in
popularity. [1]

---

[1] For the staunchest adversaries, see, notably, the contributions to *La
Technique littéraire des chansons de geste* by Riquer, Rychner, Jodogne,
Delbouille (esp. the latter's updating of the controversy in notes to his article
«Les Chansons de geste et le livre,» pp. 295-307, complemented by D.
McMillan's review in *CCM*, IV [1961], 67-71). I. Siciliano's presentation
of theories and counter-theories (*Les Origines des chansons de geste: théories
et discussions* [Paris, 1951] makes short shrift of the oral theorists, according
to R. Menéndez Pidal, in a mordant review of the question (from the neo-
traditionalist point of view) in *La Chanson de Roland et la tradition épique
des francs*, 2nd ed. (Paris, 1960), Chap. I; cf. Ronald N. Walpole's review
(*Speculum*, XXXVIII [1963], 373-382), which points out some fallacies
of Menéndez Pidal's theory of slow evolution *vis-à-vis* the *Roland* and the
French epic. See also P. LeGentil's articles in which he attempts to conciliate
opposing traditionalist and individualist views: «A propos de l'origine des
chansons de geste: le problème de l'auteur,» *Coloquios de Roncesvalles* (Zaragoza, 1956), pp. 113-121, and, more recently, «Reflexions sur la création
littéraire au moyen âge,» *Chanson de geste und hofischer Roman*, Heidelberger
Kolloquium, 1961 (Heidelberg, 1963), pp. 9-20.

We should not expect a mid-twelfth century Provençal epic to enlighten us greatly on the origin of the French epic — both traditionalists and individualists agree that by 1150-1168 it would have been normal procedure for an epic *jongleur* to set down his *chanson* in writing. However, given the archaic and traditional nature of the genre, *Daurel* might still be expected to yield evidence of oral composition, improvisation and delivery if, as Rychner would have us believe, early epics were not only recited, but composed and improvised orally. A glance at the rôle played by Daurel in our poem supports the least controversial of Rychner's theses: the epic was meant to be sung before an audience by a *jongleur*. [2] Not only does the author show Daurel tumbling, reciting, playing, singing, and, finally, improvising before an audience, but he also depicts him as a loyal and devoted vassal capable of the most noble sentiments and actions. [3] In the course of the poem, Daurel is transformed from a humble minstrel to a troubadour (see pp. 183-184), and twice we see him composing or improvising: he composes and sings a *lais d'amor* about Beton's misfortunes (vv. 1180-1189) and later in the poem improvises a *chanson de geste* about Guy's treachery in order to provoke the count. The opening is typically epic in its use of the cliché request for attention followed by the statement of the subject:

> «Qui vol auzir canso, ieu lh'en dirai, so·m par,
> De tracio que no fai a celar
> Del fel trachor Guio —cui Jhesus desampar!—
> Qu'aucis lo duc quan fon ab lui cassar (1947).»

Although minstrels and *jongleurs* are frequent characters in epic, this is an example unique in the genre of a *jongleur* actually improvising a *chanson de geste* before an audience. [4] Contrary to Delbouille, [5]

---

[2] *La Chanson de geste: essai sur l'art épique des jongleurs* (Genève, 1955), p. 10.

[3] Edmond Faral, *Les Jongleurs en France au moyen-âge* (Paris, 1910), p. 83.

[4] Faral (*Jongleurs*, appendice III) cites many exs. of minstrels and *jongleurs* in epic and romance, but only rarely (e.g., *Roman de la Violette*: the hero disguised as a *jongleur* recites verses from *Guillaume*) are they depicted chanting epic verses.

[5] *Technique*, p. 361. Delbouille finds the exs. of improvisation (as cited by Gautier, *Épopées*, II, 122-23) from *Daurel* and *Beuve* (where, in one version, Josiane, disguised as a *jongleresse*, sings «.I. son novel» about the

there is nothing exceptional in this improvisation — Daurel is shown demonstrating his talent in an ingenious fashion, creating an epic-within-an-epic. In so doing he is following an illustrious predecessor — Did not Homer portray Odysseus weeping while listening to his own adventures in the Trojan War recounted by the minstrel Demodocus?

In themselves, the two examples of improvisation prove nothing about the nature of the composition of *Daurel* — an author writing the poem may have introduced this element into the plot to give a flavor of spontaneous composition (as his predecessors in the «old days» would have done), the simulation, in other words, of oral technique, rather than actual improvisation. [6] What other discernible methods of oral composition and delivery do we find in *Daurel* to support Rychner's contention that epics were not only recited aloud but actually composed anew each time they were performed before an audience? In attempting to find a satisfactory answer, we shall examine his epic technique in the light of Rychner's brilliant analysis and classification of «oral» elements, which, although debatable as far as his conclusions are concerned, nevertheless provide a useful frame of reference for discussion of the poet's style and composition.

i. RECITATIVE INGREDIENTS

Since the *jongleur* practiced his craft before an audience, we expect to find elements of oral delivery that indicate a relationship between story-teller and audience. [7] To what extent are these traits present in *Daurel*?

1) The opening request for attention: *Plat vos auzir huna rica canso?* and the introduction of characters and exposition of plot which

---

hero in order to be recognized by him), the exceptions that prove the rule of literary composition: «Autant de cas où, précisément, est souligné le caractère merveilleux de l'improvisation supposée.» The example from *Daurel* lends little support to Delbouille's argument, since Daurel had earlier in the story been shown capable of such improvisation (v. 85 [*e say*] *trobier*).

[6] While the oral theorists maintain that oral elements in MSS represent oral creation and transmission reflected from earlier, purely oral tradition, the literary partisans hold that this trait represents a simulation of improvisation rather than improvisation itself. Delbouille (*Technique*, pp. 360-361) considers improvisation of formulaic character as the work of scribes and poets writing on parchment, not of *jongleurs* reciting a memorized text.

[7] Rychner, *Chanson de geste*, pp. 10-11.

follows, immediately and explicitly expresses this bond between the *jongleur* and his public. In *Daurel* the narrator frequently addresses the listener directly (e.g., vv. 2, 37, 217, 1043, 1047, 1172, 1279), using «listen» and «see» imperatives. [8]

2) Appeals to the generosity of the audience: no direct request for payment is made in *Daurel* but the narrator repeatedly describes the *largesse* of the nobility towards the minstrel. Whenever Daurel appears, he is cordially welcomed and richly rewarded: Bove, the Emir, Charlemagne, even Guy, accord a place of honor to the *jongleur*. [9] At the end of the scene in which Bove's generosity is exemplary, the narrator turns to the audience and says, no doubt hinting that they would do well to follow the example, *ve·us pagat lo joglar* (217). [10] There is, however, no indication of any direct appeal of the sort one finds in *Huon de Bordeaux* (4976-4991) or *Couronnement Louis* (313-314):

> Com vos orrez ainz qu'il seit avespré,
> Se vos donez tant que vueille chanter.

3) Recapitulations of the story at various intervals: The first résumé (1180-1189) occurs when Daurel and Beton are on the high seas and Daurel composes a song relating the story up to that time. The second and third are found only two hundred lines apart and relate basically the same events as the first in different fashion: vv. 1641-1683 summarize the story of Beton's birth, Guy's treachery and Charlemagne's cupidity, while vv. 1810-1845 give Beton's story as told by Daurel to the Emir's court. The former is familiar in tone and tender, the latter formal and oratorical. In the fourth recapitulation, at the beginning of the fragmentary third episode (2091-2104),

---

[8] Riquer (*Chansons de geste*, p. 305) states: «Que les chansons de geste appartiennent à une littérature d'expression orale, c'est un fait qu'elles proclament elles-mêmes avec les fréquentes répétitions des impératifs.»

[9] On the relatively high status of the *jongleur de geste* (as mirrored in epic) see Raleigh Morgan, Jr., «Old French *Jogleor* and Kindred Terms,» *RPh*, VII (1954), 279-325. On the other hand, *Daurel* 1764 *fil de glojar* is cited by Morgan (¶ 15) as having (almost) the force of an insult, giving some idea of the real social status of the *joglar*.

[10] Paris (*Mélanges*, p. 148) suggests that the exaggerated largesse in *Daurel* is best explained by «le fait que le rôle attribué dans notre poème à un jongleur était rempli, dans les récits qu'a suivis l'auteur de ce poème, par un vassal de condition chevaleresque.»

Beton reminds Ermenjart of his reasons for seeking vengeance on Charles, a résumé immediately echoed by the «message» Beton delivers to Charles (2161-2180).

The first and last of these résumés occur after episodes of approximately one thousand verses, and these clearly mark divisions in the story (see pp. 81-85); the other two can only be discussed in the context of the missing section of the poem, about which we shall have more to say later, but they appear to be placed close together in what was originally the middle of *Daurel*. Since the average length of an oral recitation session was probably between one and two thousand verses, [11] the *jongleur* might well have interrupted his presentation at 1180 and 2091 (dividing the poem into roughly-equal thirds) or at 1614 (the half-way point, if we assume the total length of *Daurel* to have been 3000+ verses). These passages are not «oral» — in the sense that the narrator does not turn directly to the audience to summarize the story and to introduce what was going to happen — but are artfully and unobtrusively inserted into the story (in a manner technically similar to Homer's recapitulations in the *Odyssey*): Daurel sings a lay to the infant Beton; Beton comes of age and must be told the truth about his birth; the Emir and his court must be informed so that they will aid the enterprise against Guy; Ermenjart must be convinced by Beton of the necessity for revenge against Charles.

The résumés in *Daurel* are functional: they allow the *jongleur* to interrupt the story at various intervals, they serve to remind the changing audience of what has already transpired, and they link the different parts of the story together. They demonstrate (along with the other recitative elements we have enumerated) the bond between *jongleur* and audience so vital to oral recitation, [12] but, on the

---

[11] Cf. Rychner, *Chanson de geste,* p. 49: «...on imaginera qu'une séance pouvait comprendre le chant de 1000 à 2000 vers.» While the *Roland* contains no explicit signs of distribution into oral sessions, other poems can be broken into relatively equal segments (*Raoul* 1000, *Moniage* 2000).

[12] Although Delbouille (*Technique,* pp. 360-361) sees them as the work of scribes writing on parchment and simulating oral presentation, the recitative elements in *Huon,* an early-thirteenth century poem, are also functional (cf. Pierre Ruelle, éd., *Huon de Bordeaux* [Bruxelles/Paris, 1960], pp. 53-54), especially the famous passage (cited by Rychner, p. 49) in which the *jongleur* asks his audience to come back after dinner to hear the second half of the poem (vv. 4976-4991).

other hand, they tell us little about the composition of the *chanson*. Was *Daurel* composed, as well as recited, orally? A glance at the smaller stylistic elements in *Daurel,* the formulas, stock phrases and epithets may help provide an answer.

ii. FORMULAIC EPITHET AND HEMISTICH

According to the oral theorists, the very conditions under which the *jongleur* worked restricted his inventiveness to developing common motifs and themes along established, stereotyped lines, familiar to and easily followed by his audience. In Rychner's words, «Le métier de jongleur, le chant public, interdisent absolument la recherche patiente d'une expression singulière et originale.» [13] Just as elements of oral recitation were set down in manuscripts by scribes and adaptors long after the disappearance of the *jongleur* from the public square, [14] the basic units of oral or preliterary composition, the cliché or formula hemistich of four or six syllables, remain vital to epic technique. [15] *Jongleur* or cleric, author or *remanieur* — all depend on a rich and varied stock of hemistichs in the creation or reworking of an epic. [16] Since medieval epic depended heavily on a stock of ready-made expressions, an author's reputation was determined more by his inventiveness in deploying these elements than by his ability to create entirely new ones. Nowhere is the reliance on formula more clear than in battle scenes, where the use of cliché ranges from the smaller elements, the formulaic epithets and the stock motifs (which we will examine next), to the long descriptions of the alignment of opposing

---

[13] *Chanson de geste,* p. 126.

[14] Martín de Riquer, «Épopée jongleresque à écouter et épopée romanesque à lire,» *Technique,* pp. 75-82.

[15] Rita Lejeune, «Technique formulaire et chansons de geste,» *Moyen Age,* LX (1954), 311-334; Zumthor, *Langue et techniques,* p. 120; Riquer, *Chansons de geste,* pp. 314-321; Stephen G. Nichols, Jr., *Formulaic Diction and Thematic Composition in the Chanson de Roland,* Univ. of North Carolina Studies in Rom. Lang. and Lit., No. 36 (Chapel Hill, 1961), pp. 43-48.

[16] The individualist theory advanced by Delbouille (*Technique,* p. 361) holds that in each case «le texte était composé vers par vers, avec plus ou moins d'originalité, à l'aide d'un jeu très riche et fort variable d'hémistichs à variantes, le travail d'agencement n'étant guère compatible avec la pratique d'une improvisation permanente par le chanteur.»

forces (of which there are no examples in *Daurel*) and the mêlée (e.g., vv. 1959-1962). As Rychner has so aptly observed: «Sans les clichés, il n'y aurait pas de chansons de geste!» [17]

The Epithet

To allow comparison of *Daurel* with the genre, let us examine an epithet with a wide range of variants — the «rapid charger.» We find only six different ones in *Daurel* (all of which figure in the list of seventy-five cited by Frappier [18]):

> destrier corren (49)
> salhidor (477)
> sojornatz (946)
> corredor (346)
> liar (521)
> coredos destriers (1129)

all of which seem unimaginative, like those in what Frappier terms the secondary epics. [19] Generally speaking, the presence of a restricted number of epithets is in accordance with the older «oral» and «classical» style of the epic; the greater the variety, the more «literary» the poem. A glance at the «rapid charger» epithets in *Daurel* reveals a sobriety of style typical of our poem; the author had at his disposal one variant (with the exception of *-or* for which he had two) for each of the rhymes he commonly used.

---

[17] «La Chanson de geste, épopée vivante,» *La Table Ronde*, No. 132 (Dec. 1958), 159. In this connection, it is unwise to speak of cliché and stereotype in a pejorative sense, since there may be little in epic that would escape such evaluation when judged by modern esthetic criteria.

[18] Jean Frappier, «Les destriers et leurs épithètes,» *Technique*, pp. 85-104; see also Rychner, *Chanson de geste*, pp. 141-143; Delbouille (*Technique*, pp. 363-367) adds numerous examples to those cited by the above, but draws different conclusions: «Chaque jongleur avait ses formules, dira-t-on. Peut-être; ou chaque poète ses façons et, après lui, chaque scribe ses manies et ses préférences.»

[19] *Technique*, pp. 98-102. These poems (e.g. *Couronnement Louis, Moniage Guillaume, Charroi de Nîmes*) demonstrate a wider variety of epithet than the oldest epics (*Roland, Gormont, Guillaume I*) but lack the ornateness of later ones (e.g. *Aymeri de N., Enfances Guillaume, Beuvon de Conmarchis*). According to Frappier they mark a drawing-away from «oral» technique.

In *Daurel,* as in all epics, the majority of epithets and stock phrases are employed as rhyme-tags. For example, of the pejorative epithets directed against Guy, we find only one (*E lo fels Gui*) which occurs frequently in the first hemistich. The others abound with variety in the second:

> Guiho lo trager lauzengier (61)
> al trachor mescrezen (198)
> lo trachor renegatz (474)
> en glot lausengador (485)
> Guis lo renegatz (948)
> lo fel trachor Guio (1155)
> sel mescrezen felo (330)
> un renegat trachor (487)
> lo tracher malapres (698)

Since the author's choice of words was dictated by the rhyme, this variety was more apparent than real: in an *-atz* laisse, for example, his choice was limited to two semantically unimpressive variants, *lo trachor renegatz* and *Guis lo renegatz.*

First hemistich epithets tend to be simple, short (three- or four-syllable), adjective + noun constructions:

> Lo tracher Guis (1281)
> Lo pros duc (592)
> Lo ric duc (77)
> Lo pros Daurel (984)
> L'efas Betos (2069)

whereas most of the second hemistich epithets show the qualifier last, varying with the rhyme. Occasionally the epithet reveals a modicum of inventiveness. Each of the following describes, in a naïve manner, an essential characteristic of Ermenjart (all are at verse-end):

> ab la cara rizen (176 = the young bride)
> ab lo cors covinen (182 = physically desirable to Guy)
> la pros e la valhan (290 = the valiant and brave wife)
> dolenta e irada (684 = mourning her dead husband)
> ab la gentil faisso (1827 = noble widow and mother)

In contrast to such clichés as *ab lo vis clier* (141), which have little affective value (the same phrase refers to Charles in 156), the author uses the above to portray the character of Ermenjart while providing a requisite number of syllables for the verse.

In numerous instances, however, ready-made phrases such as double epithets are pure rhyme-tags, especially those of the redundant type:

> tost e viassamen (187)
> a tort e a pecat (899)
> es pros e cortes (708)
> lor ops e lor conres (709)
> ben e gen (1123)
> alegre e jauzen (1124)
> per forsa e vigor (1174)

and aside from reinforcing an idea to emphasize it, they add little to the narration. The antithetical doublets are amplifications: to express «everyone,» for example, the author uses the periphrastic *li peti e li gran* (276), *li gran e li menor* (644), and *li mal e li bo* (1810). Beton will be nurtured *a forsa o a gratz* (893); the traitor will be caught *en pueh o en estrada* (681).

In his use of formulaic epithet, the *Daurel* author's choice of expression is generally apt. Nor is his use of formula excessive in the context of the genre: rhyme tags are the exception rather than the rule, and the only formulas repeated with any frequency are the oaths and epithets concerning Guy (e.g., *Que lo fel Guis — cui Jhesus desampar* 263) and stock expressions (e.g., *se a vos platz, molt mi sat bo, teno·is per pagat*). Nevertheless, on occasion the author is so captive to tradition that he contradicts himself: after an emphatic description of Monclar: *ja per nulh home non er pres ni forsat* (950-953), Daurel must surrender his castle to the mere threat of fire. The example is not, however, unique in epic literature. [20]

Traditional Motif

Stereotype in epic extends to whole blocks of verses dealing with certain common motifs — the arming and disarming of a knight, battle by lance or sword, punishment of the traitor, and so on. One of the

---

[20] Rychner (*Chanson de geste,* p. 137; also *La Table Ronde,* No. 132 [Dec. 1958], 159) cites an interesting example from *Guillaume* in which the heroes are armed with horse and lance for a combat inside the keep of a castle.

best examples of such a motif, which has been extensively analyzed by Rychner, is the «attack with lance.»[21] Seven elements, each of which is expressed by a limited range of formulaic hemistichs, recur with remarkable regularity in a wide variety of epics:

1. spur the horse
2. brandish the lance
3. strike the adversary
4. break his shield
5. break his hauberk
6. pass the lance through his body
7. unhorse him, usually killing him.

Daurel has several examples of this motif, which show its dependence on formula with variations to meet needs of rhyme and context. The most complete describes the single combat in which Beton, wearing the Emir's armor, challenges a pagan knight from Gormon's army (the numbers identify the elements listed above):

1.2. Cadaüs broca ab los espiest baissatz,
3. Grans cops si fero els bos escutz listratz.
Be lo feri aicel desbatigat
4. Que entro l'auberc s'en es lo fer passatz
3. Beto fer lui coma vasal proatz,
4.5. L'escut li trauca a l'auberc l'a falssatz;
7. Vezen de tos s'es lo paias tumbatz (1750).

During the mêlée between the besiegers and defenders of Monclar, Azemar strikes Guy, but is unable to unhorse him:

1.2. Baiset sa senha, laissa·l caval anar,
3. E fer Guio, mas no·l pot daroquar (1321).

In the same section of the poem occur two stylistically similar passages in which Guy is taunted into attacking Bertran, whom he unhorses, and a young knight, whom he kills. The author compresses the action into blocks of five verses, varying the elements in such a way that not a single rhyme is repeated, although both passages occur in an -*ar* laisse:

---

[21] *Chanson de geste*, pp. 139-150; a more concise version is found in *La Table Ronde*, No. 132, 159-162. Cf. Delbouille's critique, *Technique*, pp. 354-370.

1. Au o lo coms: sul caval va pujar
   E venc vas lui lai on lo vic estar,
3.4. Grans cops si fero pels escutz pessejar.
6. Bertran l'enpeih que·l cujet degolar
7. E·l coms Guis lui, que l'a fah darocar (1311).

   ... ...

   Au o lo coms: cujet enrabiar
1.2. E trais s'espeia, laissa·l caval anar,
3.4. Fer .i. donzel desus son elme clar,
6. Entro la[s] dens ne fes lo bran passar,
7. Mort l'en trebuca, que anc non poc levar (1328).

Although the motif is the same, the author uses wide variations of expression to fit the context; only one formula *Au o lo coms* is repeated to link the two passages. When, later in the story, Daurel jousts with Beton to test his readiness for knighthood, the elements of the motif remain relatively unchanged, but the expression, as befits the tone of the passage, is once again different:

   Cascus se lonja .i. mezurat arpen
2.3. Baisso las astas e fero·is duramen
4. Per los escut que·l fers es intra dedins
5. Entro·ls aulbertz que de mort los defen.
   Daurel l'espenh molt vertudozamen
7. E l'efan lui, qu'a terra l'en dissen
   E passa d'oltra e fetz son torn mol gen (1627).

In his treatment of stereotyped motif, the *Daurel* author drew freely on ready-made phrases in order to produce the sort of tableau his audience expected and appreciated. That he dealt skillfully with this «fixed» form is demonstrated by the variety and lack of repetition in the examples above, and these compare favorably with those cited by Rychner and Matarasso. [22] There are no identical or near-identical blocks of verses in *Daurel,* where the use of formula and stock motif is limited, but varied. It would seem that, in its present form, *Daurel* was composed verse by verse in the manner outlined by Delbouille (see note 16). Earlier versions of the poem may have been improvised and composed orally, but of this we have no proof.

---

[22] Matarasso (*Recherches,* pp. 261-270) analyzes the same mechanism of battle in *Raoul;* noting that the traditional element is considerable, she remarks: «Comment en eut-il été autrement? Il n'y avait pas mille façons de se battre avec épée et lance, et le chant oral, de par sa nature, tend vers des formes fixes.»

The author's stylistic apparatus was to a great extent traditional, rooted in time-honored epic convention. The choice of emotional epithets (e.g., *tira sa barba* 1143, *a romput son gan* 299 to express anger and sorrow), the frequent use of oaths (*cui Jhesus desanpier!* 817, *cui Jhesu ampar!* 934 to signify disapproval or approval), as well as the more obvious dependence on formula, all point to a «preliterary» technique, echoed by the author's limited use of rhetorical devices.

Figures of Speech

The only figures used with any frequency are antithesis and comparison: The *Daurel* poet is fond of juxtaposing contrasting attitudes and actions, and in so doing, creates a few artistic verses. At the beginning of the poem, when Guy and Bove have sworn companionship, the author remarks: *Et l'us ama per fe, e l'aute per trasiho* (30). When Bove asks his murderer to take care of Beton, Guy answers: «*Ieu ai vos mortz; el non es acabatz* (425).» After the murder, Guy conceals his true emotions: *Ri ne el cor, mas de guah a ploratz* (475). Charles marries his sister to her husband's assassin:

> Guis pren la dona a joi et a baudor
> Et ela lui ab ira et ab plor (649).

When Aisilineta reveals the identity of Beton to the fisherman Ebrart, she swears him to secrecy, reminding him of his duty to his lord and placing the safety of the child in his hands: «*Per vos es mortz o per vos aribatz* (801).» The author uses antithetical simile to contrast Guy's ferocity with the almost saintly demeanor of the dying Bove:

> Guis lo regarda cum leos cadenatz
> E·l duc lui cum angils enpenatz (219) [23]

The only other clear example of simile is a commonplace description of Ermenjart: *Sa color fresca cum roza de rozier* (144).

Since metaphor in its various forms was relatively rare in epic, this poverty of «literary» invention in *Daurel* does not surprise. But,

---

[23] Although v. 218 is perhaps an echo of the Albéric *Alexandre,* where we read: *Tal regart fay cum leu qui est preys* (v. 61), these are among the best verses in *Daurel.*

of the three figures usually associated with the genre — hyperbole, litotes and antithesis — only the last is used with any frequency by our author. [24] There are, however, a few weak, quasi litotes:

> Non i a .i. no·is plore de dolor (654);

> E lo duc Boves non o pot plus durar
> Del goifano de l'empeyraire portar (221);

> Tro a Paris el no s'es restancat (545)

> No la refut nien (1855)

One example of hyperbole (*ab vos iran .c. melia cavalgador* (2116) occurs near the very end of the extant poem.

Daurel was written by an epic *jongleur*, if we are to judge by the author's dependence on an arsenal, small but sufficient for his needs, of epic cliché and formulaic expression, and his rudimentary, but effective use of antithesis to the exclusion of other figures of speech. All told, it is difficult to conceive of our author as a learned cleric. [25]

iii. THE LAISSE

The *Daurel* story is presented as a chronological sequence of events with infrequent repetiton and very few halts in the narrative for poetic résumés (e.g., the lay sung to Beton in laisse XXXI), lamentations, or other passages lyrical in nature. While the laisse is the functional narrative, dramatic and lyric unit of the *Roland*, it plays only a limited structural rôle in a poem like *Daurel*. [26] This

---

[24] Zumthor, *Langue et techniques*, p. 118, distinguishes two nuances of medieval poetic style: the one (non-courtly) dominated by these three tropes; the other by allegory and metaphor.

[25] Although a cleric must have been responsible for the transmission of *Daurel* in MS. We have already seen (pp. 17-19) the intervention of a *remanieur* who did not hesitate to tamper with rhyme and meter. M. Delbouille, «Dans un atelier de copistes,» *CCM*, III (1960), 14, insists on the need to study MSS more closely for possible answers to the oral versus literary question. O. Jodogne (*Technique*, pp. 37-56) reveals the importance of cliché to the adaptor who was putting an assonanced poem into rhyme. One cannot, in the case of *Daurel*, attribute certain stylistic elements to the author and others to the adaptor.

[26] And none at all in such poems as *Moniage Guillaume* and *Couronnement Louis* which are almost purely narrative. In the *Roland*, the laisse is «l'élément, le matériau élémentaire,» according to Rychner (*Chanson de*

is only natural since the mid-twelfth-century epic is essentially narrative, not lyric, and as it followed a tendency to take on larger and larger form, the tightly-knit, measured epic strophe of the *Roland* gave way to the variable and amorphous laisse, [27] an evolution that exemplifies the transformation of epic from song to narrative.

In *Daurel* a few tightly-constructed laisses contrast sharply with the episodic and narrative nature of the rest of the poem, consisting of extensive dialogue. [28] Approximately three-fifths of the poem is told in straight narrative style. Of the fifty-two laisses in *Daurel,* only six are predominantly descriptive in content: of those that can be so qualified two (XXIX, XXXVI) recount the preparations for the siege of Monclar, one (XXXIX) recites Beton's accomplishments at the age of nine, another (XV) describes the lamentations over the dead Bove, and a fifth (XXI) tells of the nurse's devotion to Beton. The last two may also be termed lyric, along with the «lay» sung to Beton in XXXI.

Typically, the author uses a few descriptive verses at the beginning of a laisse to set the scene, as in the following example (IV): [29]

> [G]rans fo la cortz en Fransa sus el palais ausor
> Del [duc] Boves d'Antona e de l'empeyrador;
> Tan duc, tan comte i ac, tan home de valor,
> Avesques e arsebes, de cavaliers la flor (129).

Exceptionally, the author inserts a descriptive reprise to recall the action of the previous laisse. The sole example in *Daurel* is found near the beginning of the poem:

---

geste, pp. 124-125), whose distinction between «horizontally» structured poems (e.g., *Roland*) and «vertical» ones (e.g., *Moniage Guillaume*) implies a relationship between the narrative character of a poem and its structure: the more narrative the poem the less firm its strophic structure; the epic with a weak strophic structure cannot employ the means of lyricism inherent in the strophe.

[27] See Angelo Monteverdi, «La laisse épique,» *Technique,* p. 138, who maintains that «le poème narratif en France est né strophique... parce que destiné à être chantée (p. 135).» Cf. J. R. Smeets, «*Alexis* et la *Bible* de Herman de Valenciennes: le problème de l'origine de la laisse,» CCM, VI (1963), 315-325.

[28] In a random sampling of two 200-verse passages, 86 of the first 200 lines, and 99 within vv. 1000-1200 are in dialogue.

[29] Ten laisses (I, II, III, IV, V, XVIII, XIX, XXXI, XL, L) contain two to six descriptive verses each, usually placed at the beginning to set the scene for the action to follow.

[I]

... ...

Juran si companhia amdoy li compaho,
Can si foron juratz lhi bauzo sus el mento
Et l'us ama per fe, et l'aute per trasiho.

[II]

Lo duc Boves d'Antona a fah lo sagramen
Ad Antona el palais si c'o viro .v.c.
L'us es fizels amicx et l'audre mescrezens (33)

... ...

The linking together of consecutive laisses by means of «enchaîne-ment» is a common mnemonic device to facilitate the *jongleur*'s recitation. [30]

Besides the reprise already cited, *Daurel* presents a few rather mechanical examples: the last verse of laisse XVI (*Parlem de Guis cui Dieus puesca azirar!*), for example, makes a crude transition into the following laisse, and the slightly less pedestrian ones at the end of laisse XXXII:

... ...

Laissem Daurel e Betonet em patz
E tornem sai a cels qu'avem laissatz (1280).

Only in the early part of the story does the author make use of laisse division in an effective manner, and it is here that we find the sole example of repetition for dramatic effect in *Daurel*. In a sequence of three laisses, the traitor, Guy, reveals his growing jealousy by repeating his threat to destroy Bove:

<hr />

[30] C. A. Robson («Aux Origines de la poésie épique romane: art narratif et mnémotechnie,» pt. 1, *Moyen Age*, LXVII [1961], 41-84) has advanced the theory that, as an aid to memory, eleventh-century *jongleurs* grouped their laisses in a certain order, each group of three consisting of assonances in -*a*-, -*e*-, -*o*-, or -*i*-, a system which «se trahit le plus facilement dans les poèmes occitans (p. 54).» Although we find in *Daurel* what may be a few vestiges of such a system, notably towards the end of the MS: e.g., laisses XXXVIII-XL -*a*-, -*ie*-, -*i*-; XLIII-XLV -*a*-, -*e*-, -*o*-, XLVIII-L -*a*-, -*ie*-, -*o*-, they seem more coincidental than systematic.

[IV]

[Charles offers Ermenjart in marriage to Bove]
E Guis entendec o —dis c'om no·l pot auzir:
«Companh, per cela dona vos covenra murir!» (125)

[V]

[Charles grants Bove a large dowry]
E Guis a dih tot suau cum fels e traïdor:
«Per aqueta molher molra el a dolor!» (138)

[VI]

[The wedding takes place]
So dis don Guis lo tracher lauzengier:
«Compans, per cesta dona vos vendra destu[r]bier!» (154)
[They prepare to leave Paris]
Lo tracher Guis —cui Jhesu desamper—
A encobida na Esmenjartz sa molher. (173)

The poet's repeated statement of Guy's motivation (foreshadowing the tragedy to come) recalls the «laisses similaires» so typical of the *Roland* and older epic tradition. Guy's words, said between clenched teeth, sound a striking contrast to the picture of joy and harmony so manifest at the court of Charlemagne. In the ensuing laisses, Guy's whispered threats are gradually transformed into action, culminating with the murder of Bove.

It is significant that the stylistically well-conceived laisses are concentrated in the first section of the poem, where the most traditional and archaic themes occur, while in the remainder of *Daurel* the laisse is amorphous. Does this pattern suggest that the part of the poem dealing with Boves d'Antona was composed earlier than the rest? We will return to this question after a closer analysis of the structure of the whole poem; however, we can tentatively answer that it does not. The differences in technique enumerated above do not warrant the conclusion that *Daurel* was pieced together by two separate authors. They indicate, rather, a conscious effort on the part of one author to create a «classic» epic by simulating the «oral» style traditionally associated with the genre, but it is not long before he lapses into the easier and more natural «contemporary» style. We can locate this transformation roughly at laisse XIV or XV. Thereafter the style and versification become clearer and more regular, the laisses longer, and the author, finally, seems to be at ease in his narrative.

iv. THE EPISODE

While the poem can be divided into episodes of nearly even length (approximately 200+verses), the size of the laisses fluctuates widely. The average number of verses in a laisse is forty-two, but the longest (XLVII) has 122, the shortest (V) thirteen. In addition to being uneven in length, the laisses in *Daurel* frequently perform no narrative function,[31] while there is an organic unity in the typical episode which transcends laisse divisions.

The episode which relates Ermenjart's attempt to save Beton from Guy covers four complete laisses (XX-XXIV) and continues unbroken for over 200 verses. The scribe, failing to put indentations at each rhyme change, obviously was aware of this continuity. It is interesting that there are two transitional verses in the passage (735-736) which are found in the middle of a laisse. Except to change the rhyme, therefore, the laisse has no dramatic function here; the narrative flows smoothly on, unbroken by laisse division, as an analysis of laisses XX-XXIV will demonstrate. The passage opens with two lines that serve to link it to the previous one, in a typical «enchaînement» (cf. pp. 75-76).

[XX]

Lo rey s'en vai a·l tracher Guis ab els,
Qu'el le ssolassa tro es vengutz los ses. (687)

The next forty-eight verses are predominantly descriptive and lyrical and set the scene for the rapid chain of events that follows:

La franca dona trames per .i. borgues (688)
... ...
N'Aisilineta que mol jauzenta n'es (716)
Noiri l'enfan tan solamen .ii. mes.

[XXI]

Al filh del duc an facha tal maio
Dedins non a ni lata ni cabiro,
... ...

---

[31] e.g., laisses XV and XVI, which form a continuous episode. The mixed -*ier* and -*ar* rhymes in XV show how arbitrary the division at v. 511 is.

Pro lei aporta vi et pa a bando
E draps de Fransa colque l'enfanto. (734)

After two verses to make the transition from Beton's island hiding-place to Guy's castle:

Laisem l'estar a Dieu benedisio, (735)
Parlem del trage de Guio.

the remainder of the episode (148 verses) is purely narrative:

«Dona Esmenjartz, ben aves lo cor felo
Car vos per mi m'aves fugit Beto.»
... ...
Estai la dona que no i dis oc ni no. (743)
El cor sab ben c'aisi a trasio.

[XXII]

Pueis li respon: «Mas tan lo·m demandatz,
Ben es raizos que vos o sapiatz;»
... ...
«.M. martz d'a[r]gen ay uei en mar trobatz.» (815)
Daz els se partz, es en corren anatz.

[XXIII]

Lo fers pescayre — cui Jhesus desanpier! —
Entro a Guio, no se vols estancar,
... ...
«Senher,» dit el, «pessem de l'espleitar.» (852)
Abtan Daurel ven·s a la nau intrar.

[XXIV]

Ab mol gran cocha s'en so d'oltra passatz (854)
E n'Aicelina Daurel n'a rayzonatz:
... ...
Tuh n'an gran gauh et teno·s per pagatz. (897)

The last two verses end the episode by anticipating the next one:

De la noirissa foro mal oblidatz
Que·n fon destreta a tort e a pecat. (899)

This long episode of 200 verses is similar in structure to some of the short, well-constructed laisses in *Daurel*. Laisse **IV**, for example, contains in miniature the same development found in the episode: a transitional verse, two lines of description to set the scene, eleven of narrative, and two final lines that anticipate future action.

The basic structural unit in *Daurel* is the episode, not the laisse. The episode appears to have assumed the role of the laisse, perhaps because the narrative epic required a larger mold which would permit a more cohesive development of the story, uninterrupted by the repetition and transition inherent in the use of the more isolated laisse. As a glance at *Aye d'Avignon, Orson de Beauvais,* or to cite more extreme examples, *Parise la Duchesse* and *Doon de Mayence* will show, this tendency towards dilation of laisse into episode [32] is symptomatic of the general drift of epic from *chanson de geste* to *roman d'aventures*. The *Daurel* author is astride two techniques; his use of the laisse at the beginning of the poem represents, as we have said, the «classical» approach to the genre. This does not conceal the essentially novelistic nature of his narrative technique: he was composing a «canso» which required the use of the laisse, but the laisse is not the important narrative unit.

In calling this basic narrative unit an «episode,» I am not suggesting that *Daurel* is episodic, but merely that *Daurel* is told in segments of relatively equal length which one can superimpose on the formal division into laisses, and which correspond to the narrative elements in a romance (cf. *Jaufré,* for example, where each episode is very clearly delineated, or *Parise,* where epic technique has all but given way to the romanesque). [33]

We have seen how most of the traditionally epic elements associated with oral composition and delivery are concentrated in the first section of *Daurel*. In spite of this, the first 1172 verses fall into approximately equal segments, each of which could be shown to correspond in structure and to fulfill the narrative function of a laisse:

---

[32] This «dilation épisodique» of which Menéndez Pidal speaks (*La Chanson de Roland et la tradition épique,* p. 463) is reflected in the fact that, generally, later epics tend to be substantially longer than earlier ones (see René Louis, «Qu'est-ce que l'épopée vivante?» *La Table Ronde,* No. 132 [Dec. 1958], 11-12).

[33] In *Parise,* a long (300 +) laisse habitually alternates with a short one (20 + or —), serving to break the monotony of the predominating -*e* rhymes.

vv. 1-223 Brotherhood of Bove and Guy
Marriage of Bove and Ermenjart
Daurel granted fief by Bove

224-533 Jealousy and treachery of Guy
Birth of Beton and Daurelet
Murder of Bove

534-685 Injustice and cupidity of Charles
Forced marriage of widow to Guy

687-899 Guy's brutality to Ermenjart
Guy's pursuit of infant Beton
Ebrart's betrayal

900-1172 Daurel's sacrifice of Daurelet
Guy murders Daurel's son
Flight of Daurel and Beton
Monclar prepared for siege

To take another example from the section of *Daurel* in which the laisse structure is strongest — in the second episode, Guy sets the tragic events in motion by his improper advances to Ermenjart, thus destroying the outward harmony that has prevailed up to this point. Guy's motivation, an undercurrent in the first segment (see pp. 75-76), provides a transitional link to the second, in which it comes to the surface as the dominant theme. In the same manner, Guy's threat to murder Bove within two months in order to possess Ermenjart leads to the climax of this episode, the murder of Bove, and provides the nucleus of the following one (the marriage of the widow to her husband's assassin). Ermenjart's denunciation of Guy, her reiterated warnings unheeded because Bove cannot believe his sworn companion capable of infamy, heighten the sense of impending tragedy. The scene is set for the confrontation we know must come, which occurs in the dark forest far from the eyes of witnesses. Bove, praying to God for the safety of his son, dies by the hand of the man he most loved. This prayer, as well as Ermenjart's unheeded accusations against Guy, provides the transition to the next episode. Thus, action leads into action in an unbroken chain of events, a cause (Guy's jealousy) leading to an effect (Bove's murder) which is, in turn, cause of what follows. The other major episodes in this part of the poem invite similar appraisal, as does the second section. [34]

Now the question arises, how did the author fit these smaller narrative elements into his over-all plan?

v. NARRATIVE UNITY

The narrative framework of *Daurel* is clear-cut and logical: three great divisions which can be entitled «Boves d'Antona» (vv. 1-1172), «Enfances Beton» (vv. 1173-2089), and the fragmentary «Chevalerie Beton» (vv. 2090-end). Each episode, each incident, is subordinated to this over-all plan, revealing a sense of balance and unity. These divisions are not in any sense «cantilènes» linked together by scribe or adaptor to form a more substantial work; they are, like the acts in a play, useful and perhaps functional parts of the whole epic. We cannot, of course, in the absence of a complete redaction, draw definitive conclusions: we have proposed a tri-partite construction for a poem which, in its extant form, contains only two parts.

Let us examine the concrete evidence of the extant poem. The chronology admirably fits our proposed schema:

«Boves d'Antona»

Start — swearing of brotherhood
10   — ten years pass (v. 34)
12   — children born to Ermenjart and Beatrix (275)
13   — murder of Bove; exile of Daurel and Beton (1115)
       total — 13 years

«Enfances Beton»

16   — Beton aged four (1260)
24   — Beton aged twelve (1600)
25   — Beton aged thirteen (1686)
26   — return to Monclar and Poitiers after three-month
       voyage (1896)
       total — 13 years

---

[34] The thousand verses can be divided as follows: 1173-1280, 1281-1405, 1406-1640, 1641-1898, 1899-2086.

«Chevalerie Beton»

vv. 2087-2089 indicate the passage of an unspecified time
between Beton's return to Poitiers and the opening of this
episode.

The first part, as we shall demonstrate in the next chapter, is dominated by Bove. The tone is tragic and somber, the themes primeval
and universal, the style archaic and «oral». The transition between
this section and the following one, «Enfances Beton,» may appear
somewhat arbitrary at first glance,[35] but is clearly delineated by the
recapitulation in laisse XXXI, which, in the form of a *lais d'amor*
(1180) inserted into the narrative, occurs at a logical break in the
story. Even if the author had not placed this revealing lay at this
point in the text, a dramatic change in tone, style and content would
quickly apprise us of the transition. The main theme of this section
is not, as one might expect, exile and vengeance taking place against
the background of the hero's youthful adventures. The «Enfances Beton»
are like no other in epic: Beton's vengeance is compressed into a mere
200 verses, while 500 are used to describe his upbringing in the Emir's
court. «Enfances» in epic (cf. *Enfances Guillaume, Enfances Vivien,
Mainet*) meant the youthful exploits of the «anfes»; genealogy, birth
and baptism are generally mentioned, but there is no interest in the
infancy and childhood of the hero. The *Daurel* author makes this
his major theme, and in a refreshingly realistic fashion, lingers over
the growth of Beton from infancy to knighthood.

All sense of tragedy has vanished from the story at this point,
with the result that the episodes, while sustaining interest, lack dramatic
effect. Also missing are the cruelty and vigor of the first section.
The confrontation of rightful heir and usurper, the dénouement so
long awaited, the logical outcome so carefully prepared, disappoints
because it is anti-climactic. Guy, who has been depicted as a re-
doubtable adversary, is vanquished far too easily. However, these
faults are unimportant compared to the novelty of seeing a real flesh-
and-blood child in epic literature.

------

[35] It may be argued that the first section more properly ends at v. 1091
(burial of Daurelet, departure of Daurel and Beton, death of Daurel's
wife) but I prefer to include the siege preparations in the first part (relying
on the transitional recapitulation).

Chevalerie Beton

The «Enfances» ends with the banal but unmistakable «and they lived happily ever after:»

Tostemp estero ab mot gran alegrier (2086).

The fragmentary third section follows with a new laisse (L) and the conventionally transitional lines:

So es en mai quan li ram per la flor
E li boisso recobro lor odor (2088).

The remaining hundred verses suggest that a new story is beginning, one that is a logical continuation of what has gone before:

2087-2121   Recapitulation of story
Count Beton decides to seek redress
    from Charlemagne
Ermenjart counsels him to be prudent

2121-end   Beton sends ambassadors to Charles
They refuse to salute the emperor
Ambassadors recapitulate story
[MS breaks off]

Since the remainder of the manuscript is missing (and we have no idea of the extent of the loss), we can only guess at the rest of the story.

There are two possibilities:

(1) the loss is a minor one. The *jongleur* added a short epilogue to awaken interest in a sequel he had not yet composed, in the manner of *Orson de Beauvais,* which ends with the promise of a continuation about Milon de Beauvais. [36] There is one overriding reason for not accepting this possibility: a four-verse epilogue at the end of an intact MS is not analogous to a hundred-line story which starts

---

[36] Which Gaston Paris (ed., *Orson de Beauvais,* SATF [Paris, 1899], p. lxxx) doubts was ever composed, since Milon is already a major character in *Orson.*

with all the traditional elements of narration and then trails off into illegibility at the end of an obviously damaged MS.

(2) The lost conclusion comprised as many as a thousand or more verses: we are lacking the «Chevalerie Beton.» Even if as many as 2000 verses were missing, *Daurel* would still have been a relatively short poem, like the *Roland*, whereas in its present state it is slightly longer than *Guillaume* I. [37] We have seen how the author balanced the first two sections of the poem, how he constructed his episodes in a measured fashion, how he set off these sections by recapitulations. Would he have composed a third section drastically shorter or different in structure from the others? Why would he have placed three reca-pitulations (vv. 1641-1683, 1810-1845, 2091-2104) at such short intervals if he were nearing the end of his story?

There is another factor that supports our hypothesis: everything in *Daurel* tells us that this is an epic of revolt, yet revolt is precisely what is missing. If *Daurel* was influenced by earlier and contemporary feudal epics, it would certainly have reworked the fundamental themes of revolt and repentance that are of such importance in *Girart de Roussillon* and *Raoul de Cambrai*. It cannot be mere coincidence that the opening of the third section is identical with the obligatory scenes that begin *Ogier, Renaud, Garin,* and *Girart* (the spring *topos*, the messengers arriving at the emperor's court, the provocation). [38]

The tragedy of Bove, Daurel's sacrifice, Beton's upbringing must lead to something more significant than the punishment of Guy. In the final fragment, Beton challenges the might and authority of the emperor. Here is the suggestion of the real dénouement which, unfortunately, we shall never know. Is Beton to be guilty of the same *démesure* that brings about the destruction of Girart and Raoul? Or will he, like Ogier, force Charlemagne to pay for his wrong-

---

[37] The length of the epics studied by Rychner (*Chanson de geste,* p. 37) varies from 870 (*Pèlerinage de Charlemagne*) to 18,000 (*Renaut de Montau-ban*): «Dans l'ensemble de la littérature épique, nos chansons sont courtes... Cette relative brièveté doit avoir quelque rapport avec la relative ancienneté des chansons choisies.»

[38] Reto R. Bezzola, «A propos de la valeur littéraire des chansons féodales,» *Technique,* p. 193. To his examples, we may add *Doon de Mayence,* where a similar episode is introduced by the following verses:

Chen fu u temps de mai, que flourissent rosier
E flourissent li pre, verdoient li vergier, (p. 183).

doing? In my opinion, the author meant Beton to follow in the footsteps of his grandfather, Ogier. [39]

vi. CONCLUSION

From a stylistic point of view, the poem's main shortcoming is its lack of lyricism, its laconicism in potentially poetic and poignant situations. Its value, on the other hand, lies in the author's ability to weave a convincing tale out of what could have been merely isolated episodes borrowed from other epics. Although the structure of *Daurel* is narrative and episodic (in the sense that episode, rather than laisse, is the basic unit), each element is subordinated to an over-all plan, a clearly-perceived tripartite construction comprising sections which might be entitled «Boves d'Antona,» «Enfances Beton,» and «Chevalerie Beton.»

The first section of *Daurel* exemplifies the transition of epic from «song» to narrative. Although the shorter, often functional laisses, the presence of «oral» techniques and the primitive atmosphere seem to suggest an earlier epic tradition, there is no convincing evidence that «Boves d'Antona» was composed separately from the rest of the poem. It is true that the romanesque atmosphere of the «Enfances Beton» is in great contrast to the archaism of the first, but neither is inconsistent with the *ethos* of the mid-twelfth century, and the underlying unity of the whole poem supports our claim of single authorship. The differences in technique are, as we have seen, superficial, and there is nothing here to set *Daurel* apart from the epic tradition of this period or to cast doubt upon our 1150-1168 date of composition.

The vestiges of oral composition and presentation and the noble rôle played by a *jongleur* in the poem suggest that our author was, indeed, a *jongleur*. The fact that these oral elements are vestigial, and perhaps simulated, indicates that *Daurel* passed through the

---

[39] P. LeGentil traces the psychological verity of the rebel in two distinct manifestations, either of which may have provided the model for Beton: Ogier, like Raoul, superhuman in his *démesure* and fury («Ogier le Danois, héros épique,» *Romania*, LXXVIII [1957], 199-233); Girart, whose character is drawn on a realistically human scale («Girard de Roussillon: sens et structure du poème,» *Romania*, LXXVIII [1957], 328-89, 463-510, esp. 503).

hands of an adaptor; in its present form, the poem is neither «literary» nor «oral,» but these are, at best, relative terms. *Daurel,* like its contemporaries, can probably be characterized as decadent in technique: form, style and content are midway between *chanson* and *roman.*

Chapter VIII

CHARACTERS AND THEMES

While W. W. Comfort's division into six types — king, hero, traitor, woman, bourgeois, Saracen — [1] offers a somewhat oversimplified view of the characters in epic, it nevertheless will provide a useful starting-point for determining what is commonplace and what is original in *Daurel*. A brief glance at the plot (see **Summary**) makes it clear that our poem contains much that is commonplace both in treatment and content. This epic stylization, especially apparent in the author's delineation of secondary characters and motifs, is much less so in his creation of major characters, proving that, although he freely made use of epic tradition, he was original, even unique, in many ways.

In our study of secondary themes and minor characters, it is necessary to stress the distinction between analogue or parallel and source or imitation. In most cases the *Daurel* author reflects and continues prevailing mid-twelfth-century literary tradition, although there is seldom sufficient evidence to prove imitation or even derivation from a specific source. He would not, for example, have had to know the *Chanson de Roland* in order to make use of the names Roland and Olivier; the mere fact that he places Charlemagne's court in Paris may be advanced as evidence that his knowledge of the *Roland* was indeed second-hand.

Although important and often striking analogues exist between *Daurel* and other epics, given the uncertainty of dating and diffusion,

---

[1] «The Character Types in the Old French *Chansons de geste*,» *PMLA*, XXI (1906), 279-432. Cf. Ewart Lewis' critique, «Personality in the *Chansons de Geste*,» *Philological Quarterly*, XV (1936), 273-285.

the question of which poem is source and which imitation cannot in most cases be answered. The theme of child sacrifice, for instance, can hardly have been transmitted from *Jourdain de Blaye* to *Daurel,* since there is no indication that *Jourdain* existed before 1200. On the other hand, given the limited diffusion of our poem, we have no certainty that the *Jourdain* author knew *Daurel.* Nevertheless, the analogue is such a strong one that we can rule out coincidence and go on to seek a common literary source probably familiar to both authors — in this case *Amis et Amiles* (of which *Jourdain* is the tardy sequel). Now child sacrifice is a widespread theme in folklore,[2] but since it is unlikely that our medieval poet from Poitou knew either Sanscrit or Korean, our search for analogues can be limited to twelfth-century literature in which these common themes appear.

We shall start our examination with the secondary characters — the more conventional aspect of *Daurel* — showing the author's use of stereotyped material in often banal, occasionally original fashion. We will then turn our attention to the author's more original handling of the major characters and themes, and conclude with a summary of the evidence concerning sources and originality.

i. Secondary Characters

The Feudal Suzerain: Charlemagne

The emperor-figure in *Daurel* is a composite of stereotypes drawn from epic rather than from actual historical tradition. At the opening of the poem, when Charlemagne rewards Bove for his loyalty by granting him Ermenjart in marriage with a huge fief as dowry, he enacts the traditional rôle of emperor. Although his actions are those of feudal suzerain rather than imperial sovereign, and his court is situated in Paris rather than Aix, the author conveys the aura, dim but still tangible, of the legendary Charlemagne surrounded by Roland, Oliver and the rest of his court:

> Tan duc, tan comte i ac, tan home de valor,
> Avesques e arsebes, de cavaliers la flor (129).

---

[2] See Stith Thompson, *Motif-Index of Folk Literature* (Bloomington, Ind., 1957), V, 361; esp. K.512.2.2 and S.260.1.4.

But the portrait changes radically after the death of Bove. Charles is now depicted as a petty and heartless tyrant, who accepts a large bribe from Guy and forces his sister, Ermenjart, to marry the traitor. Here in this episode the motivation of Charles is guided by the most practical of considerations: having paid his mercenaries, his treasury is depleted and he is in need of money. Charles' hypocrisy is expressed in these verses:

> Cant au l'aver que es tan desmesuratz,
> Lo dol del dux es trastot oblidat (581),

And, since only he remains unmoved by Ermenjart's poignant plea for justice, Charles is not rewarding evil-doing either arbitrarily or on the basis of evil counsel. He has, as we are reminded by this cruel portrait, sold his sister for money:

> «Aital ric rey si fo en bon ponh natz
> Que per aver de sa sor fai mercatz (623).»

In contrast and apparent contradiction to this unflattering characterization, we have another portrait of Charles. Daurel in exile never speaks ill of the emperor, and in fact, praises his generosity and greatness to the Emir. Not until the final verses of the extant poem is there any indication of Beton's intention to rebel against Charles and then only if the emperor does not make redress for his dishonorable actions. What at first glance might appear puzzling or contradictory in the characterization is actually nothing more than unoriginal handling of a stereotyped character whose actions are tailored more to demands of plot than to historical prespective. The relationship of the historical Charlemagne to the Charlemagne of the *roman d'aventures* is tenuous indeed: [3] while the Charlemagne of the *Roland* is a great and wise ruler, a king and warrior of heroic stature, the saintly leader of an elite people, [4] twelfth-century epics often depict him as a weak-willed and ineffectual monarch. As Reto Bezzola, in his study of the transformation of epic into romance, points out, the degradation of the emperor-figure in epic was due

---

[3] Joseph Bédier, *Les Légendes épiques* (Paris, 1913), IV, 437 ff.
[4] Bédier, *Légendes épiques*, IV, 458. Cf. Matarasso, *Recherches*, pp. 149-158 («Le Roi et la Royauté»).

in no small part to the contrast of the fading ideal of Charlemagne as the powerful and just sovereign with the historically closer reality of the rather pathetic descendants of Charles who ruled France in the ninth and tenth centuries and, even closer at hand, the despised twelfth-century Capetians. [5] Unfortunately, and somewhat unjustly for the memory of Charlemagne, the weak and tyrannical king-figure in epic literature is identified not merely with Louis, his descendant, but with Charles himself.

The literary evolution of Charlemagne from the majestic figure of the *Roland* to the *fainéant* king of the thirteenth-century *Gaydon* and *Fierabras* has been traced by Gaston Paris in his *Histoire poétique de Charlemagne* [6] and need not be repeated here. The king-figure in the feudal epic is more a universal character-type than a literary descendant of the historical or Rolandian Charlemagne; called variously Charlemagne, Louis, Charles Martel, Carloman, or Charles the Simple, according to the poem, he is generally portrayed as a feudal suzerain, easily won over by flattery or money, capable of committing acts of flagrant injustice towards his most loyal nobles, and often guilty of starting fratricidal feudal wars between his vassals. In short, his presence in the story serves as an indispensable catalyst for the novelistic themes of the persecuted wife, the unjustly exiled hero, and other common motifs which abound in the feudal epic.

This characterization of the emperor-figure is perfectly legitimate in the context of the feudal epic where the absolute ruler is wont to use his power despotically and destructively, and «in no way represents a 'degeneration' of the Rolandian type, as Comfort would have us believe.» [7] In *Girart, Raoul, Orson, Aye, Amis, Daurel* and others of the genre, the actions of the suzerain turn the most capable and deserving of his vassals into outlaws and rebels, while traitors reap undeserved rewards and honors for their misdeeds. The feudal baron, forced to rebel against an authority he is duty-bound to respect,

---

[5] *Les Origines et la formation de la littérature courtoise en occident* (Paris, 1960), II, 496-497.

[6] 2nd ed. rev. by Paul Meyer (Paris, 1905). Cf. Karl H. Bender, «Les métamorphoses de la royauté de Charlemagne dans les premières épopées franco-italiennes,» *Cultura Neolatina*, XXI (1961), 164-174.

[7] Or so says Wm. Calin (*Epic of Revolt*, pp. 161-162) referring to Comfort's oversimplifications (*PMLA*, XXI, 286-287, 295). In the context of the feudal epic, Calin's point is well-taken.

becomes a disturber of the social order and must eventually bow to this authority by reaching a reconciliation with his suzerain, thus restoring peace and harmony. [8]

Injustice

The power of the feudal suzerain to cement alliances by granting of fiefs and the arranging of marriages provides the pretext, in epic fiction as well as in history, for much injustice and strife. When the holder of a large fief died, it was often to the ruler's advantage to marry off the widow or appoint a guardian for a surviving child as quickly as possible, so as to have the fief tenanted. [9] If someone usurped the fief by force before the arrangements were made, it was often the wisest course for the suzerain to accept the *fait accompli,* thus avoiding a test of strength with the intruder. Injustice to a widow or infant heir could thus on occasion be justified by the larger interests promoting the welfare of the kingdom. In epic, of course, such moral compromise leads inevitably to bloodshed and rebellion. It is Louis' rash promise to Raoul that he will grant him the first fief to become vacant, (since he cannot dispose of the hero's hereditary Cambrai) that causes the war over the Vermandois. [10]

The power of investiture carried with it the right to choose a husband for a female vassal, in effect to safeguard the right of a woman left without male heir by allowing her to inherit a fief, but only on condition that she marry «afin d'avoir un répondant et c'est sur ce motif que le suzerain fond son droit d'épouser lui-même ou de marier à son gré la fille vassale.» [11] Although in actual practice

---

[8] According to G. Paris (*Histoire poétique,* p. 460): «La poésie féodale ne fait pas à la royauté une guerre d'extermination. Les barons sont dominés par le sentiment de la suprématie du roi, et ne songent pas à faire la révolution. Le rôle d'ennemis acharnés de Charlemagne est laissé à des traîtres... Mais les grands révoltés que soulèvent les injustices de l'empereur lui font une guerre loyale et presque toujours défensive; la sympathie est pour eux, mais elle ne vas pas jusqu'à les délier de leurs devoirs.»

[9] Léon Gautier, *La Chevalerie* (Paris, 1884), p. 342. A new ed. by J. Levron (Paris, 1959) has an excellent iconography, but is abridged.

[10] See Matarasso, *Recherches,* pp. 107-126 («Le Problème de l'hérédité du fief»).

[11] Joseph Calmette, *Le Monde féodale,* pp. 162-163. See also Charles Petit-Dutaillis, *The Feudal Monarchy in France and England from the Tenth to the Thirteenth Century,* «Harper Torchbook» (New York/Evanston, 1964 [1936]), pp. 305-306.

women were admitted as rightful heirs without a guarantor as early as the eleventh century, [12] the abuse of this marriage right provided an eminently suitable theme for the feudal poet. Far from finding it strange «that the king should be represented as forcing a woman to marry a man who murdered her husband,» [13] one can see how historical reality, manipulated by the epic *jongleur,* grows into a commonplace theme divorced from that of reality: the king forces a widow to marry a traitor in *Aymeri de Narbonne, Orson, Aye* (for money), *Elie de Saint-Gilles,* and *Raoul* (twice). [14] Typical of the genre is *Aye,* in which the heroine, daughter of Duke Antoine, killed in the war against the Saxons, is brought to court. The barons, in the midst of the lamentations over the dead duke, request the king to give his niece in marriage and thus serve the fief, since it is fruitless to go on lamenting the dead:

> «Tot ce lessiez ester,» dist Bertran de Léune,
> «Ja ne gaura de mort ne chauf ne chevalu
> Mais mariez vo niece et n'i attendez plus (p. 3).» [15]

Aye's marriage to Garnier provokes the enmity of Beranger and his family, and, later in the poem, at Garnier's death, Charles forces Aye to marry the traitor Milon, but allows her to escape by according her a respite of one year.

In *Aye,* the emperor is depicted as a noble figure, betrayed by those who, since the death of Roland and the peers, have assumed honored positions in his court. As old Girart remarks: «*Trop ont li traïtor en grant cort conversé* (p. 11).» While the Charlemagne of *Daurel* is a much less noble character (since he is guilty of selling

---

[12] F. L. Ganshof, *Feudalism,* «Harper Torchbook» (New York, 1961 [1952]), p. 124, cites an example of how this could be done (and was done under Henry I for Countess Adela).

[13] as does M. Skidmore, *The Moral Traits of Christian and Saracen as Portrayed by the Chanson de Geste* (Colorado, 1935), pp. 112-113. Cf. Jackson (*Literature of the Middle Ages,* p. 82) who suggests that this sort of marriage is a Celtic motif (e.g., *Yvain*). Whether Celtic or not, the theme has been a favorite one of dramatists from Euripides (*Hecuba, Trojan Woman, Andromache*) to Shakespeare (*Richard III*).

[14] Matarasso (*Recherches,* pp. 110-112) demonstrates how closely the situation of Aalais corresponds to feudal law. She has three years to remarry or give up the fief.

[15] Cf. *Daurel,* vv. 616-617, 633.

his own sister's honor for money), his motivation is basically the same: he must remarry his sister as quickly as possible in order to tenant the important fief now lying vacant and undefended. In view of the lack of proof that he murdered his companion, Guy is the logical and legal heir, and Charles actually has little practical choice in the matter, since Guy is already in command of the situation. All this would be sufficient motivation for Charlemagne's action. Why then does the *Daurel* author emphasize the greed and dishonesty of the emperor by having him accept the bribe offered by Guy? We are reminded of *Raoul*, where the characterization of the king is even more ambiguous: Louis has no redeeming quality at all and embodies all the defects ever attributed to sovereigns in epic literature: [16] among his other faults, he is weak, capricious, unjust, malicious, acts without thinking, lacks imagination and common sense. The *Daurel* author does not go quite so far, since our first impression of Charles is favorable, but he is obviously influenced by an anti-imperial literary tradition. As in *Girart*, the view of Charlemagne is two-sided: he is capable of evil actions, but he is nonetheless divinely ordained and must be honored and respected. The *Raoul* author had no such compunctions in dealing with Louis, whose name obviously lacked the imperial magic.

The emperor-figure in *Daurel* reflects two stereotypes, the first being a rather weak echo of the Rolandian Charlemagne, the second representing the detested suzerain of the feudal epic. The author, by employing the former, links his poem to the greatest *geste* of all, but the latter better satisfied the exigencies of his story. He makes no attempt to reconcile what appear to a modern reader as two contradictory portraits.

The Heroic Wife: Ermenjart

Ermenjart, *la pros et la valhan* (290), is a touching portrayal of feminine fidelity and constancy. As a woman, overshadowed at every turn by the men around her, her rôle in *Daurel* is secondary. She is incapable of direct, effective action — her warnings to Bove go unheeded, her attempt to slay Guy is thwarted, she cannot obtain justice from her own brother — but her very vulnerability makes of

---

[16] Matarasso (*Recherches*, pp. 154-155) sees Louis as a marionette, a caricature of the king-figure.

her a noble and even tragic figure. Her love for Bove and her loyalty to his name demand the utmost sacrifice on her part; whatever the cost to her, their infant son must be saved. Imprisoned, mistreated by her husband's murderer who has been forced upon her by her own brother, she remains steadfast, and Guy must finally concede defeat in his attempt to win her by guile, threat, and when these have failed, force. Her very existence, moreover, is a constant reminder to him of impending vengeance. Her presence lends courage to the defenders of Monclar and poisons whatever enjoyment Guy might have hoped to obtain from the fruits of his treachery.

Like Aalais (*Raoul*), she represents moral right held captive by unjust legalism. Charles has wronged her, but the law, as an instrument of his power, supports him and leaves her no recourse. As a woman, she cannot take up the sword against her enemy; words are her only weapons, and her lament on the death of her husband, her confrontation with Charles and Guy are scenes which are eloquent expressions of passion, grief and anger. Powerless to act, she expresses her anguish and frustration in what are among the best lyrical verses in *Daurel*:

> «Lassa, caitiva, d'un renegat trachor
> Que mi a tolta trastota m'amor (488).»

> «L'autrier mi venc, pres mi a menassier
> Qu'el me tolria mon senhor e mon pier;
> Ara·l vei mort, mos cors mi vol crebier!
> Vieus es Betos que·l sabra be vengier (509)!»

Although the description of the physical manifestations of grief in these verses is pure convention (rending of clothing, tearing at hair and flesh), and the physical portrait of Ermenjart quite banal (see p. 68),[17] the passage is not without power; since the author has gradually developed the character of Ermenjart by portraying her as the victim of a series of events which turn her happiness into sorrow and which she is unable to prevent. After her second warning to Bove goes unheeded, she foresees the inevitable tragedy: «*Mon essien n'aurai lo cor dolan* (309).» Her reaction when she is informed of her husband's death by none other than the murderer himself:

---

[17] Cf. the similar portrait given by Matarasso of Aalais (*Recherches,* pp. 231-232).

Sospira fort e mena gran dolor,
Ca enblesmada de dol e d'ira e de plor (490).

is saved from triteness by the dramatic intensity of the scene. It is in this section of the poem that Ermenjart plays an important role: she gains the sympathy of the burghers (and, by identification, of the audience); since everyone must submit to Charlemagne's will, she is left a lonely and tragic figure, victim of male injustice, bound over to the hated Guy. Courageously, if only symbolically, she defies them both by cursing Charles and throwing the wedding ring into the fire. [18] She will live to see the vindication of her sacrifice when, at the end of his long exile, she is reunited with her son.

The heroic, long-suffering wife-widow-mother is another commonplace character-type in the feudal epic. Sometimes a relatively unimportant minor figure (as in *Jourdain,* where she is barely mentioned at the beginning of the poem, or in *Doon,* where the mother-figure is little more than the pretext for a few scenes of sadistic eroticism), she is, on occasion, the heroine of the poem (e.g., *Aye* and *Parise*). However, neither Aye nor Parise dominates the stories to which they give their names, as does, by way of contrast, Kriemhild in the *Nibelungenlied.* [19] The French feudal heroine is overshadowed by male characters — hero or traitor. Ermenjart is, in turn, under the tutelage of her brother, dominated by her husband, at the mercy of Guy, and finally, dependent upon Beton. For one brief moment (at the death of Bove) she is free to speak and act in her own right, but to no avail, since no one dare openly be her champion against Guy and Charles.

With the exception of Guibourc (*Guillaume*) and Berthe (*Girart*) who with their husbands form closely-knit couples, the epic heroine is a passive character, reflecting the traditional rôle of woman in medieval society, [20] where she was relegated to secondary status, and was little more than a legal minor always in the tutelage of some

---

[18] Vv. 639-649.

[19] According to M. O'C. Walshe (*Medieval German Literature: A Survey*) Cambridge, Mass., [1962], p. 229), Kriemhild, unlike her French counterparts, «dominates the tale from first to last and gives it unity.»

[20] Cf. Joseph Coppin, *Amour et mariage dans la littérature française du Nord au moyen âge* (Paris, 1961), chap. 1.

male; [21] she was treated with an often unjust contempt, often with indifference and brutality. [22] Woman was, of course, slowly emerging from this rôle during the twelfth century, but this aspect of contemporary life seems not to have been mirrored in epic, an essentially masculine genre. [23]

The plight of the widowed Ermenjart, stripped of the legal right to rule Bove's fief for her son, Beton, is in conformity to the traditional treatment of the subject in the twelfth-century epic. The *Daurel* author chose to ignore the history of his own province where, from the beginning of the eleventh century, the wives and mistresses of the dukes of Aquitaine played important political roles. [24] The persecuted-widow motif appears even more archaic and ambiguous when we take into account the agreement, so primitive in nature, that gives Guy a legal (and moral, insofar as Bove was concerned when he made it) claim to the possession of Ermenjart and the fief.

While one might justifiably expect a southern author to be an innovator in his creation of female characters, or at least not to have been altogether immune to courtly influence, our *jongleur* echoes the robust male tone of his northern models; of the courtly aspect of his Poitevin environment, we find no trace in his characterization of Ermenjart.

Cruelty

Since cruelty was part of the medieval *ethos*, we are not surprised to find women abused and beaten in epic; this is one of the less attractive, although most typical aspects of the feudal *chanson*, where sadistic brutality is a prime characteristic of the traitor, permitting the author to portray the cliché motif: «feminine virtue, defenseless and outraged.»

---

[21] Sidney Painter, *French Chivalry*, «Great Seal Books» (Ithaca, N. Y., 1957), p. 102.

[22] Matarasso, *Recherches*, p. 231.

[23] Bezzola, *Origines*, II, 461-485, «les moeurs et le rôle de la femme.»

[24] Bezzola (*Origines*, II, p. 462) cites several examples, among them Agnès de Bourgogne who, governing Aquitaine for her son, managed to keep it out of the hands of her second husband, Geoffroi Martel Ier.

There are two instances of blatant cruelty to women in *Daurel*: Ermenjart is beaten with spurs by Guy [25]

> .I. espero de fin aur ten caussatz,
> Pren la pels cavelhs, tans colps li a donatz
> Que·l vermelh sanc ishi pels costatz (763).

causing her to confess that Beton is indeed alive and will avenge her; Aisilineta is thrashed on the breasts with nettles in order to force from her the whereabouts of Beton (917-922). Both scenes are necessary to the story and are not, in this context, excessive — domestic mores in the epic often displaying the same barbarity that was practiced on the battlefield. [26]

Ermenjart's situation is typical of the feudal epic stereotype where the wife is forced to marry the traitor against her will and is mistreated while trying to protect her virtue. In *Orson*, for example, Aceline is repeatedly beaten by the traitor Hugon, who has her buried in a filthy ditch up to her waist: *Puis li fait giter aigue et escucin au vix* (854). The brutality perpetrated by the traitor in *Doon* would be even more horrible, were it not for the almost ludicrous exaggeration of these passages, in which Herchambaut drags the countess into court by her hair, binds her hands so tightly that the blood spurts from under her fingernails, strips her naked and prepares to burn her alive (pp. 15-28). The *Jourdain* author shows more originality in the sadistic genre: [27] Eremborc is seized by Fromont's men, who threaten to rape her. She is thrown into a dark, stinking prison with her husband, where, for over a year they are beaten and starved. Only after great privation and torture (Eremborc's breasts are cut off), do they give in to the traitor. Here, as in *Daurel*, the cruelty is necessary to plot

---

[25] The use of spurs to punish a woman occurs in *Eledus et Serene* where, in the last three verses of the extant poem, the lady tells how she was beaten with spurs by a rejected suitor (*Des esperons me baty tant / Que de tous lieux sally le sanc*). Cf. *Mio Cid*, where the Infantes de Carrión beat the hero's daughters *con las espuelas agudas* (2737).

[26] Cf. exs. cited by Skidmore, *Moral Traits of Christian and Saracen*, chap. 12 (*Daurel* cited p. 113).

[27] According to Walter H. Bishop («A Critical Edition of *Jourdain de Blaivies*, with Introduction, Notes and Glossary» [unpub. diss., Univ. of North Carolina, 1962], p. xxiii) the prison scenes form the most original part of the poem.

and motivation and therefore more effective than the romanesque amplifications of *Doon*.

Not that the novelistic is completely absent from *Jourdain*: at a later point in the story, Gaudiscete, daughter of Jourdain and Oriabel, has refused the love of a prince; in a scene reminiscent of the *Sainte Agnès* and the *Historia Apollonii*, she is about to be delivered to a *bordel*, where a hundred men are to have their will of her, when Jourdain arrives and saves her.

Only exceptionally is the female the cruel one: in a reversal rare in epic, Biatris (*Beuve*) beats her vassals with spurs and clubs when they beg her to spare Beuve's tutor, Sobaut. [28]

The women in *Daurel*, whatever their rank, are heroic, loyal, virtuous, long-suffering. Beatrix, wife of the *jongleur* Daurel, and Aisilineta, daughter of a wealthy burgher, play small, but significant, rôles which emphasize these virtues. Respect for womanhood is discernible in the *Daurel* author's treatment of his female characters penetrating the surface cruelty and brutality typical of the genre. There is nothing in *Daurel* to compare with the erotic scene in *Amis*, for example, between Bellisant and Amile (vv. 623-694), or with the charming love affair between Nicolette and Doon de Mayence. In *Daurel*, women play secondary but virtuous roles.

Saracens: The Emir and Erimena

The exile of the young hero often took him to the court of a Saracen ruler, where love would blossom between the handsome young Christian and the beautiful Saracen princess (e.g., *Mainet*, *Jourdain*, *Orson*, *Beuve*, *Horn*). [29] In *Daurel*, the Emir of Babylonia is portrayed as a friend to those whom Charles has indirectly caused to be exiled, thus providing both a counterpart and a contrast to the figure of the emperor, emulating his glorious reputation, but outdoing him in generosity, kindness and justice. Since the Emir is a minor character, the real significance lies in the author's portrayal, not of him, but of his court, which is all that a medieval court was supposed to be: the

---

[28] Even further removed from French epic tradition is Brunhild's cruelty to Gunther: she ties him up and hangs him on a nail in their wedding chamber.

[29] Paris, *Mélanges*, p. 145; Comfort, *PMLA*, XXI, 420 ff. Our list is only a partial one.

Saracen lords and ladies are indistinguishable from their Christian counterparts in Monclar or Paris. In fact, the question of different faiths does not arise until the marriage of Beton and Erimena is proposed by the nobles of the Emir's court.

The portrait of the Emir (and his queen, who is also nameless) is concisely drawn: here is a ruler without a male heir who, out of kindness and generosity provides a home and an upbringing for the son of a *jongleur*. As the boy grows, the Emir is sensitive to his innate quality and sees in him everything he desires in a son:

> «Volgra·m costes .xiii. de mas cieutatz
> Qu'eu agues fil que fos de molher natz
> C'aquest sembles, qu'el fora amiratz (1270).»

This idealized portrait of life in a Saracen land is not uncommon in the epic, and is carried to even further heights in *Aye*, where the figure of Ganor is the archetype of the «noble Saracen.» Ganor raises Guy (Aye's son) in his court and, in a reversal of the usual Saracen princess theme, is converted to Christianity in order to marry the heroine of the poem. In later poems such as *Jourdain* and *Beuve*, the hero's exile becomes the pretext for innumerable fanciful adventures in which the character and motivation of a Saladin, Marco, or Hermine do not go beyond the grossest stereotype. The motif is constant: the young hero saves the kingdom and marries the princess, who may have offered herself to him beforehand, unable to resist his charms. [30] In *Beuve, Gaydon, Gui de Nanteuil, Floriant, Huon* and other *romans d'aventures*, the Saracen princess offers herself to the hero, boldly and shamelessly, thus allowing the *jongleur* to introduce an erotic element into his poem without offending Christian morality. But these romanesque adventures of Josiane (*Beuve*), Oriabel (*Jourdain*), Esclaramond (*Huon*), and their many sisters have little to do with epic literature. Like the passionate Christian maidens Bellisant (*Amis*) and Nicolette (*Doon*), they are types drawn from romance.

---

[30] W. W. Comfort has aptly pointed out («The Literary Rôle of the Saracen in the French Epic,» *PMLA*, LV [1940], 657-658) that in none of these cases is the love affair consummated until baptism of the maiden: e.g., Orable (*Prise d'Orange*), Mirabel (*Aiol*), Rosamond (*Elie de St. Gilles*), Flordepine (*Gaufrey*), Floripas (*Fierabras*).

Erimena is depicted as a chaste girl, whose love for Beton has roots in their childhood spent together, and is reinforced by her admiration of his manliness and good character. The author tells us that by the age of six, Beton is already loved by the princess. A year later, when he is called upon to entertain her as a pretext to test his nobility, she is described in the following manner:

> Ela es joves et es grans sa beutat
> Non a .x. ans enquara acabat (1492).

Thus, according to the author, she is two years older than Beton. Although the ripening of this mutual affection into love is not described in any detail, the gift of a set of finely-worked dice (the only payment Beton will accept from the princess for his singing) symbolizes the tacit bond between the two young people. A few verses later, when Beton is nine years old, we are reminded of Erimena's love:

> Ama·l lo rei, la regina a sobriers,
> Sa genta filha que lo te motz en chiers (1571).

When the Emir's barons demand that Erimena be married to Beton as reward for his courage and in accordance with his noble lineage, the young couple readily, but modestly acquiesce in terms which, though typical of the laconicism of our author, have a touch of realism about them. How prosaic, but true-to-life for the youth to accept with these words:

> «Senher,» dit el, «no la refut nien;
> Si o vol mos paire que m'a datz garnimen
> Ieu la prendrai mol voluntieuramen (1857).»

or for Erimena to accept Daurel's only reservation and agree to be baptised, in these words to her mother» «O ieu, ma domna, a totz lo sieu talen (1870).»

Although hardly original, the Daurel author's treatment of the Emir and Erimena does not fit into the cliché. The psychological verity of his portrayal, although rudimentary, transforms what might have been mere caricatures into convincing characters.

Minor Characters: the Lower Classes

One would hardly expect the burgher or villain to play a signifi-cant role in the essentially aristocratic *chanson de geste*. Representing the mass of followers, townspeople and peasants held little interest for the epic *jongleur* (or for his audience) concerned with the heroic deeds of great leaders. The stereotyped portrait of the burgher was that of the lawabiding but cowardly citizen, neither good nor evil, but easily swayed in his opinions and actions by the desire (under-standable enough in the rude context of feudal life) to retain life and possessions.

Daurel is noteworthy in its portrayal of middle-class heroism in the persons of the rich burgher and his family (it will be recalled that Daurel and Beatrix are also burghers) who risk their lives to help Ermenjart save Beton from Guy. The burgher's daughter, young Aisilineta, who cares for the baby with the love and tenderness she would have lavished on her own dead child, is a memorable character in spite of the brevity with which she is sketched by the author. This demonstration of heroism and loyalty on the part of a burgher is rare in epic, where townspeople are seldom depicted as individuals. More typically, they act as a group, offering their support or withdrawing it from a leader. In *Parise*, the townspeople refuse to serve Raymond against Clarembaut, an old knight faithful to Parise, and repudiate Raymond for having unjustly exiled his wife. Similarly when Doon de Mayence returns home as the rightful heir, the burghers quickly desert the usurper Herchambaut. *Daurel* is not without its example of this motif: the citizens of Poitiers show genuine grief over Bove's death, but are unwilling to challenge Guy, the usurper forced upon them by royal authority. The author accepts this behavior as normal and does not castigate the burghers for their obedience to the law of self-preservation. On the other hand, he points to the individual examples of heroism on the part of the wealthy burgher and his daughter, the seneschal Azemar, and most importantly, Daurel's entire family. Having accomplished noble deeds, they are fittingly rewarded by grants of land that elevate their status accordingly.

The serf, of whom neither loyalty nor nobility of sentiment was expected, is another matter. In epic, he is often the willing tool of an evil master; like the twelve serfs who welcome the usurper Fromont

(*Jourdain*), he is an extension of his master's evil, an instrument of torture and murder. The type is represented in *Daurel* by the fisherman, Ebrart; it is he, not Guy, who beats Aisilineta. Ebrart shares Guy's duplicity; while professing his devotion for the infant, Beton, whose hiding-place he has discovered, he is inwardly counting the reward he is to get for betraying the boy:

> Respon lo tracher: «Per mi er molt amatz.»
> Entre sas dens dis lo vilas malvatz:
> «.M. martz d'a[r]gen ay uei en mar trobatz (815).»

The fisherman ordered to kill the young hero is a stock character: in *Haveloc,* Grim saves him instead (a variation on the faithful servant theme); in *Doon,* Salemon is killed by the child Doon, after he has brutally murdered Doon's brothers.

Although there is a vague hint of Judas in the figure of Ebrart selling his rightful lord for gold, and although the name, like Salemon, is Hebrew in origin, there is no indication that these characters were meant to be Jews, nor is there any other apparent anti-semitism in *Daurel.* Ebrart is merely the lower class counterpart of Guy, reflecting his villainy much as the burghers reflect the noble qualities of Bove and Ermenjart.

ii.   THE TRAGIC HERO: BOVE D'ANTONA

L'us es fizels amicx e l'audre mescrezens (30). In these words the *jongleur* states the theme of the first 475 verses of his poem: it is this stark contrast that reduces the plot, motivation and characterization to a simple black-and-white confrontation between hero and traitor, between blind loyalty and unredeemed villainy. Bove's virtue is such that it blinds him to Guy's evil-doing, but the audience sees clearly both this blindness to evil (Bove's tragic flaw) and Guy's true nature: an unworthy and recreant knight who would rather stay home and gather wealth than serve the emperor as duty and honor demand. As the author, re-emphasizing the contrast, states:

> E lo coms Guis cui ja Dieus non ampar
> Pessa de l'aur et de l'argen amassar.
> E lo duc Boves non o pot plus durar
> Del goifano de l'empeyraire portar (221).

Is Bove a stock character? As a paragon of knightly virtues, he resembles many an epic father: Guy (*Beuve*), Girart (*Jourdain*), Garnier (*Aye*), Guy (*Doon*), Elyaduc (*Floriant*), Sigmund (*Sigfridtrilogie*). However, of these, only Bove, Guy (*Doon*) and Orson are important characters; the remainder disappear early in the story and are of minor significance, and this is only natural, since the traitor invariably survives to play a greater rôle than the father he has murdered. [31] Bove, like the fathers in *Beuve* and *Jourdain*, is murdered by a traitor; but there the resemblance ends, since nowhere do we find precisely the same relationship between hero and traitor that is portrayed by the *Daurel* author. Nowhere (except in *Orson*) is feudal *compagnonnage* the basic theme. Nor does the author of *Orson* make of the father a tragic example of the «friendship betrayed» motif. [32] Orson, unlike Bove, survives his companion's treachery but when he reappears in the narrative, his rôle is decidedly secondary to that of his son, Milon, more comparable to Daurel's rôle as tutor of Beton than to Bove's as father. Orson and Hugon are sworn brothers, but Hugon, unlike Guy, cannot bring himself to murder his companion; thus the dramatic effect of the brotherhood theme is vitiated. When Guy kills Bove, a sacred relationship is being flagrantly violated, and the tragedy takes on a universal dimension. Guy, like Cain, «was moved by that diabolical, envious hatred with which the evil regard

---

[31] Since in *Doon* and *Orson*, the fathers are only thought to be dead, but actually reappear later in the story, they assume roles of greater importance than the fathers in *Beuve* and *Jourdain*, who are murdered at the very outset. In these poems, where characterization depends more on action than on insight, the traitor, by remaining in the story and participating in the action, is due to be in the forefront of the narrative. This does not make him necessarily more complex or interesting than the hero, although, as W. P. Ker (*Epic and Romance: Essays on Medieval Literature* [New York, 1957 (1908)], pp. 300-301) has remarked, there is often a stronger interest in the adversary than in the hero (e.g., Fromont [*Garin le Loherain*] who is a «half-hearted traitor, trying to be just, but always dragged further into iniquity by his friends.»).

[32] Orson, like Bove, has carried Charlemagne's standard into battle and is rewarded by the emperor, but unlike Bove, he is sold into slavery by his false companion, Hugon, his adventures eventually leading to a dramatic reunion with his son Milon. Returning home together, they enter Hugon's company disguised, confront the traitor. Both sides plead their case before Charles, who accepts Hugon's word. Milon vanquishes Hugon, who finally confesses his crime to Charles.

the good just because the good are good while they themselves are evil.» [33]

Sworn-brotherhood

The bond of *compagnonnage* was apparently widespread under the Merovingians and seems to have been a milder form of Germanic and Scandinavian blood-brotherhood, which demanded that the surviving companion join the other in death — hardly a custom likely to endure. The survival of the more primitive forms of brotherhood is attested by numerous examples in the *chanson de geste*. Bédier remarks that the twelve peers, who formed the inner circle of Charlemagne's court, form at least five fraternal couples: besides Roland and Oliver, Berengier and Haton are two inseparables, as are Anseïs and Samson, Gerin and Gerier, and Ivon and Ivoerie. In the primitive tradition they choose to die together in battle. [34] The bond between warriors is found in the earliest epic literature — Achilles and Patrocles, David who loved Jonathan «as his own soul» [35] — therefore it is no surprise to find good and bad companions in the *chanson de geste*. We have already mentioned the traitor Hugon, who sells Orson into slavery; Godard, who betrays his companion the king of Denmark (*Haveloc*), and Raoul, who forces Bernier to break their pact, are typical of the genre. [36] On the other hand, Amis and Amiles, like the fraternal couples in the *Roland*, represent the loyalty of *compagnonnage* carried to its noblest degree. [37] Few epics, however, are as explicit as *Daurel* (15-25) on the juridical nature of the bond of sworn-brotherhood. Turold, for example, does not tell us *how* Roland and Oliver become companions, although we do find a description of the ceremony in *Girart de Vienne* (vv. 5935-5967) written a century later, where the

---

[33] St. Augustine, *The City of God*, XV.

[34] *Commentaires*, p. 306. Bédier questions the supposed Germanic origin of the «fraternité d'armes,» since the words expressing it (*compagnon, nourri, fidèle, mesnie*, etc.) have nothing Germanic about them. The institutions in question appear nonetheless to be Germanic in origin (e.g., the relationship between *cumpainz* and OHG *gileibo*).

[35] *I Samuel*, 18.

[36] Cf. Matarasso, *Recherches*, pp. 182-183. The *Daurel* episode is cited, p. 183.

[37] Cf. MacEdward Leach, *Amis and Amiloun*, EETS Orig. Series, No. 203 (London, 1937), pp. lxv-lxxi. It should be noted that Amis and Amiloun are not blood-brothers (the same is true of Bove and Guy), but *compagnons* in the eleventh-century French conception of the term (p. lxxi).

pact between them is sealed with a handshake and a kiss.[38] In *Amis*, the two heroes are sworn to loyalty in every important version of the poem from that of Radulfus Tortarius to the Middle English, but the *chanson* barely hints of this relationship (vv. 16-18).[39]

Although the various forms of brotherhood are often presumed to be of Germanic origin,[40] German epic literature is not especially clear on the juridical nature of the relationship. There is, nonetheless, an analogy between *Roland, Daurel* and the *Nibelungenlied* that serves to demonstrate the essential unity of the concept, seen here in three works widely separated in time and place: the overlord (Charlemagne/ Gunther) binds his «family» to him in what may be called *compagnonnage* of the lower degree. In this relationship the vassals (Roland, Oliver, Ganelon, the Peers) are bound to each other in their devotion to the emperor, but this bond does not preclude a stronger and more personal one, the companionship of higher degree, typified by the couples Roland and Oliver / Bove and Guy / Sigfried and Hagen.[41] This particular form of brotherhood involves a bond which may never

---

[38] Jacques Flach, *Les Origines de l'ancienne France* (Paris, 1893), II, book 2, chaps, ii, iii, vii; see esp. pp. 472-474, where *Girart de Vienne* and *Daurel* are cited. Cf. the critique of Flach by George B. Fundenburg, *Feudal France in the French Epic* (Princeton, 1918), pp. 79-84.

[39] Leach, *Amis*, pp. lxv-lxvi. The Anglo-Norman version is only slightly less laconic:

> Tant s'entreamerant durement
> Ke freres se firent par serment.
> As autres ne feseint semblant
> De compaignier tant ne kaunt (v. 20).

The Middle English is much more explicit (cf. vv. 145-156).

[40] See George Fenwick Jones, *The Ethos of the Song of Roland* (Baltimore, 1963), pp. 106-109, on the derivation of the *comitatus*, of *cumpainz* (< OHG *gileibo*), and on the semantics of «peace, love, and friend» in this context; on Germanic oath-brotherhood (Schwurbruderschaft) p. 143. See also R. Boutruche, *Seigneurie et féodalite* (Paris, 1959), I, chap. 2 and «Documents» esp. Tacitus' description of Germanic *compagnonnage*; W. W. Comfort, *PMLA*, XXI (1906), 318-319; W. A. Stowell, «Personal Relationships in Medieval France,» *PMLA*, XXVIII (1913), 410; M. Bloch, *La Société féodale*, I, 237-241.

[41] D. von Kralik, *Die Sigfridtrilogie im Nibelungenlied und Thidrekssaga* (Halle, 1941), pp. 845-860. Kralik notes this similarity between *Daurel* and Germanic legends, which I have expanded to include the *Roland*, earlier than any of the poems cited by Kralik. While not entirely analogous, the situation in which Gunther needs Sigfried's help to tame (and in the *Thidrekssaga* to deflower Brunhild) is suggestive of the same primitive concept of wife-sharing.

be broken or repudiated. The brothers share property in common, may not marry without each other's permission, and, at the death of one partner, the survivor, if legally free to do so, often marries the widow. This institution, as mirrored in epic literature, was already archaic in the twelfth century, but had never completely died out: [42] male comradeship has always accompanied the danger and privation of battle and adventure.

Daurel provides a most complete statement in feudal terms of the significance of this relationship between men: the tragedy of Bove is none other than that of sacred friendship betrayed. In swearing companionship with Guy, an impoverished knight, Bove establishes a community of wealth, even stipulating that, should he die childless, Guy is to inherit all his property, including his wife. Guy profits from this arrangement so advantageous to him, yet not content with money and power, he covets Bove's wife, and in the absence of the duke, attempts to seduce her. His surprise and anger at her refusal is interesting, since one could interpret it as a subconscious survival of a custom that still prevails among certain semicivilized peoples which holds that the blood-brother, in the absence of the husband, has the right to possess the wife — and this may explain Bove's refusal to take seriously Ermenjart's accusations against Guy. [43] Clearly, Bove's love for his companion outweighs his affection for his wife; he might well have said, in the words of David: «thy love to me was wonderful, passing the love of women.» [44]

What other explanation for Bove's repeated attempts to excuse Guy's treachery? Even as Bove lies dying with Guy's spear in his body, he begs Guy to look after Ermenjart and Beton, cautions the murderer to avoid detection of his crime, and, in a final, impassioned exhortation, realizing that nothing will touch his false companion's heart, he pleads with Guy to eat of his own heart: «*Prendes del cor senhe, ni ne manjatz* (434)!» Were it not that Bove's love for Guy (*«Nulh hom non es qu'ieu pusca tant amar* [272]!») epitomizes the ideal of masculine friendship, and that Guy, driven by blind envy, is so patently unworthy of this love, the scene itself would be little

---

[42] Leach, *Amis,* p. lxx.
[43] René Nelli, *L'Erotique des troubadours* (Toulouse, 1963), p. 284. The same analysis appeared earlier in *Cahiers du Sud,* No. 347 (1958), 1-37.
[44] *II Samuel,* 1.

more than melodrama. The confrontation between two powerful motives — love and envy — makes the tragedy: when Bove begs Guy to eat his heart, when all else has failed, he is trying desperately to transfer his virtue, loyalty and courage to Guy, so obviously in need of them, in the hope of changing Guy's character. [45] He has offered Guy his wealth, his land, his wife, yet Guy is not content: Bove's ultimate gift to Guy is the chance to become a worthy man. In other words, if his courage and virility were to survive in the person of his assassin, he would reconcile himself to dying. [46]

The confrontation between hero and villain in *Daurel*, stripped of all courtly trappings, of all external circumstance, is basic and elemental. The tragedy unfolds in a wilderness, remote from the eyes of witnesses; thus Guy, although implicated and strongly suspected, cannot legally be accused of murder: his word as a knight weighs more heavily in Charles' judgement than Ermenjart's tearful pleas. Murder will out, the crime will be punished, but not by juridical procedure; in the feudal world order, blood must be avenged by blood, and Guy will eventually meet death at the hands of his murdered companion's son.

iii. THE TRAITOR: GUY D'ASPREMONT

Traitor and hero are portrayed with a black-and-white, good-versus-evil contrast that leaves little room for depth of characterization. Neither Guy nor Bove «evolves» during the course of the story: the audience

---

[45] Thompson (*Motif-Index*, V, Q 478.1) cites numerous exs. of the Eaten Heart theme in folk literature, as well as exs. of sworn-brotherhood (p. 311) and blood-brotherhood (p. 312), and refusal to believe that a friend will harm one (p. 317.1). One is reminded of the verses in Sordel's poem «*Planha vuelh En Blacatz*»:

Qu'om li traga lo cor, e que·n manjo·l baro
Que vivon descorat: pueys auran de cor pro.

which suggest the mystical communion Bove may have had in mind when he uttered the words in v. 434.

[46] As René Nelli suggests in his analysis of the passage (*L'Erotique*, p. 285): «Il tient à communiquer après sa mort à son ami félon les vertus qui lui manquent, et pour cela il l'exhorte à manger son coeur, c'est-à-dire à parfaire — plus réellement cette fois — l'affrèrement déjà contracté par serment, (remplaçant l'échange des sangs) qui s'est révélé si peu efficace. Il mourrait tranquille s'il était sûr de pouvoir survivre ainsi, de quelque façon, *en son meurtrier*.»

is aware from the outset that the worthy Duke Bove will be murdered
by the villainous Count Guy; the interest lies in how and why it will
come about. Before the events narrated in the story, Guy's qualities
have already won for him the steadfast friendship of Bove: outwardly
then, Guy is a good knight and companion, until the appearance of
Ermenjart puts his character to the test. Desire is stronger than loyalty,
and the author depicts the gradual falling-away of Guy's mask of
honor and respectability (cf. pp. 75-76): muttered threats become overt
actions, which in turn become open deeds of villainy, but there is
no real change in his character, no internal struggle between his desire
for Ermenjart and his loyalty to Bove.

Why it comes about is equally simple: since Ermenjart does not
return his affection, this desire cannot be resolved within the context
of Provençal *fin'amors,* although Bove would have almost certainly
accepted such a solution. [47] Although *Daurel* is in no way a courtly
novel, our twelfth-century author was certainly not ignorant of the
courtly love tradition: Guy's destructive passion is what the troubadours would call *fals'amors,* the equivalent, in courtly love, of treason
in the feudal world-order. Guy's misguided love is the direct cause
of his treachery, which destroys the equilibrium (the «normal» feudal
order of things) prevailing up to that point: the eternal triangle in
one of its numerous variations (Ermenjart loves Bove, Bove loves Guy,
Guy loves Ermenjart). The situation, viewed in this manner, is courtly;
the author's treatment is not: he resolves the triangle by destroying
it quickly and brutally.

Guy's motive is envy. As Bove's sworn companion, he has a right
to share all of Bove's possessions, and he enjoys this right freely until
Bove's marriage. In sinister jest, he asks Bove if he is prepared to
share Ermenjart with him:

> «Bela es madona ab lo cors covinen,
> Dares m'en partz si co m'aves coven (183)?»

Bove's ironic reply whets his appetite and arouses his envy:

---

[47] His dying speech (esp. vv. 408-410) is explicit on this point: had he
known of Guy's desire, he would have given up Ermenjart to his companion
and become a pilgrim.

«Companh, pregat lo payre omnipoten
Que·m do la mortz tost e viassamen;
Pueis l'aures vos, pus vos ve a talen (188).»

At this point in the story, Guy is willing to take his share in secret, but Ermenjart's refusal to submit to him transforms his passion into a rage against his companion, whom he eventually slays. Guy's envy moves him to commit the worst form of treason: the betrayal of the sworn bond between two individuals, the basis of the legal and moral order of feudalism. [48] Having broken the most elemental feudal law, he must support his crime by further evil deeds in order to legitimize his legal position as heir to Bove's fief. His first task is to stamp out Bove's lineage — to destroy his heir, Beton. By so doing, he is able to harm the woman who has spurned him while freeing himself of the threat of vengeance, a sword hanging over his head as long as the boy lives.

Guy differs from the Ganelon-archetype in that he is not portrayed as a renegade who aids the enemies of his overlord. He never, as do the rebels of the feudal cycle, sides with Saracens against his own countrymen. His crime is that of an evil and treacherous man, a traitor, but he is neither renegade nor rebel. [49] Unlike the traitors in *Amis, Aye* and *Parise,* Guy is not linked genealogically to Ganelon, nor is there any mention of Roland's nemesis in *Daurel.* There is, however, a certain evil grandeur, an epic *démesure* in Guy and his crimes that likens him more to Ganelon than to Hardré or Béranger; the similarity is limited to depth of motive and validity of psychological characterization. As the *Daurel* author was a lesser poet than the author of the *Roland,* further comparison would be out of place. It suffices to say that the *Daurel* author, unlike the authors of *Amis, Aye* and *Parise,* is more concerned with motivation than with imitation (through genealogy). In *Amis,* for example, Hardré is a conscious borrowing from the tradition, though in an obvious and superficial manner. As the chief steward of Charlemagne, he is envious of the honors shown to Amis and Amiles, and his desire to harm them is enflamed by their refusal to accept his offer of friendship. Although he belongs

---

48 Adalbert Dessau, «L'idée de la trahison au moyen âge et son rôle dans la motivation de quelques chansons de geste,» *CCM,* III (1960), 23.

49 See the distinction made by Karl Plath, *Der Typ des Verräters in den älteren Chansons de geste* (Halle/Saale, 1934), pp. 3-4.

to the «family of traitors,» his treachery has nothing in common with that of Ganelon; it belongs, instead, to romance tradition: betrayal of lovers, juridical combats, etc. [50] In *Aye*, Béranger, identified clearly as a relative of Ganelon, betrays Garnier through jealousy over an honor shown Garnier by Charles. Although Béranger's motivation is justified, [51] his characterization is conveniently accomplished by the expedient of genealogy: we are told of his «bad blood,» and we therefore know what to expect of him. This genealogy is elaborated even further in *Parise* (the sequel to *Aye*), where Béranger is identified as one of twelve traitors (a sort of evil peerage has replaced the traditional one) of Ganelon's race.

The «jealous seneschal» type represents a further degradation of the traitor in epic. Fromont, for example, although identified in *Jourdain* as the nephew of Hardré and Ganelon, is an uncouth and cowardly usurper who has Girart and his wife murdered in bed by serfs. [52] Herchambaut (*Doon*) is another typical «jealous seneschal,» who covets his master's wife and wealth. Absent are motivations such as the blood feud, honor refused or unjustly awarded, friendship or love spurned, which gave convincing motivation to earlier traitors (such as Ganelon and Guy, and, to a lesser degree, Béranger and Hardré) and made them plausible characters. Absent also the nobility (external) and the valor (misdirected) that make the Ganelon-type traitor an adversary worthy of the epic hero. [53]

As we have seen, there are remarkably few parallels in the French epic to the Bove-Guy couple: *Orson* and *Haveloc* contain similar situations, but the most striking analogy is found in the *Nibelungenlied*,

---

[50] Cf. Leach, *Amis*, pp. lxxii-lxxiii. The episode in which Hardré attempts to deliver the heroes to Gombault, the enemy of Charles, by leading them into a prearranged ambush, is a meaningless episodic adventure imitated from the *Roland*. He is a descendant of Ganelon: this is sufficient to type him.

[51] Charles had granted Aye to Garnier, unaware that Aye's father had already promised her to Béranger, thus explaining Béranger's anger.

[52] Herman J. Green («Fromont, a Traitor in the *Chansons de geste*,» *Modern Language Notes*, LVI [1941], 329-337) suggests that Fromont and others of his ilk had counterparts in history, citing a Fromont of Sens, who unseated an archbishop in 941, and other evidence, including a proposed model for Ganelon. The traitor stereotype is so commonplace (especially in the case of Fromont) that Green's argument seems unconvincing.

[53] The traitor-figure in adventure romances (e.g., *Doon, Beuve, Huon, Joufrois, Macaire, Reine Sibille*) is generally depicted as an ignoble character, devoid of redeeming qualities, whose crimes are of base nature and motivation.

where Hagen (Guy's counterpart) is the *Gefolgsmann,* the companion of inferior rank to Sigfried (Bove's counterpart). Gunther (Charlemagne), the overlord to whom both owe allegiance, is the companion of superior rank to Sigfried (Bove) and grants his sister Kriemhild (Ermenjart) in marriage as a reward for faithful service. Hagen (unlike Guy) is motivated by loyalty — he mistakenly believes that Gunther is being deceived by Sigfried, [54] though greed and envy are secondary motives for his betrayal of Sigfried. Some scholars have theorized that *Daurel* and *Haveloc* reflect, in their treatment of this theme, Germanic legend, [55] although the post-1200 date of the *Nibelungenlied* suggests that this betrayal motif was drawn by the German author from French sources. [56] Whatever the original source, which is probably lost in a common Franco-germanic feudal tradition, the parallel is a welcome one, since it demonstrates the persistence of a primitive feudal theme in two epics composed long after the institution they are describing had disappeared. *Daurel* and the *Nibelungenlied* are unlike in language, style, form and content; Hagen and Guy (and the theme they represent) are alike in motive and crime.

When Guy is finally cast down, he confesses his crimes and, resigned to his fate, meets death without fear or remorse. [57] He is executed by being flayed alive, dragged by a horse, and hanged — the classic punishment for traitors. [58] All seems of a kind: the character, the crime brought about by the narrative necessities of the characterization, and the inevitable and, perhaps, predictable punishment of the crime. [59]

---

[54] Walshe, *Medieval German Literature,* p. 234.

[55] Kralik, *Die Sigfridtrilogie,* pp. 854-860; Richthofen, *Estudios épicos,* p. 21, p. 80, pp. 125-126.

[56] As suggested by Jackson (*Literature of the Middle Ages,* p. 209), and certainly valid in terms of the *literary* treatment of the motif, as opposed to the actual historical bases. *Daurel,* in any event, cannot be used as evidence to prove otherwise (cf. Kralik and Richthofen, note 55).

[57] Since Bove was murdered in secret, the punishment for treachery is carried out by the feudal pattern of vengeance (Cf. Carl F. Riedel, *Crime and Punishment in the Old French Romances* [New York, 1938], p. 22).

[58] During the thirteenth century, common criminals not only were drawn asunder by horses, but were also hanged, burned and mutilated (see exs. cited by M. Skidmore, *Moral Traits,* p. 88), but in literature this punishment was reserved for the traitor.

[59] In *Jourdain, Haveloc, Doon,* as well as *Daurel,* the traitor is variously flayed alive, dragged by horses, and hanged. Other epics contain similar punishments (cf. Riedel, *Crime and Punishment,* p. 38, p. 89, p. 102; Skidmore, *Moral Traits,* p. 88), and this method of execution is common to many

In his cruelty, greed, envy, volatile temper, and duplicity, Guy is one of many. But, surpassing the stereotype, he is an accomplished knight, a competent leader of men, courageous and able in battle, and these virtues emphasize the tragic nature of his wrong-doing.

iv. THE FEUDAL HERO: BETON

The young hero, rightful heir banished by treachery from his heritage, grows to knighthood and returns to reclaim his fief — this, essentially, is the story of Beton and his numerous epic brothers: Jourdain, Beuve, Haveloc, Girart (*Amis*), Guy (*Aye*), Milon (*Orson*), Hughes (*Parise*) and Doon de Mayence. The motif is a venerable one, drawn more or less freely from the popular and well-known Apollonius legend: [60] good, in the person of the handsome and noble youth, conquers evil, represented by the villainous usurper. In the over-all feudal context, this moral triumph assumes added significance, since the ability of the legal heir to prevail against the power of the usurper is essential to the preservation of the rightful and legitimate lines of inheritance upon which the whole feudal structure rests.

In many feudal epics, the rightful heir is an innocent and vulnerable child who would perish were it not for the loyalty and devotion of a faithful vassal or servant who saves him from the traitor. The greater the sacrifice made by the loyal servant, the more magnanimous will be his reward when the heir eventually regains his fief. The treacherous vassal who aids the usurper will, on the other hand, inevitably be punished. Thus, the moral in the feudal epic is as explicit as an *exemplum*: the duty of the vassal is loyalty to his rightful lord, whatever the cost and through all vicissitudes. Exemplary also is the concern shown the formation of the child into knighthood, since the youth of noble blood takes naturally to the diversions and duties of his class, regardless of obstacles and tribulations such as banishment and the loss of identity. In this respect the feudal epic is a primitive

---

widely-separated societies (cf. exs. in Irish, Icelandic, Indian, Hebrew and Lithuanian folk literature cited by Thompson, *Motif-Index*, V, Q 416, S 117).

[60] The *Historia Apollonii Regis Tyrii* MS dates from the ninth or tenth century, but the story was composed as early as the third, according to Rodolfo Oroz, ed., *Historia de Apolonio de Tiro* (Santiago de Chile, 1954), p. 8.

Bildungsroman, following the development of the young hero from birth through maturity.

By illustrating the rewards of loyalty to the overlord, the epic *jongleurs* were in a sense preaching adherence to the feudal system; in the feudal epic, loyalty to church, suzerain and nation were all secondary in importance to the great bond between lord and vassal. If we recall that the *jongleurs* who composed and sang these epics were patronized by feudal lords, it is easy to understand how these works fulfilled, although perhaps unintentionally, a didactic function by preaching the importance of loyalty. If, on the other hand, these epics simply reflect society as it was in actuality, then it would not be accurate to call them «didactic.» There is, of course, some truth in both conjectures.

Infancy

Since rarely did the *jongleur* describe children under the age of seven, apart from the commonplace scenes of birth and baptism, the term *enfans* in epic usually denoted adolescent, bachelor, and, on occasion, knight. [61] Beton, for example, is sent to be baptised by Roland, since a noble child should have god-parents of the highest rank. [62] At this point, however, our poem parts company with most epic and romance literature by depicting Beton as an infant. While it is true that certain poems, those of the feudal cycle, the *Alexandre,* and Arthurian romances such as the *Perceval,* are partially biographical in nature and discuss the education of princes or the formation of knights, [63] it is rare for an epic poet to speak of an infant, [64] beyond a brief statement to the effect that the child was, for example, «well-nursed.»

---

[61] Jeanne Lods, «Le Thème de l'enfance dans l'épopée française,» *CCM,* III (1960), 58.

[62] Gautier, *La Chevalerie,* p. 108 ff (chap. V) «L'enfance du baron.»

[63] See G. Raynaud de Lage, «Les Romans antiques et la représentation de l'antiquité,» *Moyen Age,* LXVII (1961), 262-263.

[64] Cf. exs. cited from *Sept Sages, Raoul, Jourdain,* etc. in H. A. Smith, «La Femme dans les chansons de geste,» II, *Colorado College Studies,* X (1903), 24-40. Gautier (*La Chevalerie,* p. 118) deplored the fact that so few epic mothers nursed their infants, and cites *Daurel* as an «excusable case where the mother was unable to do so, since the child was taken from her.»

In *Daurel*, the scene in which Aisilineta, Beton's wet-nurse, lovingly cares for the infant, is unique in epic:

> N'Aisilineta, cui Jhesu Crist ben do,
> Molt gen lo bauza cant es ben de sazo,
> Pueis lo envolopa en .i. bel cisclato,
> Pueisisas li vet ermi pelisso,
> Et en aprot ela·lh ditz .i. bel so,
> Bauzan los uelhs e tota la faisso
> E prega Dieu que longa vida·l do (730).

That Beton is a helpless infant adds to the pathos of his disinheritance and his mother's degradation, since, unlike the superhuman child, Beuve de Hanstone, he is entirely incapable of any action on his own behalf. This vulnerability enhances the value of Daurel's sacrifice of his own infant son to save Beton, his rightful lord, in spite of the apparent futility of hoping to preserve this fragile child who can know nothing of what has passed and whose ability to avenge these wrongs is fifteen years distant. Now, the author of *Daurel*, in distinct contrast to most feudal epics where the child is old enough to realize the wrong being done him and strong enough to attempt to take matters into his own hands,[65] felt that it was important to his story to depict Beton as an infant. The exploits of Jourdain, who cuts off Fromont's nose, of Doon, who kills the traitor Salemon, of Beuve, who assaults his step-father with a club and calls his mother a «pute orde prové» (albeit justifiably), are colorful, but make mockery of the feudal ideal so coherently expressed in *Daurel*. In these epics, the hero springs from infancy to the age of reason (seven) without any transition: the epic *jongleur*, his primary focus on plot, was not (nor, apparently, was his audience) interested in realistic portrayals of charming, though hardly singular, infants and children.

Unlike other *jongleurs*, the *Daurel* author chose to depict the formative years of a very charming child. Indeed, he devotes more

---

[65] In *Doon, Beuve* and *Jourdain*, typical of the genre, the child is, upon the death or disappearance of his father, mistreated by the «jealous seneschal» or the wicked stepfather. Protected by a faithful servant or vassal, the child comes out of hiding and assaults the traitor with fists or clubs, in a preliminary attempt at revenge, after which the young hero goes into exile (usually in a Saracen country) where he will further exercise and develop his skills. In these poems, the exile and subsequent return home provide the pretext for innumerable fabulous adventures.

space to the child Beton than he does to battle scenes. One wonders how the audience reacted to this novelty — indifferently, if we are to judge by the poem's lack of success.

The poet's treatment is always gracious, never passing beyond the bounds of realism. He is describing a real infant when he depicts Daurel presenting Beton to the Emir:

> Daurel lo·l baila et el lo pren viatz;
> Ausa·lh lo pali, l'efas a·ls silhs levatz,
> Geta .i. ris, e·l rei es ne pagatz (1234).

The baby looks into the Emir's eyes and laughs happily. The Emir, charmed by the infant, orders the queen to look after Beton. She is very pleased:

> «Tam be sera noirit et alautat
> Cum s'ie·l agues e mon ventre portat (1243).»

At the age of three, he is brought out of the queen's chambers for everyone to admire, and the poet gives us a stereotyped, but, in this context rare, description of Beton; rare, because the child is only three years old, commonplace in the language used: «charming face, blond hair, eyes like a falcon's, skin white as snow (vv. 1248-1252).» Even more striking is the poet's portrayal of Beton at four, five and six, ages which do not figure in other epics, with the exception of a brief passage in *Jourdain* where Eremborc laments the sacrifice of her young son; she will surely die in the years to come, when she sees boys of his age playing under the walls of the city:

> A la quintainne et a l'escu jouster
> Et corre as barres et luitier et verser (661).

Jourdain, however, like most epics, says nothing else about the upbringing of a child before the age of seven. [66] The author is content to say that Renier brought him up as his own son:

> Or croist li anfes en joie et en sante,
> Quant ot .xv. ans, si ot bel bachelier (767).

---

[66] See W. C. Meller (*A Knight's Life in the Days of Chivalry* [New York, 1924], pp. 17-18) who cites at length (paraphrasing Gautier) these passages in *Daurel,* which he finds unique in epic.

This is all we are told about Jourdain between infancy and the age of fifteen: *Jourdain* is typical of the genre.

Blood-will-tell Motif

Part of the author's purpose in describing Beton's character at progressive stages of his development is to demonstrate the inherent nobility and virtue of the young hero. It is an essential feature of the exile theme that «blood will tell,» whatever the circumstances. The child may be raised by a poor fisherman (*Haveloc*), may be cast adrift in a boat to fend for himself (*Doon*), or, more typically, will be brought up as an exile or foundling in the court of a rich Saracen (*Aye, Beuve, Jourdain,* etc.). Whether clothed in rags or finery, he will always have the instincts of a noble child, and his physiognomy will further distinguish him as highborn. This motif, a variation on the Apollonius story, is commonplace in the *chanson de geste,* which is an essentially aristocratic genre, and is found in romance (e.g., *Perceval,* and to a lesser degree, *Alexandre*). In the majority of epics, it is stereotyped (e.g., *Orson, Beuve, Doon, Parise, Jourdain, Mainet*), the author stating simply that the lord in whose court the boy was raised recognized him as noble, before or after which the youth saves his kingdom from an aggressor. Some authors embellish the motif: Jourdain, who is sent (incognito) to Fromont's court as a squire, is twice mistreated by the traitor, who sees in him a disturbing resemblance to Girart, the boy's father. The *Daurel* author does more: he lingers over the theme, develops it, and makes of it a central idea. At the age of three, when Beton is shown to the Emir, he remarks to his nobles:

> Anc aquest efas non fo de Daurel nat,
> Ges no·l ressembla.»... (1255).

Soon after, the child steals the Emir's gloves and presents them to the queen. The king laughs over the incident and maintains that he would give thirteen of his cities to have a son like Beton:

> «Miel li covengra que fos fil d'amirat
> Que [de] joglar de paucas eretat (1272).»

The inference is clear: were Beton really a minstrel's son, he would have the coarse, lower-class features of his father and the cupidity of a *jongleur*. Stealing the gloves to give to the queen was a charming, noble gesture; a minstrel's son would have stolen them and kept or sold them. [67]

Beton's first real test occurs at the age of seven; he gambles with some noble children, wins their shirts, but, in keeping with his inherent nobility and in contrast to his apparent status as the son of a *jongleur*, he gives away his winnings. This generosity, inconceivable in a mere minstrel, convinces the Emir that Beton is not Daurel's son. Determined to find out the truth, the queen suggests that they test the boy: Beton will be asked to play and sing for the princess Erimena, who will offer him payment for his services. If he accepts, he is clearly the son of a minstrel. Beton, of course, refuses the money and accepts only a token payment, a pair of finely-worked dice, thus establishing beyond a doubt his real nobility. [68] The Emir repeats his statement that the boy could not be Daurel's son, and the nobles reply: *«Fils es de duc, de ric o d'amiratz (1550).»* The episode is very freely adapted from the Apollonius legend: In the *Historia Apollonii*, the shipwrecked hero astounds King Archistrates' court with his lyre playing, singing, and acting. Apollonius gives the rich presents received for his singing to the servants, a gesture which is interpreted as incontrovertible proof of his nobility. The king's daughter requests that Apollonius teach her the art of music and, as is to be expected, she falls in love with him. [69]

Generosity, then, is the *sine qua non* of nobility, the virtue that separates the high-born from the serf or burgher. [70] Beton gives away his gambling winnings and his war booty; he will accept only token payment for his singing; thus, regardless of external appearances, he cannot be the son of the minstrel Daurel. Similarly, when Josiane, in

---

[67] The word *eretat* refers not only to material wealth but also to the qualities transmitted from father to son («heredity» in the modern sense).

[68] Franz Semrau (*Würfel und Würfelspiel im alten Frankreich* [Halle, 1909], p. 39) cites this verse in *Daurel* among other exs. of finely-worked dice (*Daurel* is the sole ex. cited in epic).

[69] *Jourdain* follows the Apollonius story very closely, and *Beuve* contains much that is directly attributable to this source, but *Daurel* owes only this scene to the tradition, and even it is not directly borrowed.

[70] Cf. Thomas McGuire, *The Conception of the Knight in the Old French Epics of the Southern Cycle* (Lansing, Mich., 1939), pp. 86-95; Marian P. Whitney, «Queen of Mediaeval Virtues: Largesse,» *Vassar Mediaeval Studies* (New Haven, 1923), p. 187; Painter, *French Chivalry*, pp. 30-32.

the English *Sir Bevis,* sends a message to Bevis, he rewards the servant with a fine cloak, thus giving further proof of his nobility to the love-struck princess:

> For it was nevure churlis dede,
> To give a messingere suche a wede (938)!

In *Daurel,* all those of noble blood, even, paradoxically, the traitor, Guy, are generous. By his largesse then, Beton demonstrates his worthiness to become a knight.

Education

We have already seen how the *Daurel* author develops Beton's character from infancy and early childhood, depicting the games, pastimes and duties learned at each step of the way. [71] Unlike other authors who bring the child to the age of knighthood at a bound, [72] he describes the intermediate stages, telling us, for example, at what age Beton learned to ride a horse, how he was trained in the use of arms, and what his duties were as a squire. These vignettes of Beton at different ages are plausible and ring true — the author is depicting a precocious, though normal child (compared to the superhuman Beuve and Alexander). From the age of five, when Beton:

> Fon ben cregut et pros et essenhat;
> Pueja cavals et a los abrivatz,
> Fon bels parliers e gen enrazonatz,
> Joga a taulas, ad escax et a dat[z] (1278).

to the age of eleven, when Daurel furnishes him with weapons small and light enough for him to handle and hires a Saracen master-at-arms to teach him how to use them in a tourney (vv. 1564-1640), the way is being prepared for young Beton's entry into knighthood. By way of contrast, few epics give any realistic details on the education of a noble child. Although the *Alexandre* romance tells about the hero's

---

[71] See **Summary,** pp. 56-59.

[72] Most epics describe the entry into knighthood at the age of thirteen to fifteen (e.g., *Amis, Beuve, Doon, Jourdain*); those that give details on education relate them to fantastic feats of arms (Beuve and Jourdain defeat the leaders of a powerful army).

mentors and recounts his fabulous exploits, these are of classical and supernatural nature and not germane to our poem, which is a relatively faithful reflection of twelfth-century life. *Doon* and *Perceval* describe youths whose inherent nobility is sufficient to instruct them in the use of arms far from masters-at-arms, court, and jousting-grounds, but the motif is not at all analogous to *Daurel*, where Beton receives a normal education into knighthood. [73]

Also in contrast to most epics where the entry into knighthood is accompanied by ceremonial arming, dubbing and jousting, the scene in *Daurel* is one of effective simplicity: far from the eyes of the courtiers, Daurel forces the boy to joust with him, and Beton proves able to unhorse his «father.» The boy descends from his horse weeping only to find Daurel laughing and giving thanks to God:

> «Bels filhs,» dis el, «aras sai veramen
> Que seret pros se vivet longamen.»
> Las armas pauzo amdoi cominalmen,
> Van se ceze sus en l'erba verden (1640).

The boy has become a man, and Daurel can now reveal the truth to him as they sit together on the grass — without ceremony, the *jongleur* relinquishes the rôle of father and becomes Beton's mentor and vassal — soon, after his first real test against two knights from Gormon's army, he will seek vengeance on Guy and be no longer *l'efas Betos* (2069), but *lo coms Beto* (2089). Thus the *Daurel* author gives validity to the cliché father-son speech which accompanied the coming-of-age ceremony. [74] Daurel does not have to advise Beton on what is expected of a *chevalier* — he has conscientiously seen to the boy's education — but can instead counsel him on the strategy to be used in regaining his fief. For unlike poems such as *Jourdain, Beuve, Doon*, revenge — the essential motivation that knits the poem together — is never

---

[73] In *Floriant*, the Arthurian epic, vv. 733-812 are devoted to the education of the hero at the age of seven by the fairy Morgan (an echo of *Perceval* and *Tristan*), but this is hardly a knightly upbringing in the epic tradition.

[74] The *Amis* author parodies, in an amusing and telling fashion, the advice given by father to son on knightly behavior, by depicting the lesson delivered by the traitor Hardré to his god-son, which ends:

> «Ardez les villes, les bors et les maisnils,
> Metez par terre autex et crucefiz,
> Par ce serez honorez et servis (1636).»

lost from view in *Daurel*. There are no endless adventures and fabulous encounters (on the model of *Apollonius*) to divert the hero from his duty. [75] Since Beton must reach manhood to accomplish this vengeance, his exile will last twelve years, after which he will return home, lift the siege of Monclar, and regain his heritage. The theme is commonplace; but in *Daurel* it is repeatedly given unity and meaning by a pervasive motif: the bonds between men are sacred; whoever destroys them is shaking the very foundation of feudalism and must be punished so that the social order may be restored. The disequilibrium caused by the murder of Bove can be repaired only by the restoration of Beton to his rightful heritage. Beton alone, the legal heir, can right the wrong; for should anyone else depose Guy, the disruption of the normal order would be perpetuated and the original wrong compounded rather than set right. [76] The *Daurel* author never loses this ideal from sight and does not blur the issue with superfluous and distracting adventure. The quasi-novelistic aspect of the exile (if indeed there is one in *Daurel*) is subjugated to its importance in feudal terms (the preservation of the rightful heir). With each episode, the author constructs the character of Beton, preparing him for his confrontation (in the manner of Ogier, Raoul, Girart or Renaut de Montauban) with royal authority in the person of Charlemagne. [77]

v. The Faithful Servant: Daurel

A contrast to the «jealous seneschal» or treacherous serf character-type, the faithful servant is a familiar figure in epic and an ancient one in literature, often, as in *Daurel*, related to the child-sacrifice motif. In one group of folk-tales, the child is sacrificed so that a

---

[75] There is a misconception, reflected in even the most recent manuals, that «le jeune Beton reviendra, après *maintes aventures*, venger son père, et recouvrer ses droits» (Jean Rouquette, *La Littérature d'oc*, Coll. Que Sais-je? [Paris, 1963], p. 29). There are, of course, no shipwrecks, no pirates, no kidnapping of wife or child, nothing, in short, between Beton's first taste of battle and his revenge.

[76] As is the case when King Louis wrongfully disposes of fiefs in *Raoul*: attempting to right the wrong done to Raoul, he wrongs the innocent Vermandois.

[77] In the missing third section of *Daurel*. See p. 84.

ruler, father or friend may be restored to life or health. [78] Although this version of the theme (represented in epic literature by *Amis*) is quite dissimilar to the treatment in *Daurel*, we can see how appealing it was to an author desiring to depict the highest forms of feudal loyalty. Instead of having a father sacrifice his children to save his companion (as in *Amis*), the *Daurel* author portrays a vassal sacrificing his own son to save his lord's son, thus according greater importance to the traditional faithful-servant character-type by elevating the servant-master relationship to the stronger feudal bond between vassal and lord. Along with Renier (*Jourdain*), Daurel, the ennobled *jongleur*, exemplifies the highest devotion and fidelity to the feudal ideal. Daurel is both servant and vassal; he is courageous and wise, yet retains a sense of humility — never losing sight of his lowly birth, yet taking pride in his craft. As a substitute father for Beton he sees that the boy receives all the elements of a noble education, nor does Daurel neglect to teach him how to sing, play and compose:

«Bels filhs Beto, apendet d'esturmens,
D'arpa e de viola, seres ne plus jauzens (1415).»

When Beton becomes a knight, he is ready, through Daurel's capable stewardship of his affairs, to win back his heritage. Daurel and his family are, to be sure, richly rewarded for their sacrifice, but the sacrifice itself has been made without any thought of recompense.

The situation in *Jourdain* is strikingly similar: Renier raises Jourdain as his own son, having sacrificed his real son to the traitor Fromont. His wife, Eremborc, is a more important figure than Daurel's wife, Beatrix, but their rôles are similar in that both wives suggest to their husbands the cruel sacrifice that must be made as the only honorable solution to their dilemma. Jourdain is raised incognito in the traitor's court and goes into exile when at the age of fifteen he learns the truth about his birth from Renier. Daurel and Renier stand apart from the more typical epic servants such as the fishermen in *Beuve* and *Haveloc* who save the rightful heir although ordered to kill him and dispose of the body, and their villainous counterparts

---

[78] See Leach's analysis (*Amis and Amiloun*, pp. xlix-lxv) of the twelfth-century Indian story *Vivavara* and the «Faithful John» tale (Grimm, No. 6). These analogues are valid for *Daurel* and *Jourdain*, but are too late in date to have influenced *Daurel* or *Amis*; cf. p. 88.

in *Doon* and *Daurel* (Ebrart) who attempt to do him in. In a romanesque reversal of Daurel's sacrifice, young Beuve de Hanstone gives
himself up to the traitor Doon in order to save Sabot, his tutor.[79]
The consequences of Beuve's sacrifice are in no way catastrophic but
merely serve as pretext for fabulous adventure.

The extraordinary nature of Daurel's sacrifice is expressed in the
words of Ermenjart:

> «So aves fait que a[n]c hom mai non poc far,
> C'om des so filh per so senhor salvar (1064).»

She has Daurelet buried next to Duke Bove: *Per luy es mort, ben
deu ondrat estar* (1069).[80] In the context of the feudal epic, Daurel's
action is the apotheosis of the feudal mystique,[81] the demonstration
that vassalic bonds are stronger than blood.

The Jongleur-hero

At the climax of the second part of the poem, Daurel and Beton,
disguised as minstrels, enter Guy's camp. The count invites them to
join him at dinner, but Daurel says: «We want to entertain you first.»
With Beton accompanying him on the *vielle,* Daurel sings:

> «Qui vol auzir canso, ieu lh'en dirai, so·m par,
> De tracio que no fai a celar
> Del fel trachor Guio — cui Jhesus desampar! —
> Qu'aucis lo duc quan fon ab lui cassar (1947).»

Thus, in an epic within an epic analogous to the Elizabethan «mouse-
trap,»[82] Daurel provokes Guy by confronting him with his crimes

---

[79] Sabot had been bribed to kill Beuve, but had instead disposed of a
blood-covered dummy and raised the boy as his own son. As a result of
Beuve's indiscretion in revealing his existence by attacking the traitor, Sabot
is captured and tortured by Doon.

[80] One is reminded of the verse in Corneille's *Heraclius* (II, v) «Mon
fils fut, pour mourir, le fils de l'empéreur.» A mother substitutes her child
for that of the emperor and delivers him to the tyrant to be killed.

[81] As Smith expresses it: «C'est le comble de la féodalité.» (*Colorado
College Studies,* X, 33).

[82] Rudolph Zenker, «*Boeve — Amlethus*: Das Altfranzösische Epos von
Boeve de Hamtone und der Ursprung der Hamletsage,» *Literarhistorische
Forschungen,* XXXII (Berlin, 1905), 277-279. Zenker suggests this parallel

dramatized. The scene is unique in epic; [83] it sets *Daurel* apart from the stereotyped servants and vassals of the genre by his talent: skilled in his profession, ennobled by Bove, rewarded by Beton, Daurel represents the very apotheosis of the *jongleur* in a literature which often depicts the *jongleur* as a minor figure, but seldom as a vassal of noble instinct and character. Having been made a landed vassal, Daurel does not lay aside his instruments, but takes up a sword to become, like Volker in the *Nibelungenlied,* a *jongleur*-warrior. Unlike Volker or the courageous Taillefer (*Roman de Rou*) who sings of Roland and insists on striking the first blow at the battle of Hastings, Daurel is not an «amateur» troubadour. Nor is he a minor character in the poem like the *jongleur* in Guillaume. [84] Guillaume's minstrel, Taillefer and Volker, like the historical figures Richard the Lion-hearted and Guillaume IX are nobles who sing, rather than *jongleurs* who fight; Daurel, a *jongleur* of lowly birth, plays a predominate rôle in our poem.

What, precisely, is the engagement between Bove and Daurel? At the opening of the story, the author does not feel compelled to elaborate beyond Daurel's statement,

«E son, senher, vostre om, d'un riche castelier
Que hom apela Monclier (87).»

an utterance doubly significant: first of all, Daurel and his family are vassals of the duke of Poitou; this bond having been stated, the author feels further explanation unnecessary, but we can surmise that Daurel's elevation stems not only from his ability to entertain but

---

in *Daurel* (not valid between *Boeve* and *Hamlet,* a fact that he does not make clear) in an attempt to prove, through *Daurel,* the «Germanic» origin and the antiquity of the *Beuve de Hanstone* tradition.

[83] The episodes in *Beuve I* (v. 10,046) and *Beuve III* (v. 12,800) are obvious borrowings from the Apollonius-legend (cf. *Historia Apollonii,* XLI, where the hero hears his lost daughter, Tarsia, singing about their adventures) involving as they do Josiane singing about Beuve's noble deeds. The episode is not germane to *Daurel* or *Hamlet* and is not found in the older Anglo-Norman version of the poem. See also R. Menéndez-Pidal, *Poesia juglaresca y orígenes de las literaturas románicas* (Madrid, 1957), pp. 31-32, p. 41.

[84] The sorrow and concern voiced over the unnamed *jongleur,* when Guillaume appears to be carrying his dead or wounded minstrel from the battlefield (vv. 1253 ff): *En tote France n'ad si bon chantur, / N'en bataille plus hardi fereur.* shows that the *jongleur de geste* was held in high esteem by the knight.

also from some previous service on the part of Daurel or his family to Bove's family; secondly, from a textual point of view, truncated v. 87 (above) is suspect and may indicate a lacuna at this point, although the following verse (*Per so t'en deh may amier*) seems to follow naturally enough in this context. Bove appreciates Daurel's talents; upon finding out that the *jongleur* is his «man,» he loves Daurel all the more. In an epic composed in twelfth-century Languedoc by a man of the craft, it would be surprising not to find some glorification of the *jongleur*; in this respect, Daurel's ennoblement does not appear excessive, nor does his admission into noble company by virtue of his inventiveness (e.g., Bernart de Ventadorn) seem fabulous or unusual in the culture of southern France, where the ability to compose and sing often transcended class distinctions; [85] the *jongleur* or troubadour, accompanying the knights into battle, could further distinguish himself with the sword (e.g., Bertran de Born, Marcabrun). This would seem to be one of the rare cases where a man could move out of the class into which he was born — an idea of social mobility made all the more interesting and striking by its occurrence in that most traditional of genres — the feudal epic. In *Daurel*, the metamorphosis from lowly minstrel to knight is accomplished in a single generation: a minstrel who sings, plays and does acrobatic tricks becomes, after his ennoblement, a troubadour, a composer as well as singer of lays and epics (as a landowner, he need no longer earn his living from his craft and is thus free to practice the higher forms of the art). When, in Babylonia, Daurel teaches Beton the art of music, the vocation of the minstrel has already become the avocation of the noble: Beton learns these arts as part of his knightly education, to make him (as Daurel explains in v. 1415) a happier person, not to earn his livlihood. Although Daurel's exploits with the sword are left to the imagination, his sons perform noble deeds on the battlefield against Guy: all traces of their humble lineage have disappeared.

---

[85] Faral (*Les Jongleurs en France,* pp. 80-81) affirms that the classification of *jongleurs* according to class — popular or noble — does not suffice. It is closer to the truth to say that in each *jongleur*, lowliness and nobility are mixed. «C'est ce que nous apprennent un certain nombre de textes, la pièce des *Deux bourdeurs ribauts,* par exemple, ou l'épopée de *Daurel et Beton,* ou d'autres encore.»

vi. Sources and Originality

The themes and characters in *Daurel* are, for the most part, drawn from the mid-twelfth-century milieu in which the poem was composed (pp. 43-44). In spite of several archaisms (e.g., the relationship between Bove and Guy, the setting of the poem in the time of Charlemagne), there is nothing in *Daurel* to preclude the proposed date of composition, 1150, or the *terminus ad quem*, 1168 (pp. 34-37). Given the uncertainty of dating (pp. 36-37) it is impossible to indicate with precision the sources with which the *Daurel* author was familiar, but it is apparent that he knew in some form *Roland, Gormont, Girart, Amis, Apollonius, Aye, Ogier*, and, possibly, *Raoul*. For the first three epics, the evidence is circumstantial (pp. 37-43):

1) Through the personage of Charlemagne, the author makes a transparent attempt to link his poem to the *geste du roi*. That he refers to Paris, rather than Aix-la-Chapelle,[86] as the capital of Charlemagne may indicate that he borrowed the emperor-figure from other feudal epics rather than from the *Roland* itself. While he mentions Roland and the peers, he makes no reference to Ganelon, no attempt to link Guy to this most infamous of traitors. The superficiality of these borrowings indicates that, although the *Daurel* author knew Rolandian tradition, the filiation between *Daurel* and the *Roland* is tenuous and indirect. By using famous names the author is echoing a respected but vaguely conceived tradition.

2) As in the case of the *Roland,* there are no close analogies between *Daurel* and *Gormont*: the evidence that our poet knew the oldest feudal epic is limited to one allusion; the name of the Saracen who attacks the Emir of Babylonia, of uncertain, but probable significance, since the name Gormont is not common in epic (p. 42, note 26).

3) If we are to judge by personal and place names, the *Daurel* author was patently familiar with the *Girart de Roussillon* legend. The linguistic similarities also indicate a closer filiation between *Daurel* and *Girart* than is apparent from the plots, which are quite dissimilar (although Girart might conceivably have provided a model

---

[86] As do the oldest poems. See Paris, *Histoire poétique*, p. 368.

for the missing section of *Daurel* involving the struggle of Beton against Charlemagne).

Amis, Aye and *Ogier,* although northern poems, relate more closely to *Daurel* in form and content, have southern locales and, along with the Apollonius legend, were known in the South at the time *Daurel* was composed:

4) *Amis* is an old legend, known to have existed in an early twelfth-century version (Latin hexameters of Radulfus Tortarius),[87] in which the child-sacrifice theme is presented in an heroic and primitive manner — stripped of all feudal or romanesque trappings — the motivation for the sacrifice is the bond of blood-brotherhood between Amis and Amiles: «This is the strongest exhibition of fidelity to the brotherhood vow,»[88] since the children are sacrificed (with no hope of miraculous restoration) so that their blood may cure Amile of his fatal disease. The theme of friendship is never lost from view in this early version, and remains vital in the feudal cadre of the epic *Amis.* In the poem of Tortarius, Charlemagne plays no rôle, but his name is mentioned in passing as the uncle of Gaiferus of Poitiers, whose court is visited by the heroes of the story.[89] The many analogues between *Daurel* and *Amis,* the fact that the legend is attached to Poitiers, and the early date of composition indicate that the *Daurel* author knew *Amis* in one of its versions.

Jourdain, the sequel to *Amis,* is based on a combination of the *Apollonius* legend, *Amis* and other *chansons* (including, possibly, *Daurel*), and the Bible. A late poem, it could not have had any influence on *Daurel,* although the analogues are, as we have seen, striking. The *Daurel* and *Jourdain* authors, separated by time and place, drew from the same sources, but composed epics quite different in style and tone. *Jourdain* is modelled closely on the *Apollonius,* for example, and contains several episodes clearly borrowed from that tradition; the *Daurel* author, on the other hand, although probably familiar with the legend in one of its many forms,[90] uses only one

---

[87] Cf. Konrad Hofmann, *Amis et Amiles und Jourdains de Blaivies,* 2nd ed. (Erlangen, 1882), pp. xxi ff.

[88] Leach, *Amis,* pp. xxiv-xxv.

[89] Leach, *Amis,* p. xxxi.

[90] References in Cabrera and *Flamenca* indicate possible Provençal versions of *Apollonius,* known as early as the sixth century in the South (the Bishop of Poitiers refers to it [*Carm.* VI, 8, 5]); See Oroz, *Historia de*

scene from it, which he freely adapts to his narrative requirements (p. 117).

5) *Aye d'Avignon,* like *Amis,* contains many broad analogues with *Daurel*: the exile and upbringing of the young hero, the southern locale of the poem, the probability that it existed in some version as early as the mid-twelfth century (although the extant poem is relatively late in date), indicate a relationship to *Daurel,* although the two poems are quite dissimilar in most respects (*Aye* contains for example, elements of courtly love completely absent in *Daurel*). We cannot be more precise about the relationship: if the Daurel author used *Aye* (or *Amis*) as a model, he did so with great originality and cleverness, changing and adapting to an extent that defies all attempts to establish filiation: we can see similarities, but we cannot say that a specific episode or theme in *Daurel* is borrowed from a specific episode in these other poems.

6) Since we know very little about the early versions of the *Ogier* legend, the debt of *Daurel* to *Ogier* is tenuous and hypothetical: Bove is identified as the son of Ogier, but this allusion could just as well be drawn from the *Roland* tradition. However, the *Ogier* legend appears to have an historical basis in the South [91] and may well represent one of the archetypes of the feudal hero. The legend had a very wide influence and, in its Catalan and Castillian versions, resembles a typical feudal epic of the *Daurel* type. [92] In the French *chanson,* Ogier, driven to rebellion by Charlemagne's injustice, kills all the best French knights, is finally captured by Turpin, who refuses to kill his prisoner as Charlemagne had ordered. Charles, besieged by Saracens who have attacked him upon hearing the false news of Ogier's death, is forced to bind over his son Charlot (responsible for the unjust accusations that have caused Ogier's predicament) to Ogier before the hero will consent to lead the imperial armies to victory

---

Apolonio, pp. 7-8; C. Carroll Marden, ed., *Libro de Apolonio,* Elliot Monographs, No. 6 (Baltimore, 1917), pp. xxvi-xl.

[91] See p. 38, note 15. Cf. also Jean Frappier, «Reflexions sur les rapports des chansons de geste et de l'histoire,» *ZRPh,* LXXIII (1957), 5.

[92] Riquer, *Chansons de geste,* pp. 248-249. Reference is to the *Romance* which begins: *De Mantua salió el marqués Danés* (Duran, *Romancero,* I, 207-217 [no. 355-357]). Baldovinos, nephew of Danés Urgel, marries a Saracen princess named Seville. Prince Don Caroloto makes advances to her, which are repulsed. He decides to kill Baldovinos in order to marry Seville, carries out his plan as they are travelling through a «desert.»

against the Saracens. Charles humbles himself before Ogier, who (unlike most rebellious barons) wins out in the end. From this brief outline it is obvious that *Ogier* in the form that we know it had no direct influence on *Daurel,* although, as in the case of *Girart,* there may be similarities with the missing part of our poem. Did the *Daurel* author intend to make of Beton an Ogier, a rebel baron whose adversary is Charlemagne? This we cannot know, but the onomastic evidence indicates that our author did indeed know something about the *Ogier* legend.

7) *Raoul* and *Daurel* are quite different in character and plot, but they both reflect the problems of feudal society in that they examine the two powerful forces which form the backbone of that society: blood and vassality. In *Raoul* every major character is linked by family, and the act of the individual engages the whole clan. [92] The only bond stronger than blood is the vassalic relationship of one man to another; thus, only the murder of his mother can cause Bernier to break his bond with Raoul, and this mainly because of the sacrilegious nature of Raoul's act. In other words, Raoul must murder *and* blaspheme God before he becomes an unworthy companion. *Raoul,* like *Daurel,* is intimately concerned with feudal relationships, duties and obligations, and presents a strong case for the preservation of feudal order. There is in these poems no facile motivation, no handy traitor upon whom to hang the blame — the cruelty and injustice brought about by the disruption of feudal order is laid bare.

In postulating these seven epics as likely sources of *Daurel* — all were composed by the mid-twelfth century or earlier, all appear to have historical antecedents, and all contain characters and motifs mirrored in our poem — we are not suggesting that they were models consciously copied by the Poitevin *jongleur* who composed our poem. They represent, rather, the epic tradition familiar to our author. Though it is true that *Daurel* appears at times strikingly similar to other feudal epics like *Orson, Doon* and *Jourdain,* nevertheless these *chansons,* later in date than *Daurel* (pp. 36-37), could not have influenced it. *Romans d'aventures* such as *Huon, Floriant, Doon* or *Beuve* appear even less probable as models for *Daurel* (pp. 43-46).

Daurel, a northern-influenced poem, retells much that is found in other epics, but its individual handling of this common material offers

---

evidence that it is an original work. The seven epics enumerated represent a tradition transformed by the freshness and originality of a southern poet into a poem which resembles many other epics but still remains unique. Too late in date to support the argument for the existence of a Provençal epic tradition which may have pre-dated the northern feudal epic; [93] too devoid of tangible historical references to suggest the origins of a meridional epic stemming directly from the struggles between feudal lords and royal authority; *Daurel* with its elements of originality proves to be essentially southern. Let us briefly review the evidence:

1) Language: *Daurel,* like *Girart* and *Aigar,* is written in a literary *koiné,* apparently created expressly for the epic in southwestern France (see p. 25). The northern flavor of vocabulary and rhyme is superficial, an obvious attempt to render the «atmosphere» of the *chanson de geste* in a «foreign» language. Conversely, the southern personal and place names found in *Daurel* would be out of the ordinary in a northern epic where the author would use the North-French forms of southern places and characters (p. 43). Since the *Daurel* author did not hesitate to use northern name forms for his most conventional characters, the presence of southern forms for the major ones is proof that the poem was an original composition, not a copy or translation of a northern *chanson.*

2) Geography: Although topological accuracy is generally absent from adventure stories such as *Beuve, Orson* and others, [94] the place names in *Daurel* are, as we have seen (pp. 39-41), significantly linked with the Midi. The mention of Saint-Hilaire of Poitiers, unique in epic, is especially interesting in view of the important school connected with this church, which had a rich library and was particularly brilliant during the twelfth century. [95] The Count of Poitou was, in fact, hereditary abbot of Saint-Hilaire; Bove and Beton are, in fiction, counts of Poitou: Bove is buried there and Beton is married there. Although no connection between our fictional heroes and the historical counts can be discerned from the meager evidence, the poet's link

---

[93] Cf. Lejeune, *Recherches,* pp. 156-157.

[94] according to Bédier (*Légendes épiques,* IV, 404) who includes *Daurel* in this category.

[95] Robert Favreau, «Les écoles et la culture à Saint-Hilaire-le-grand de Poitiers des origines au début du XII siècle,» *CCM,* III (1960), 473-478.

with Poitou is too obvious to be merely coincidental and *Daurel* may well have been composed to please or flatter one or another ruler of that province.

3) The anti-Carolingian character of the poem: *Daurel* reflects, although faintly and distantly, the rebellion of the Aquitanian nobility against the Carolingians, a struggle carried on almost continuously since 768, when Waïfre, Duke of Aquitaine, died after a lifetime of warfare against Pepin.[96] There is an absence in *Daurel* of any sentiment of national patriotism (Charles is depicted as a weak suzerain), crusading zeal or intolerant fanaticism (the Saracens are portrayed as noble and good and no attempt is made to convert them, except for Erimena who is to wed Beton).

4) Saracens: The favorable literary treatment of the Saracens may reflect the ties of Languedoc to the Orient, which remained un-broken from the early twelfth century when Raimond de Saint-Gilles conquered the kingdom of Tripoli.[97] The civilization of the Midi had much in common with the Arabic and Byzantine cultures, and it is likely that certain themes, especially the ideal of blood-brotherhood as mirrored in *Daurel,* derive in part from these civilizations.[98]

5) The amenities of life: There is in *Daurel* a concern with com-fort more typical of the Midi than of the spartan North (as reflected in epic). The knights are often *a taulas* (Bove, when Ermenjart de-nounces Guy; Guy, when Daurel and Beton arrive disguised as min-strels), and it is significant that Guy abandons his quest for Beton because it is dinnertime and his men haven't eaten. When Monclar is being prepared for siege,[99] when Daurel's boat is being readied for sailing, the greatest detail is given over to victuals. French and

---

[96] Ernest Lavisse, *Histoire de France illustrée* (Paris, 1911), II, pt. 1, 276; see also Lejeune, *Recherches,* pp. 154-155.

[97] Lavisse, *Histoire de France,* II, pt. 1, 305-306.

[98] Nelli, *L'Erotique,* pp. 278-283.

[99] *Daurel* is enumerated in a list of epics contained in a document dealing with the objects needed to defend a besieged castle. This document, addressed to Alfonso X, contains words in *langue d'oc,* and it is probable that it came from the Midi in the time of Alfonso, but there can be no certainty about its date. The document is reported in Manuel Milá y Fontanals, *De la poesía heroico-popular castellana,* Vol. I of *Obras Completas,* re-ed. by Martín de Riquer (Barcelona, 1959 [1874]), p. 336 (new ed. p. 423). Meyer, *Daurel,* p. xxxii, gives wrong volume and page in citing this passage, which begins «Item sint ibi romancia, et libri gestorum, videlicet Alexandri,... et de Otonell et de *Bethon...*»

Saracen nobles are depicted playing dice, chess and backgammon (e.g., the charming scene in which Beton gambles with the noble children and wins their shirts). One expects scenes like these in courtly literature, but they are surprising in epic. The point is a minor one, but does cast some insight on the mentality of our author and, if we are to give any credence to the old saw «les Francs à la bataille, les Provençaux aux vivres,»[100] on his southern origin.

6) The *jongleur*-hero: Although there are numerous examples of minstrels in epic, they are almost without exception minor characters.[101] As we have seen, Daurel represents the glorification of the *jongleur*, ennobled by virtue of his talent; capable, in spite of his humble birth, of the highest devotion and loyalty.

7) Sworn-brotherhood: The loyalty of Bove to Guy, the masculine love that is the dominant theme of the first part of the poem, goes beyond the simple bond between warriors to symbolize the ideal of virile fraternity destroyed by a betrayal of this most sacred trust. The tragic nature of this relationship is fully explored by the *Daurel* author in a manner unique in epic.

8) Lord and vassal: *Daurel* dramatizes the vertical links in feudal society from burgher to emperor by portraying Bove's devotion to Charles, paralleled by Daurel's and the burgher's loyalty to Bove. The fact that in *Daurel* the dividing line between noble and commoner is indistinct, reflects a viewpoint of social mobility (and a modest sense of liberalism) more generally typical of South than of North.[102]

9) Childhood: No other epic depicts the upbringing of a child in such detail. Brief references to a youth's education are found in other *chansons*, but as Gaston Paris remarked: «L'auteur de *Daurel* s'y complaît, s'y arrête, lui qui d'ordinaire est si pressé, y montre une

---

[100] Raoul de Caen's stereotyped (and biased) description of the Provençal crusaders, cited by Paul Meyer, «L'Influence des troubadours,» *Romania*, V (1876), 261, who adds: «Les Provençaux se soucient peu d'entendre conter des prouesses pour lesquelles ils n'ont pas de goût, et voilà pourquoi ils n'ont pas d'épopée.»

[101] Faral, *Jongleurs*, p. 79, p. 83; Menéndez-Pidal, *Poesía juglaresca*, p. 77.

[102] See for example, the existence of the Languedocian communes in the eleventh century, which demonstrates the historically more liberal nature of the Midi (Lavisse, *Histoire de France*, II, pt. 2, 205).

certaine grâce, qu'on ne rencontre pas souvent dans les poèmes de ce genre.» [103]

It is apparent that the *Daurel* author's originality lies neither in his poetry nor in his choice of matter. It does lie in his dramatic ability, his brevity, his clear unencumbered narrative style, his vigorous spirit that infuses new life into commonplace themes, rendering the motivation of his characters convincing. Had *Daurel* been written in a North-French dialect, it would, in my opinion, have been considered among the better works in its genre, the equal of *Aye d'Avignon, Orson de Beauvais,* or *Amis et Amile;* but written as it was in an obscure Poitevin border-dialect, it has been largely ignored or misjudged, often by scholars who have barely glanced at the text: no one who has read it could possibly consider *Daurel* an imitation of *Beuve de Hanstone* or *Doon de Mayence. Daurel,* whatever its faults and weaknesses, is a *chanson de geste,* not a *roman d'aventures;* it is, furthermore, neither a copy nor a reworking of any northern poem. Taken individually, the nine motifs enumerated in this conclusion provide only fragmentary evidence that *Daurel* is indeed an original work, very much a product of the Midi; taken as a whole, these motifs demonstrate that *Daurel* is an anomaly — an epic written on a normal human dimension — a worthy representative of an isolated epic tradition which was able to produce one masterpiece — *Girart de Roussillon* — before it died out in the political and religious upheaval of the early thirteenth century.

---

[103] *Mélanges,* p. 149.

Chapter IX

TEXTUAL METHOD

In presenting a new edition of *Daurel et Beton,* I have reproduced the text of the MS as faithfully as possible, given the limitations imposed by working with a photographic copy, indicating all divergencies from it in the textual notes, where attention is drawn to deletions and erasures made by the scribe and to words or letters added by him above the line (in superscript) or overlying other words. All indentations are reported in the notes and all illustrations are described.

The text is emended under the following circumstances:

1) Obvious error: Scribal omissions are emended in brackets (e.g., ca[ste]l) if support for the emendation can be found elsewhere in the text or if both sense and meter call for it. Dittographies and words that spoil sense and meter are eliminated in the edited text only if they appear to be the result of scribal error. All such deletions are reported in the notes. Orthographic blunders are emended only when they are obviously gross scribal errors of no linguistic interest and interfere with the comprehension of the verse. The rejected reading is found in the notes.

2) Doubtful readings: Italics represent readings supplied by conjecture to partially destroyed or illegible parts of the MS, which may or may not be verified by ultraviolet examination. Brackets, on the other hand, indicate the addition of material omitted by the scribe, and are also used to expand words shortened by syncope and to provide capitals left uncompleted by the scribe. Suspension points represent lacunae or omissions in the edited text due to illegibility of the MS and not subject to fairly certain conjecture. Doubtful readings

caused by letters or words overlaid by scribe, similarity of certain letters, imperfectly formed letters, etc., are resolved on the basis of usage elsewhere in the text whenever possible. Alternative interpretations are discussed in the notes after the following abbreviations which indicate their nature and source:

MS: lesson found in manuscript, but rejected by editor.

ALT: a possible alternate reading of the MS, rejected in favor of another which appears more favorably adapted to the context (e.g., *cant a·n* is alternate reading of *cant au* 580).

Meyer: the reading found in Paul Meyer's edited text (*Meyer suggests* refers to a conjecture made by Meyer in his notes or glossary).

Chab.: remarks made by Camille Chabaneau in his review of *Daurel* (*RLR*, XX, 246-260).

3) The solutions of the abbreviations are as follows:

K.: only two solutions are found in the text, *Carles* (subject) 416 and *Karlo* (object) 1819. Therefore, the solutions are made on the basis of case.

G.: there are numerous solutions in the text, *Guis* (subj.) 416 (obj.) 370 *passim; Guio* (obj.) 4 and *Guiho* (obj.) 46 *passim*.

Other abbreviations (e.g., *S., Jhũ, oĩpoten, tostp̃s*) have been solved in the usual manner, and the usual modern distinction is made between *i* and *j,* and *u* and *v.* The sign of nasality is replaced by *m* or *n.*

4) The divergencies between my edited text and Meyer's are too numerous to list, but are for the most part concerned with the addition or deletion of readings in the edited text based on emendation of meter or grammar. All important differences have been reported in the notes. Meyer's reading of the MS differs from mine in numerous cases involving error on his part or mistakes in transcription. I have corrected these in my text without noting them.

5) Emendations: since the unique *Daurel* MS is often faulty and ambiguous, I have felt it necessary to make many emendations. But in all cases where the MS reading has not been respected in the edited text, the original reading is reported in the notes. I have emended prudently when confronted with manifest errors in sense and meter or faults of orthography representing obvious scribal error or causing confusion due to possible misinterpretation.

In the following verses, names of characters confused by the scribe have been emended: 119, 149, 316, 1006.

Lacunae or possible lacunae are found after the following verses: 14, 121, 735, 1730 (?), 1917.

Misplaced hemistichs or verses are found as follows: 28-29 second hemistich (emended in text); 143-144 second (emendation suggested in note); 150-151 second (emended); 204-205 first (doubtful: see note); 1732-1733 second (emendation suggested in note); 1095: verse inserted by scribe in anticipation of 1126 (omitted in edited text); 1585: misplaced verse (sense of passage required it after 1587).

6) Concordance between Meyer's edition and my edited text:

Numbering of verses: 1946 is omitted from Meyer's edition by error, therefore his numbering differs from mine from this point on. Add one to the verse number of the present edition to get the corresponding verse in Meyer's.

Numbering of laisses: XIII-XVI differ from Meyer's edition (see note on v. 491). Meyer numbers a laisse at the very end of the poem, which I have omitted since it is undecipherable.

THE TEXT
OF
DAUREL ET BETON

SO ES LO ROMANS DE DAUREL E DE BETO [76ᵛ]

[I]

Plat vos auzir huna rica canso?   1
Entendet le, si vos plas, escotas la razo
D'un rich duc de Fransa e del comte Guio,
De [D]aurel lo joglar e de l'enfan Beto   4
Que en sa junbentut tray tan gran pasio.
Lo duc Bobis d'Antona se sazia en un peyro,
Et entorn lu son Franses, tuh li melhor baro,
Aqui fo lo coms Gui cui Donedieu mal do!   8
Cel que no n'a vila ne valor
Mas sol hun ca[ste]l c'om apela Aspremont.
Lo duc pres lo pel ponh e mes lo en razo:
«Sira d'aut parayge, vos et mon paube hom,   12
Be sai que et mos [hom] ses tota mentizo.»
«Seher,» dit Guis, «vers es, ses contradicsio.»
«Lo meu alue vos solvi, e au o [mei] baro,
E seret engau mi seger de ma mayzo;   16
Jurat mi companhia a totz jornz que vivo.
Mas s'ieu prengui molher e [no mi] venh enfanto,
S'ieu mori denan vos, companh, ieu la vos do;
Mos castels e mas vilas, ma tera e maio   20
Vos solvi, bels companh, e·us meti a bando.»
«Senher,» dis lo coms Gui, «vos mi donas gran do,   [77ʳ]
Et ieu pren lo, si vos plas, ab tal gaserdo;
Gardaray vostras ostz e[·m] metray a bando   24
Pertot hom vos volres e lai on vos er bo.»
So respon lo duc Boves: «Lo sagramentz farom.»
Fac aportar .i. libre on lhi evangeli son,

Juran si companhia amdoy li compaho,   28
Can si foron juratz lhi bauzo sus el mento
Et l'us ama per fe, et l'aute per trasiho.

[II]

Lo duc Boves d'Antona a fah lo sagramen
Ad Antona el palais si c'o viro .v.c.   32
L'us es fizels amicx e l'audre mescrezens.
.X. ans complitz estero en bon acordamen
E mesclero lor teras e lor ost assimen
Tro que Dieu trames a Boves .i. gran isassamen,   36
Que estava el palaes ab lo mels de sa gen,
E jutgava .i. plah; e ve·us vengutz corretz
Le messagie de Karlo; dissen el païmen
E pueissas venc avan e saludec lo gen   40
Etz a·l pres per la ma e trais lo parlamen:
«A vos mi trametz Carles, lo rey a qui Fransa apen,
Que vos anes a lui e vostre bevolen,
Car tal plah vos vol far don tuh sere[m] manenh.»   44
So·l respon lo duc Boves: «Irai lei veramen
E meneray Guiho mon compaho valen.»
Motz s'i fiza lo duc; peuis lhi·n pres malamen.
«A vos,» fay cel, «amix, donara[y] .i. prezen,   [77ᵛ]   48
Mon ric pala[f]ren e mon destrier corren,
Etz anas vo·nh al rey cui gar Dieu de turmen
Digas lhi qu'ieu verray abans del mes pasen.»
«Senher,» dis lo mesagier, «voste comadamen   52
Faray mol volonties et gran grat vos en ren
Del do que m'aves datz e de l'arculimen.»

[III]

Lo mesage de Carles se pres a retornier;
Lo duc Boves d'Antona apela .i. trotier: 56
«Vay me ad Aspremon, no m'o velhas tarzier
A mon companh Guiho c'am me venga parlier.»

«Senher,» dis lo messauge, «so faray volontier.»
E vinc ad Aspremon dejos .i. olivier; 60
Aqui trobec Guiho lo trager lauzengier
Que jogava a taulas et vi lo messagier.
«Senher,» dis lo messaigeus,» ab vos vol parlier,
Say me evia lo duc que li aves mestier.» 64
Lo coms Guis apela Bertran son escudier:
«Vay me metre la cela a mon destrier,
Anem saber del duc que vol ni ha mestier.»
E dobero se cadaüs vol[on]tiers, 68
E vengro ad Antona so el palais plenier
E Bobes quan [lo] vi si lo vay abrasier:
«Dieu vos sal, amicx, e mon bon compagier!
Carles mannes mi manda qu'eu an ab lui parlier; 72
Menar vos ay, cum companh, a Paris cortegier.»
«Senher,» dis lo coms, «cum vos plara si er.»
Lo duc Boves si pres de la cortz ad alier
E fon en sa compahia .ii. melia cavalier, [78ʳ] 76
Lo ric duc ac grah car va al rey parlier.
Abtan vec vos vengut devant .i. joglier,
E viueulet agradable e gueiamen e clier,
E fo paubres d'aver, ma be·is sap deportier. 80
Lo ric duc d'Antona li pres a demandier:
«Cum as tu nom, amicx? garda no m'o v[e]lhas celier.»
Daurel li respon, que bo sap motz gensier:
«Senher, Daurel ay nom, e say motz gen arpier, 84
E tocar vihola e ricamen trobier
E son, senher, vostre om, d'un riche castelier
Que hom apela Monclier.»
«Amic,» so ditz lo duc, «per so t'en deh may amier; 88
En seta cortz ab me·us volray mener.»
«Senher,» ditz Daurel, «ges no lei puesc alier,
Ca si ay ma molher e .ii. fils a cabdelier;
Non ay aur ni argen que lor pusca laysier.» 92
Lo duc Boves apela son vayley Azemier:
«Amic,» so ditz lo duc, «fe que·m deves portier,
Gardas li sa molher, vestir la deberetz chier,
Et d'aquest .ii. enfans vos prec del norriger; 96
Tot aquo lor me donatz que sabran demandier

Ce el mon, per nulh aver, tu o pots trobier.»
«Senher,» ditz n'Azemars, «Dieus vos lais retornier!
Ja non auran frachura de re qu'i puscam fier.»   100
«Daurel,» so dis lo duc, «tenes per cavalgier
Aquest palafre blanc que be·us poyra portier.»
Tal joia n'ac Daurel que motz non potz sonier;
Baysa·s al sabato, cuja·l lo pe bayzier.   104
Lo ric duc l'en leva, be·l fay a pe paregier.
«Senher,» so dis Guiho, «trop nos podem tradier;
Bels amix duc companh, pensem del esperonier.»
Dresadas an las rennas e prendo·is az anier,   [78ᵛ]   108
E vengro a Paris lo sapte a l'avesprier.

[IV]

Lo dimenge mati can pres a l'esclarier
Le duc Boves e Guis se prendo a vister;
Cadaün vest bliautz d'un bon pali de Tir.   112
Lo duc Bobes d'Antona si fes Daurel venir,
Vai ab el a la cortz e violar e bordir.
L'emperaire de Fransa, can vi lo duc venir,
Leva·is de la cadieura e va lo arculhir   116
E pres lo pre la ma, josta se lo fai sezir,
Mes li lo bras sus col, e pueis pres a dir:
[Dux], jes vos no sabes per que ie·us ay fah venir,
Mas sabres ho en breu, ans que·ns vos layse tornier;   120
Ans que vos en tornes vos volray requerir…»
«Sira,» lo dis lo duc, «so vos dei mol grazir,
Be·m podes en requir mas vos ve per plazer.»
E Guis entendec o — dis c'om no·l pot auzir: 124
«Companh, per cela dona vos convenra murir!»

[V]

[G]rans fo la cortz en Fransa sus el palais ausor
Del [duc] Boves d'Antona e de l'empeyrador;
Tan duc, tan comte i ac, tan home de valor,   128
Avesques e arsebes, de cavaliers la flor.

Lo duc Roulan i fo que es de gran valor,
E·lh dotze par i foro que so de gran vigor.
Adonx dis Carles magnes: «Escoltas mi, senhor; 132
Aminas mi seror genta — donar l'ay per amor
Maritz lo ric duc Boves se [de] vos n'ay lauzor,
E donar l'ay Peutieus, lo solier e la tor;
De Bordels atresi lo vulh faire senhor.» 136
E Guis a dih tot suau cum fels e traïdor:
«Per aqueta molher molra el a dolor!»

[VI]

Pueisas escria Carles magnes lo bavier: [79ʳ]
«Levas en pes, sira coms Olivier, 140
Amena mi ma seror ab lo vi[s] clier.»
El la·lh amena ab molt gran alegrier
Ela fo fresca, fes la bel esgardier,
Sa color fresca com roza de rozier. 144
Lo rey si leva, vay Boves apelier:
«Duc de bon aire, filh del amic Augier,
Levas en pes e prendes [a] molher
Ma seror genta que ieu vos vuelh donier.» 148
S[o] dis lo [dux]: «So fay mal refugier.»
Pren la lo rey; Carles la·lh fay donier
A l'arcivesques que .iii. ves la·lh fay bayzier.
Las nosas fan sus el palais plenier, 152
Ab mot gran joy los i veiras ajustier.
So dis don Guis lo tracher lauzengier:
«Compans, per cesta dona vos vendra destu[r]bier!»
«Ai! sire duc,» dis Carles al vis clier, 156
Mon gonfaino vous autrei per portier,
E mas grans ost menar e capdelier.»
Lo riche duc li vay la ma baier
E pren lo gan de sa senha portier. 160
Lo duc sogorna .i. mes tot entier,
Pueis vay a Karlo ab son compagier:
«Reys, empeyrayre, de Guis vos vulh preguier,
Se mi amas, que lhui tengas en quier.» 164

So dis lo rey: «Far n'au mon cossilier,
Per vostr'amor lo voldray fort amier.»
Lo riche duc tantost lo vay baier,
E pren cumjhat, e vay s'en ab sa molher;   168
E Daurel vieula e mena alegrier
Que·l rey de Fransa li a datz .i. destrier.
Et s'en vai Bobes ab mot grant alegrier,   [79ᵛ]
Lo tracher Guis cui Jhesu desamper   172
A encobida na Esmenjartz sa molher.

[VII]

Lo ric duc Boves ab gran alegramen
Vay a Peytiey ab gran joi issimen
E n'Esmenjartz ab la cara rizen.   176
Ela cavalga .i. palafre corren,
Cela ac d'eborin; lo peitral fo d'argen,
E so .ii. m. cavaliers valen;
E·l tracher Guis dis al duc belamen,   180
«Companh,» fay s'el, «diray vos mon talen:
Bela es madona ab lo cors covinen,
Dares m'en partz si co m'aves coven?»
Lo pros duc li repon en riën   184
Que no·s cujava que i agues traïmen:
«Companh, pregat lo payre omnipoten
Que·m do la mortz tost e viassamen;
Pueis l'aures vos, pus vos ve a talen.»   188
Lo trager Guis respon entre sas dens:
«Ieu v'ausirai ab mon espieyt lozen.»
Tan cavalguero tro viro a prezen
Las autas tors de la cieutat valen;   192
E lhi borzes so a l'aculhimen,
E so .v. melia, cadaüs vestitz gen.
A molt gran joia intro al païmen,
Redon la viala e l'ausor mandamen.   196
E lo franc duc totas la forsas pren,
Las rendas dona al trachor mescrezen,
Tota la tera que viro a prezen,

Trastot Bordels a l'apertenemen   [80ʳ]   200
Tro en Agen, a son comandamen.

[VIII]

Lo ric duc fay la cort ajustar.
Abtant vec vos la molher del joglar,
E Daurel vieula, ela pres a tombar   204
Denan la dona, gen si van deportar.
Bem plai al duc car los ve alegrar;
Dis a la dona: «Molt fan sist a prezar.»
«Daurel,» dis el, «a vos volrai donar   208
.I. ric castel c'om apela Monclar,
Prop es d'aisi en riba de mar,
Que del port podet ondrat estar;
Tuh silh qu'en so sio a to mandar.   212
Ab ta molher tu t'en vai lai estar,
Tan can vieurat lo te vulh autrear,
Apres ta mort a cui te vols donar.»
E li a fah lo castel autregar,   216
A lo·lh lhieurat, ve·us pagat lo joglar!
E lo coms Guis cui ja Dieus non ampar,
Pessa de l'aur e de l'argen amassar.
E lo duc Boves non o pot plus durar   220
Del goifano de l'empeyraire portar:
Can lo rey vol en loc cavalgar
Tramet per lui, e vai li ajudar.
.I. jorn lo duc fo [a]nat ribarar   224
E lo coms Guis volia ab lui parlar;
No l'i trobet, e si pres a passar
Don'Esmengars, gen lo vai covider.   [80ᵛ]
Sap que·l duc l'ama e vol lo fort onrar;   228
Pren la pel ponh, van s'en asetier,
En .i. escaun s'en anero parlier.
«Dona,» dis el, «no·us o puesc plus celar:
Amada·us ay, vulh vos merce clamar,   232
Qu'ieu sia voste e que·m volhas amar.
Colgas m'an vos, no m'o volhas tardar.»

«Glot,» dis la dona, «cum o auses pessar?
Lo duc vos ama e vos te fortz en car   236
E vos sercas co·l puscas galiar!
Nuls hom de mon en vos no i pot fier,
Que lo duc Boves vos volhas desoudier!»
«Dona,» dis Guis, «trop lo podes amier.   240
Per cel senhor que·s fes en cros lievier,
An[s] de .ii. mes vos faray a muier
Que ieu l'ausiray, e jes no·m pot escapier!»
«Glot,» dis la dona, «Dieus te puesca azirier!   244
Per sol lo dih, te farai anta fier.»
Or s'en vai Guis que no·is vol plus tardier;
E lo franx duc si ve de deportier,
Vai so falco e la perga gitier;   248
E cant el venc fo aparegat de mangier,
Lava sas mas, vai se asetier.
La franca dona si pres fort a plorier;
Vi o lo duc e laisa·s del mangier,   252
Et ac tal ira que cujet enrabier.
«Dona,» dis el, «co·us vei desconortier!
Qui vos a fah ira ni desturbier?
Fais o per so car vos cove laisier   [81ʳ]   256
Voste païs, Fransa desamparer?
Dona gentiels, voles lai retornier?»
So dis la dona: «Anc no·m venc a penser,
Mas sabres o a la taula levier.»   260
Cant ac manjat ela lo va abracier:
«Ay! sire duc, aiso vos vuelh mostrer
Que lo fels Guis —cui Jhesus desampar—
Venc non a gaire, no saup alres trobar,   264
Mes m'a razo, que·m cujet anta far;
Mal li respozi, pres mi a menassar
C'ausira vos, no·lh podes escapar,
La nost'amor el fara desevrar.»   268
«Dona,» dis el, «no·us volhas corossar,
Anc non o dis mas per vos asagar
Se ja nuls homs vos poiria enganar.
Nuls homs non es qu'ieu pusca tant amar!»   272

Dieus! Del franc duc cum s'i pot tant fizar!
Que [Guis] neis l'ausis can fo ab lui cassar!

[IX]

Al ric duc Boves donec Dieus .i. efan,
Gran joia n'an li peti e li gran.   276
El l'en evia al palazi Roulan
Que l'en bateie ab gran alegramen.
Gen l'en batie car el es sos parens;
Bel nom li mes segon son essien,   280
Beto ac nom, que pueis [ac] gran afan.
Tramet l'a·l duc en .i. bresol d'argen
Et ab lui vengro .m. cavaliers valhen,
Fon recobratz ab gran alegramen.   [81ᵛ]   284
Gran guah n'a·l duc, a Dieu grant grat ne ren;
Be fo noiritz tan solamen .i. an;
Pueissas li venc .i. desturbamen
C'anec cassar en Ardena la gran.   288
Lo ric duc Boves sezia en .i. banc
Ab n'Esmenjartz la pros et la valhan;
Abtan vec vos .i. messagie corran.
«Cira,» fai sel, «escoltas mo semblan: 292
Ins en Ardena a .i. singlar tan gran
Pertot lo·s cas e dabant tot l'aglan,
Anc nulha bestia no vi de so semblan!»
So dis lo dux: «Irai la veramen,   296
Sera cassat e farem ne prezen
Aisi a la dona et a Beto l'efan.
Menarai Guis mon compaho valen.»
Can l'au la dona, si n'a mon maltalen   300
C'ab ambas mas en a romput son gan:
«Ai! sira dux, per que·us i fias tan?
Anc no·us amet ni ja no·us ama nian,
Ausira vos, ja non aures guiren.»   304
«Dona,» dis el, «dises voste talan.
Non aur[a]i mal ni nulh desturbamen
Tan cum el puesca, a tot lo mieu viven.»

«Dieus!» dis la dona, «aujas fulia gran 308
Mon essien n'aurai lo cor dolan.»
Lo riches dux apela .i. corran:
«Vai me per Gui al castel d'Aspremon
E vai tantost e mol joliamen.» 312

[X]

Lo tracher Gui es vengut de rando
Per la causea, pesan la tracio, [82^r]
C'ausira·l duc can sera e venaro.
Ab tant intret el [palais] de [Buvo], 316
Bo[v]es lo vi e a·l mes a razo:
«Bel companh senher, .i. singlar casarem
Qu'e[s] grans e fort, e nos conquerem lo.»
So·lh respons Guis: «Senher, mot mi sat bo! 320
Non es tan ffort que be no·l conquero;
Aportar l'em e dar l'em a Beto.»
La richa dona de la cramba on fo
A entenduda de celui la razo. 324
Estrens sos det e rom son peliso,
Apela·l duc e baia·l el mento:
«Bel dos amix, que Jhesu be vos do!
Non crezas mia aquel trachor Guiho; 328
Mal aia l'ora que vostre companh fo!
Mala crezes sel mescrezen felo.
Ausira vos, non aures gerizo.»
«Dona,» dis el, «Ben tenes fol sermo; 332
Mesclar nos n'em ieu e vos de tenso.»
«Senher,» dis ela, «mas a vos sap bo,
Anatz ab lui a Dieu benedisio!»

[XI]

Guis li a dih: «Sira dux, anem nos, 336
Fais encoblar los veltres e·ls bracos,
E non aiam gaires de compahos,
Mas sol aiam .iiii. venados bos,
E nos serem els destri[e]s coredors. 340

Ferrem lo porc, senher, et ieu e vos,
El tombara, non er tan vigoros!»
Enten la dona que mala es la razos,
Vai a la cambra, geta por sos botos,   344
Plora dels uelhs e rom sos pelissos.
Al duc amenero son destier corredor.

[XII]

E can lo duc volc el destrier montar,   [82ᵛ]
Vec vos vengut Daurel, lo bon joglar: 348
«Bel sira dux, be mi dei alegrar;
.I. pauc filh ai, vuelh vos merce clamar;
Que·us plassia, senhe, lo·m anes bategar.»
So dis lo dux: «Anas lo·m aportar.»   352
Vai lai Daurel, que o volc enansar
A la porta e vai lo·lh presentar.
E mes li nom Daurelet de Monclar,
Pueis es montat e vol anar cassar.   356
La gentiel dona si vai [lo] duc baisar
(So fo·l darier que anc li poc donar):
«Senher,» dis ela, «Dieus vos lais retornar!»
Lo pros dux vai los cas apelar,   360
En Brunas Vals trobero lo singlar,
Et anc pels [cas] no si denget levar.
Lo pros dux fai los cas alagar,
Als venados si fai los corns cornar,   364
E·l porc si leva e fa·ls esparpalhar,
.III. cans a mors ab la den maiselar
Et ieis del bosc; en altre vai intrar,
So es Ardena c'om non pot adesar.   368
Los venadors lor covenc a laisar
E dis a Guis: «Anem los encaussar.»
«Senhe,» dis el, «be·l podem trabucar.»
Lo pros duc, aitan cum pot brocar,   372
Ab son espieut li vai tal cop donar
Per las esquinas que·l fer ne fai passar,
Que los budels ne fai forras anar.

«Companh,» ditz el, «venes mi ajudar   376
Que aquest porc no·is porra mai levar!»
Guis venc tantost cum pot esperonar
E fer lo duc dejos per l'espaular,
Que son espieut li fai d'oltra passar,   380
Apres lo porc fai lo duc eversar!
Lo duc s'esforsa, e cuga·s sus levar,   [83ʳ]
El cors a·l fer, non pot en pes estar;
De ginolhos comensec a parlar: 384
«Dona Esmenjartz, ges no·us en puesc blasmar,
Se vos crezes ges no i pogra pecar.
Tan gen, ma dona, mi prezes a castigar
Qu'ieu mi laisses d'a[ques]st Guiho amar!   388
Ay! cara dona, ben o vei averrar!
Ay! fals companhs, be saps lausar,
Me as tu mortz e non pas lo senglar.
Ay! fals companhs, cum te pogis pessar   392
Tal tr[a]siho ni cum la pogis far!»

[XIII]

E·l franc duc que era fort nafrat
Dis al fals Guis: «.I. petit m'escoltatz,
Gardas l'espieut del cor no mi tragas   396
Tro qu'ieu vos diga, compays, cum o fassas.
D'aqueta mort sai que seret reptatz,
Mas dirai vos, amix, cum o ffassatz;
Las dens del porc mi metres el costatz,   400
E vostes spieut e vos el porc ficatz;
Trastos diron pel porc soi afolat,
Vos non seres dementitz ni torvat.
Mos companhs eras e plevis e juratz;   404
Mortz m'as, companh, qu'ieu o sai asatz,
Per ma molher que tan cobeutavatz.
Si m'ajut Dieus ni·m perdo mos pecatz,
Se m'acces dih que tan la volias   408
Dada la·us agra ab sas grans eretat.
Oltra la mar ieu m'en fora passatz.

Per Dieu vos prec que mal no lhi volhat,   [83ᵛ]
Al bon rey Karlo e vos [la] demandat;   412
Dar la vos a, car es pros ni orratz.
De Betonet vos prec que·l nosricatz
E vostra cort, coms, se·us platz, l'amenatz;
Neps es de Carles, no i seres dissonratz.   416
De tot cant a la meitat vu·lh aiatz.»
Guis lo regarda cum leos cadenatz
E·l duc lui cum angils enpenatz;
Dis lo fals Guis: «De folia parlatz!   420
Per sel senhor que fo en cros levatz,
Ja no vieura .xv. jorns acabatz!
Se el en mas mas pot eser bailatz,
No·l pot gerir ni vila ni sieutatz.   424
Ieu ai vos mortz; el non es acabatz!»
E lo franx dux s'es vas lui regardatz
E junh las mas: «Companh, si a vos platz,
Ab de la fuelha vos me cumergas.»   428
«Per Dieu!» dit Guis, «de folia parlas;
More vos tost, per o trop o tarzas.
Del cor del ventre vos farai .ii. meitatz!»
«Companh,» fai el, «de folia parlatz,   432
Del mal que·us fi vos seret be vengatz;
Prendes del cor, senhe, si ne manjatz!
Jhesu Crist senhe que en cros fos levatz
E denhes naiser per los nostes pecatz,   436
Santa Maria Dona, ieu vos prec, si a vos platz,
Mo filh Beto d'ente sas mas gardatz,
E quere vos que·m perdones mos peccatz!»
E·l fals Guis s'es de lui aprosmatz,   440
Trais ne l'espieut e lo duc es traspasatz,   [84ʳ]
Mor es lo duc, mai non es recobrat.
E·l traher Guis al porc l'espieut a figat,
Las dens del porc mes al duc el costat,   444
Pren lo costel, l'a menut percuzatz
Coma cel porc l'ages tot mangatz.
E lo fals Guis a pueis lo [co]rn cornat,
E·lh casador so vengutz esclasan   448
E viro[·l] dux mortz et aglaziatz

Et ac saunenta la cara e·l costatz.
No·m meravilh·se foro for irat!
Lo trachor an tantost arasonatz: 452
«Digas, coms Guis, qui a·l duc afolat?»
«Senhors,» dis el, «pauc i ai guazahat,
Que perdut ai, segon lo mieu pessat,
Mon bo senhor e mon companh juratz.   456
Cant ieu vengui lo porc l'ac darocatz,
Escoisendut et aisi afolat;
Ieu cant o vi ag[u]i lo cor irat,
Feri lo porc et ai l'aisi plagat   460
Que mon espieu li ai pel cors passatz.
Ai mortz lo porc e·l bon duc ai vengat.»
«Fels,» so dis l'us, «be mal as espleiatz.
Que·l duc as mort; as fah gran pecat   464
Que tuh nosaltre ne serem reptat.
Anc no fes porc la plaga del costat
Car be vezem que .i. palm a de lat!»
«Amix,» dis el, «dizes ta volontat;   468
Non o pesera per cant Dieus a mandat.
Vec tel senhal que·l porc i a laissat
E las .ii. dens li trobas el costat.»
E·lh venador no i an plus demorat,   [84ᵛ]   472
En .iiii. pergas an lor senhor pauzat,
E lo coms Guis, lo tracher renegatz
Ri ne el cor, mas de gauh a ploratz.

[XIV]

Lo trager Guis trastotz premiers s'en cor,   476
E venc premiers el destier salhidor.
La franca dona fo el palais ausor
Que a ausida lai fora la rimor,
E cor lai foras et ac tantost pahor;   480
Troba Guiho, garda lo per feror:
«Digas, coms Guis, cum es de mon senhor?»
«Dona,» dis Guis, «mort es el bosc maior.
Mortz l'a·l sanglar, al cor n'ai gran dolor.»   484
«Mentit n'aves, en glot lausengador,

Ans as tu mort to natural senhor!
Lassa, caitiva, d'un renegat trachor
Que mi a tolta trastota m'amor.»   488
Sospira fort e mena gran dolor,
Ca enblesmada de dol, e d'ira e de plor.

[XV]

Lo [cors] duc Boves van tantost aportat,
Trastuh lei coro, et auzirat cridar   492
E caras rompre, e cabelh descirier.
Tan cavalier lei viras enblesmier,
Tan borzes lor vestirs esquicier,
Tantas pros daimas lor caras sanglentier,   496
Anc mai nuls hom no vi tal dol menier.
Done Eimenjartz revenc de l'engoisier
E vi Guio decosta ce estier;
Garda vas lu tant, e pres a ssospirier.   500
La franca dona non o pot plus durier;   [85ʳ]
Ad .i. borges vai son coltel ostier,
Cuja·l ferir, mas non o poc anc fier
Que tengo la, no la volo laisier.   504
«Senhors,» ditz ela, «volhas mi escotier.
L'autrier mi venc, pres mi a menassier
Qu'el me tolria mon senhor e mon pier;
Ara·l vei mort, mos cors mi vol crebier!   508
Vieus es Betos que·l sabra be vengier!»
Cor vas lo duc, vai lo pali levier.

[XVI]

«Senhors,» dis ela, «gardas que vos en par;
Aquesta plaga no fo anc di singlar,   512
Ans fo d'espieut, pel Senhor que fai parlar.»
Cant o ac dih, ela·is vai engoisar,
De las carns primas fai las pessas levar,
Tuh la regardo e prendo·is a plorar.   516
Mai de .x.m. l'an auzirat cridar:

«Ai! senhe dux, anc no volgis menar
Vostra mainada que·us saubro ben gardar.»
Abtan vec vos Daurel lo ben joglar,   520
Laissa·s cazer del bon destrier liar,
Geta·iss a tera, que anc no·is pot levar
E can revenet, e el pres a parlar,
Nostre senher ne pres fort a reptar: 524
«Ai! senher Dieus, aiso cum pogis far
Aital franc dux d'aquest segle gitar?
Qu'el mi donet lo castel de Monclar.
Ieu n'era paubes; el mi fes ric tornar!»   528
Tan gran dol fai no vos o sai comtar.
Tres jorns lo tengo, pueis lo van sostrar   [85ᵛ]
A Sant Alari, josta·l corn de l'autar.
Dieus pres l'arma! or lo laissem estar,   532
Parlem de Guis cui Dieus puesca azirar!

[XVII]

E can vi fels Guis que·l duc es sostreratz,
Ad Aspremont s'en es tantost anatz;
Sos melhors homes a tantost apelat: 536
«Senhors,» ditz el, «mon tesaur m'aportatz.»
Il lhi respondo: «Senher, cum a vos platz.»
Aportat n'an .xv. somies cargat.
«Baro,» fai el, «ades tot lo·m trossatz,   540
De bonas armas vostes cors adobatz.»
.III. c. n'i ac fort ben encavalgat
Ab las espezas, ab los ausberx safratz.
Guis los capdela, lo tracher renegat,   544
Tro a Paris el no s'es restancat.
Sus el palais ab Karlo es montat;
Lo rey lo vi et es en pes levatz,
Pueis li demanda co sai es aribatz: 548
«Com esta·l dux, lo mieus companh p[r]ivat?»
Guis li respon, lo tracher renegat:
«Senher,» dis el, «malvazamen assatz.
Mort es lo dux, lo mieus companh jurat;   552

Us fers singlars—que mala fos el nat!—
L'escoisendec lo ventre e·ls costatz.»
Au o lo rey, tot n'es enrabiat;
Bat ne las mas, apela·is mal fadat.   556
Per mieh la cort s'en es gran dol levatz,
E·l dux Rolan s'en es tot esquintatz.
Guis dis al rey: «Senher, set dol laissatz.   [86ʳ]
Se per dol fos, per ver o sapiat   560
Tan n'avem fah que fora recobratz.
Trazes vos sai, .i. pauc am mi parlar.»
En .i. escaun se son asetiatz.
«Rey emperaire, .i. pauc me escoltat: 564
Vostre tezaur auh dire que es mermatz,
Que aves lo als logadiers donat.
Ieu lo·s vulh creisser, senher, se a vos platz;
Ve·us vo·nh lai foras .xv. saumies cargat   568
D'aur e d'argen qu'es fis esmeratz.»
So dis lo tracher: «Ieu tenh las eretatz
Qu'ero del duc que del segle es anat.
Reis, se vos plas, a mi las autreas.   572
L'aur e l'argen vos er tot aportat.
Das mi la dona, serai vostre conhat;
Amar vos ai mai c'om de maire natz.
Ieu so rix hom, be i seres onratz;   576
Serai el loc del duc qu'es traspasatz.»
So dis lo rey: «Bel prezen m'aportatz;
Ades irem can nos cerem dinat.»
Cant au l'aver que es tan desmesuratz,   580
Lo dol del dux es trastot oblidat,
L'au e l'argent es trastot estugatz,
E lo rey crida: «Cavaliers, esselatz.»
Sol .c. n'i ac que so ab lui anatz,   584
Tro a Peutieus no si so restancat.
.I. cavalier es el palais intratz:
«Dona,» dis el, «e vos cossi estat?
Ve·us vostre frayre, encontra lui anatz.»   588
Cant ela o ausi, sos cors n'es alegratz:
«Dieus! ditz la dona, «aras sai per veritat   [86ᵛ]
C'aras mora lo tracher renegatz

E lo pros dux cre que sera vengat!»
Don'Esmenjart dissen per los degras,
Venc al rey Karlo, los uelhs li a baiatz.
E·l tracher Guis es apres montat,
Vi lo la dona, .iiii. motz a cridat: 596
«Senher,» ditz ela, «bem petit mi amatz,
C'aquel trachor e vostra cort menatz
C'aucis lo duc can fo ab lui cassar,
Que son espieut li fiquet pels costat.»   600
«Senher,» ditz Guis, «mai no l'an crezatz;
Ela es dona e ditz sas volontatz;
S'om m'o dises, be·m fora adobatz
De l'escondieire cant mi fora armat.   604
Mos companhs era e plevit e juratz,
No m'o pessera per .lx. cieutatz.»
«Reis emperaire, so que ieu dic es vertatz,
Que el l'a mort, et er be esproat.   608
La fors el pla sia·l fuoc adobatz,
Ieu passar n'ai veia o tos barnatz;
Se ja .i. pels es sobre mi cremat
Qu'eu sia asa, ja merse no·m agatz!   612
Se·m salve Dieus ni la mia verdat
Aquel tracer sia a totz rossegatz!»
So ditz lo rey: «Cest contendre laissas.
Per tot aiso non er lo duc cobrat,   616
El loc del duc, Guis vos sia donat.
Au lo la dona, .iiii. motz a cridatz:
«Ai! Senher reis, leu vos es acossellatz,   [87ʳ]
Que pel ric duc .i. trachor mi donatz!   620
Ben grans aver cre que vo·nh sia donatz!
Aital ric rey si fo en bon ponh natz
Que per aver de sa sor fai mercatz!
Si Beto vieu, que es petitz assatz,   624
Aquest mieu plah sera mol car compratz.
Mortz es son paire e vos puois mi forsatz,
Per drecha forsa a maritz lo·m donatz,
Mas ja de Dieu gracias non aiatz!   628
Fraire,» ditz ela, «cavalier mi donatz
Que mieu efanh trachor no sia apelatz

E mos coratjes tenia·is mielhs per pagatz.»
So ditz lo rey: «De folia parlatz!   632
Mai val coms que no fa postatz;
Ieu vos do Guiho, pregui que·l prengas.»
Pueis li a dih: «Coms, dese l'espozatz.»
«Senher,» ditz Guis, «volontiers, si a vos platz!»   636
Le rey meteis es sus en pes levatz,
Pren la pel ponh, .iiii. ves la·lh fai baiar.
«Fraire,» dis ela, «per forsa lo·m donatz.
Dieus vos cofonda que en cros fo levatz!   640
Flodres vos parga ans que sias tornatz!»
E pren l'anel ab que l'a espozatz,
E lor vezen el fuoc l'a getatz!

[XVIII]

Tuh la regardo, li gran e li menor,   644
Non i a .i. no·is plore de dolor,
Car a tos peza, fors [a] l'emperador;
No l'auzo dir, car de luy an pahor.
Guis pren la dona a joi et a baudor   648
Et ela lui ab ira et ab plor.
Las nossas fan sus el palais ausor.
Vec vos vengutz Dauretz lo joglar bo: [87ᵛ]
«Dona,» ditz el, «donas mi mon senhor,   652
L'enfan Beto; que paor ai del trachor
Que l'ausiza cum fes lo mieu senhor.
Ieu ai Monclar, metrai lo en la tor,
Noirirai lo ab joi et a baudor   656
Entro que sia de mot granda vigor.
Can lei sera ja non aura paor
Que ja·l mi tuelha coms ni enperador.»
La franca dona ac de l'enfan pahor,   660
Dis a Daurel, suavet, ab temor:
«Enviat l'ai ad huna ma seror
Que·l me noirira tro sia de valor.»

[XIX]

La franca dona es del mangar levada,   664
Ab tres comdessas en sa cambra es intrada.
Tant a batuda sa cara e gautejada,
Estors sos detz e apela·s mal fadada
Que per la boca ieis la sanc macada: 668
«Lassa, caitiva! en ta mal ponh fui nada!
Marit avia de que era pagada,
Cel lo·m ausis a cui ara son dada.
Santa Maria, regina coronada,   672
Das mi colssel, que non aia durada.»
E respon li .i. dona privada:
«Ieu vos darai colsel se be soi escoltada.
Vostre pauc filh fais noirir a selada,   676
C'om non o sabra en aquesta encondrada.
Can sera grans, venra ab ca[va]lgada,
En pauca d'ora aura tera cobrada;
Vengar vos a d'aisel que·us a forsada,   680
Prendra·l trachor en pueh o en estrada!»   [88ʳ]
Ditz n'Esmengartz: «Be·m aves acosselhada;
D'aquest cosseh mi tenh fort ben per pagada.»
Ieis de la cambra dolenta e irada,   684
Lo rey l'abrasa e puis l'a comiada.

[XX]

Lo rey s'en vai e·l tracher Guis ab els,
Qu'el le ssolassa tro es vengutz lo ses.
La franca dona trames per .i. borgues   688
Que amix era del ric dux marques,
Et el venc tost, que anc pon falha no i fes.
«Senher,» ditz ela, «cauzimen e merses.
Socores mi, que grans mestiers mi es.   692
Fort vos amava lo pros duc que mort es;
De son pauc filh cauzimen vos prenges.
Ve·l vos aisi en .i. pali gres,

Ben o sabes que voste senhor es;   696
Socores li e non o triges ges.
Se sa·l atroba lo tracher malapres
Ausira lo, non escapara ges!»
El li respon: «Dona, si vos voles,   700
Noyri farai ins e mar e·l gras,
Non intrara tempesta ni fret ges,
Vens ni gelada ni nulha mala res.
Dar l'am noirisa tal que bona res es,   704
Una ma filha que sos maritz mor es,
E lo cieu efas, que no·l alaita ges,
Cela·l tenra, que d'efan non a ges.
Mos magers filh que es pros e cortes   708
Lor portara lor ops e lor conres,   [88ᵛ]
No·lh falhira neguna mala res.»
La franca dona li·n ret grandas merses:
«Prendes lo donc e gardas que·n fares.»   712
E si lo pren aquel ric borges
Dedins la cambra cum se panatz l'ages.
Ben tost l'enporta en irla demanes;
N'Aisilineta, que mol jauzenta n'es   716
Noiri l'enfan tan solamen .ii. mes.

[XXI]

Al filh del duc an facha tal maio,
Dedins non a ni lata ni cabiro,
Ans es en mar on las grans ondas son,   720
En .i. roca on sol estar lo loc
Am bel mur fah, de porta, de viro;
No i intra aiga ni tempestacio.
N'Aisilineta, cui Jhesu Crist ben do,   724
Molt gen lo bauza cant es ben de sazo,
Pueis lo envolopa en .i. bel cisclato,
Peuisas li vet ermi pelisso,
Et en aprot ela·lh ditz .i. bel so,   728
Bauzan los uelhs e tota la faisso
E prega Dieu que longa vida·l do.

Aisel enfan noiri hom a lairo,
Mas lo borges e cel da sa maio   732
Pro lei aporta vi e pa a bando,
E draps de Fransa colque l'enfanto.
Laisem l'estar a Dieu benedisio,
Parlem del trage de Guio.   736
«Dona Esmenjartz, ben aves lo cor felo
Car vos per mi m'aves fugit Beto.   [89ʳ]
Tan l'am cum vos, se Jhesu Crist be·m do!
Fais lo aportar e gen noirirem lo,   740
Tota sa tera pueissas li rendro.
Gran be mi fes lo duc, rendrai li·n guazardo.»
Estai la dona que no i dis oc ni no,
El cor sab ben c'aisi a trasio.   744

[XXII]

Pueis li respon: «Mas tan lo·m demandatz,
Ben es raizos que vos o sapiatz;
Non a encaras .vii. dias acabatz
Qu'ieu Beto me trobe mort delatz;   748
A Sen Alari es l'efan sosteratz,
E ce·l voles vos laïns lo demandatz.»
«Dona,» dis el, «largamen traspasatz
Que de mentir vergoha non agatz!»   752
«Fels coms,» ditz ela, «per que contrastatz?
Major mensonga vos a mi finavatz,
Qu'ieu sai lo be e que ne vorriatz,
Que aucizes lo duc que dezias c'amat.   756
Ja non aures de mi, so vulh que sapi[a]tz,
Bona molher aitan can ja·us vivas,
Car ja tracher non deu eser amatz.»
Iratz fo Guis et es en pes levatz,   760
.I. espero de fin aur ten caussatz,
Pren la pels cavelhs, tans colps li a donatz
Que·l vermelh sanc ishi pels costatz.
«Fels,» dis la dona, «prec vos m'on ausigatz   764
Vieus es Beto, per ver o sapiatz,

Laïns en fransa es l'enfan noirigatz;   [89ᵛ]
Cant el venra voste jorn er propchat,
Pessa e pessa ne seret desmenbratz.»   768
Ieis de la cambra lo tracher renegatz,
Dos cornadors n'a a se apelatz:
«Vai baro,» ditz el, «per la tera cornatz
Que si Betos es en loc atrobatz   772
Que a mi sia ades aportatz.
Qui que·l m'aporte no s'es pas destrigatz,
.M. martz d'argen li·n pagaram e patz.»
Et elh o cornon per borc e per cieutatz   776
Cum si Beto fos .i. laires proatz.
So fo .i. jorn que·n devenc per pecatz
Que .i. pescaire fo ins en mar intrat;
Ebratz ac nom lo tracher renegatz,   780
E venc tot dret on Betos es entrat,
Fer a la porta et es intrat viat.
E n'Aissilina tenia l'efan el bras,
L'efan risia, qu'era gen alegrat.   784
«Dieus vos salv, dona, que vos tan gent obratz
E [com] molher aitan gen noirigat.»
Ela·l saluda et a·lh los uelh baisatz:
«Senher amix, vas Dieu vos regaratz;   788
Cestz pauc efan per amor Dieu selatz.
De lui vos prenga merse e piatatz
Qu'e[s] vostre senhor, valha li fizaltatz;
Car orphes es, es piatatz asatz;   792
Agardas lo cossi es faisonatz,
Grans pecatz er si el es afolatz;   [90ʳ]
Cum a fresca la boca e la fatz,
Filh foc del duc, so sabem qu'es vertatz.   796
Ay! al trachor, senher, l'ensegavatz,
El l'aucira, car vas lui es iratz.
C'el vieu a longas vos seres ric asatz
Qu'ieu li diray cum fo per vos trobatz.   800
Per vos es mortz o per vos aribatz.»
«Dona,» ditz el, «de folia parlatz,
Mo senher es, no·il faria falcetatz;
Estais ben, domna, gentamen lo gardatz,   804

Pro beves, domna, e be vos alegratz
Qu'ie·us portaray tot so que vos vulhatz.»
E n'Ayselineta porta l'efan el bras:
«Ebram,» ditz ela, «aquest efan tocatz;   808
May ne valres aytant can vivatz.»
E leva·l pali, l'efas ris li assatz,
E ditz la dona: «Ebram, ar esgardas;
Anc may no·us vi, tan gen s'es alegratz!»   812
Respon lo tracher: «per mi er molt amatz.»
Entre sas dens dis lo vilas malvatz:
«.M. martz d'a[r]gen ay uei en mar trobatz.»
Daz els se partz, es en corren anatz.   816

[XXIII]

Lo fers pescayre —cui Jhesus desanpier!—
Entro a Guio, no se vols estancar,
E cant el venc Guis volia manjar,
Garda avant e vi Ebrartz intr*ar*:   820
«Senher,» ditz Ebrartz, «ab vos volria p*arlar*:
D'aquest Beto cant me volras donar?»   [90ᵛ]
Guis ac tal gauh c'a penas pot parlar:
«.M. martz d'argen, tan cum ay fah cridar.»   824
«Senher,» dis el, «fais los me afizar.»
«Amix,» dis el, «so m'es fort bon a far.»
«Daurel,» ditz Gui, «puec me en vos fizar?»
«Ostat! bo senher, cum o pogues pessar?   828
Non a home el mon qu'ieu tan puesca amar.»
«Ad aquest home me volhatz afizar
.M. martz d'argen abans de l'avesprar
Si el me pot Betonet enssehar.»   832
So dis Daurel: «Ieu li faray pagar.»
Ebrart li ditz: «De far en re m'agar;
Vos me siatz a la riba de mar,
Qu'ieu l'i trobe cant anava pescar,   836
Qu'el es rescondutz, be·l sabray ensehar.»
E·l pros Daurel vay son caval selar;
Tro a la mar no si volc restancar,

Venc a la riba, non pot d'oltra passar: 840
«Jhesu Crist senher, tu que·m volguistz crear,
Das mi coselh cum lay puesca intrar
E mo senhor puesca de mortz garar.»
Lo joves hom que lor porta a mangar   844
Ven·s ab sa nau e pres a aribar.
Daurels lo vi e pres [a] apelar:
«Amix,» ditz el, «vinet am mi parlar;
Se·m pasat d'oltra, ben poiret cavalgar   848
Que ie·u[s] donaria aquest caval liar
Que·l filh del duc vol ducs Guis afolar.»
Lo joves hom si pres fort a plorar: [91ʳ]
«Senher,» dit el, «pessem de l'espleitar.»   852
Abtan Daurel ven·s a la nau intrar.

[XXIV]

Ab mol gran cocha s'en so d'oltra passatz
E n'Aicelina Daurel n'a rayzonatz:
«Senher,» ditz ela, «cum vos vei esclesat!   856
Frayre amix, que l'avetz amenatz?»
«Bela sor dona, ades vos er comtatz.»
So ditz Daurel: «Ieu ne diray vertatz;
Lo fil del duc sai a Guis espiatz,   860
Vendutz lo·ilh a lo pescaire Ebrar[tz];
.M. martz d'argen lh·en ai ieu afizatz
Tot per Guio, a la sua volontat.
D'aqui enant ay tan Dieu reclamat   864
Que·l mi mostres per la santa bontat,
Gran gauh ai, dona, quar l'ay trobatz,
Bailatz lo mi, que trop sai [ai] estat.»
«Senher,» dit ela, «e fol m'avet parlatz,   868
Ab lui morai, c'aissi m'es destinatz.»
Tuh trei si prendo quant an l'efan gardat
E vec enant: Daurel a·l rapat,
Fuh s'en ab el cum se l'agues panatz,   872
Mol corren d'oltra son ambidoi passatz;
Remas la dona, que i fero gran pecatz.

Ela fo lassa: quant ac .i. brieu ploratz
Adurmis se, que la nueh ac vilhatz.   876
E Daurel pueja; a tant esperonatz
E va son caval ne sancno lhi costat.
E l'efas plora et el l'a acabat:
«Ay! mon pau senher, ta lueinh vos ay cercat!   [91ᵛ] 880
Dieus cre que·us aga a bon port aribat.»
Tro a Monclar non a regna tirat.
Sa molher genta si li a demandatz:
«Ay! Daurel senher, cum vos vei ta lassatz!»   884
«Dona,» ditz el, «que bona fui a[n]c nat,
Lo fil del duc vos ay ieu aportatz,
Qu'en una riba l'ay ins e mar trobatz.»
Ve·l vos ayssi; e·ls bras lo·ilh a pauzatz,   888
Quant ela·l tenc a .i. sospir getat,
Garda vas cel, an mol fort Dieu lauzatz.
So ditz la dona: «Ben es endestinatz;
Mortz es mo senher, aquest avem cobratz,   892
Cest er noirit a forsa o a gratz.»
Met l'e la cambra et a lo asadatz.
Lih fil Daurel s'en son tant alegratz
May que s'aguesso tot l'aur del mon trobatz;   896
Tuh n'an gran gauh et teno·s per pagatz.
De la noirissa foro mal oblidatz
Que·n fon destreta a tort e a pecat.

[XXV]

[L]o tracher Gui leva tost del mangar: 900
«Ebrart,» ditz Gui, «et es ora d'anar.»
«Senher,» dis el, «no i a re que tarzar.»
«A celas!» crido, et van si adobar.
.III.c. n'i ac pel filh del duc cassar,   904
Pro n'i ac d'els que y fa forsa anar.
Tro a la mar no [se] van demorar,   [92ʳ]
Trovo la nau e van d'oltra passar.
Vengro dreh lay on l'efas sol estar,   908

E·l tracher Gui va la dona abrasar:
«Amiga dona, que vos a fayta plorar?
Dat me Beto, no lo·m volhatz selar.»
«Senher,» ditz ela, «laysat me rayzonar: 912
Per cel del cel no·l vos puec ges baylar,
Que mardiers say vengro aribar
Et an lo·m tolt e van s'en ab el per mar;
Per so·m vezet aissi desconortar.»   916
So ditz lo fels: «D'alre·us er a parlar!»
De grans espinas si fay pro aportar,
A[d]eis Ebrart las fay fort aguzar,
Per las tetinas l'en comensa a ficar   920
Que .c. aüdas lh'en fes laïns intrar,
Que [fes] sanc e lah mesclar [e] ragar.
La franca res comensec a cridar:
«Ay! senher Gui, no·m volhat afolar!   924
Daurel l'en porta no·us say plus esenhar.»
So dis lo tracher: «Aisso vertat mi par,
Qu'encuei no·l vi a la taula manjar.
Baro,» dit [Gui] «anem nos albergar,   928
Vespres [es] bas, non avem que mangar,
Al bo mat[i] nos n'irem a Monclar.
Mas sia l'efas on lo poirai trobar,
Nuls hom del mon no lo·m [pot] escapar.   932
Ad Aspremon estarem al colgar.»
E n'Aicelina —cui Jhesu ampar!—   [92ᵛ]
Tant fo batuda que·il n'ac obs a portar.
Sos frayre venc prop del vespres sonar,   936
Aporta·l an, que tant la pot amar.
E lo borgues vi sa filha intrar
Ta mal menada que s'en pres a plorar:
«Jhesu Crist senher, de Betos vueil pregar   940
Que vos, senher, lo volhat de mort garar!»

[XXVI]

Lo tracher Guis s'es be matis levatz,
.C. cavaliers dels meliors a triat.

«Baro,» fay cel, «ades vos adobat.»   944
Elh lhi respondon: «Senher, cum a vos platz.»
El pla amenero los destiers sojornatz,
Et cilh i monto per les estrieups dauratz.
El premier cap foc Guis lo renegatz,   948
A Monclar vengo quant meydia fo pasatz,
Als pes del mur de Daurel aribatz,
El [es] veltitz e de voltas talhatz,
A y .iii. tors ab denteilh cayrat,   952
Ja per nulh home non er pres ni forsat.
La porta es clauza; Guis lo[s] a apelat
Et cilh l'entendo e foro esariat.
Dizo sielh filh: «Payre, vas lui anat,   956
Per nulh home aquest enfan no·ilh rendat;
Aur e argen aven nos pro assat.»
«Ay! mieu bo filh, tan gentamen parlat.
Ieu isiriey; vos las portas sarrat.   960
Per nulh destret que vos far mi vegat,
Mon car senhor vos no li prometat.
C'el m'auci, diray vos que fassat:
Tenetz vos be tro·l jorn sia passatz,   [93ʳ]   964
Quant sera nuich de las cordas aiatz,
Per mieh la roca ins e mar vos n'intratz,
Ab la naveta mo senhor ne portatz
E lais on Dieus volra, bels fils, vos aribatz.»   968
Daurel ieis forras e lh'an l'us estanquatz,
E Guis li ditz: «Mos amix vuelh siatz;
Dat mi Beto que·s laïns albergatz
E dar vos ay .i. de mas sieutatz.   972
Far l'ay noyrir; per mi er mot amatz.»
«Sen[her],» ditz el, «per ver o sapiatz:
No·l vos rendray per aver que aiatz,
Se pessa e pessa tot mi pessejatz.   976
Mo senher es, e noirir l'ai em patz.»
E lo fels Gui .iiii. motz a cridatz:
«Miei cavalier, lo castel m'abrazatz.»
Li cav[a]lier volo far so mandatz,   980
Prendon del fuoc, mas Daurel ditz: «Estatz!
Intraray lai, aportar l'ay viatz.»

E Guis respon: «Be·us es acoselhatz.»
Lo pros Daurel es el palais intratz 984
E lo fels Gui remas forras irat.
Daurel si es el banc asetiatz,
Plora del uuelh, a sos cabelh tirat,
Tant s'a batut lo pieh e lo costat 988
Que per la boca lh'en es lo sanc ragatz.
Aiso ditz el: «Cautieu, mal aÿratz,
Ta mala fuei en cest loc aribatz! [93ᵛ]
Se·lh do l'efan tost seray pessegatz, 992
E s'ieu·l retenh, el er saïns crematz.»
Ploro li filh c'on son esblasmatz
La molher plora, venguda lh'es de latz:
«Amix,» ditz ela, «fort vos desconortat.» 996
«O ieu, ma dona, que mala fui anc natz;
Ben conoc aras que soy descoselhatz.
Amica dona, quinh cosselh mi donatz?»
Ditz Biatris: «Filh e vos autres [aujatz] 1000
So qu'ie·us diriei e vos altres fasatz.»
Tuh li respondo: «Dona, que·ns so celatz?
Que anc digas ve·us nos aparelhatz;
Nos o farem si cum vos comandatz.» 1004
«Vec vos aissi aquest efan que jatz?
Vostre [senher] e mos filh propiatz
En una nueh ambidoi foro natz.
Batejet lo lo duc qu'es traspasatz 1008
En aicel pali; e vos l'evolopatz
E Betonetz el bresolet colgatz,
E nostre filh al traïdor portat
E de luy fasa totas sas volontatz. 1012
Morra mos filh, mo senher er salvatz!»
Tuh tres respondo: «Dieus ne sia lauzatz!
D'aquest coseilh be·ns tenem per pagatz.»
Daurel ieis foras, so filh porta el bras; 1016
L'efas fom bels, car fon be aleutat.
Daurel dit a Guis: «L'efan m'aseguratz,
Que negun mal vos n'oqu'a lhi·n fassat.» [94ʳ]
So ditz lo tracher: «Ben per ver sapiatz 1020
No·ilh farai mal, ans sera be gardatz.»

Daurel lo·ilh baila et el lo pren viatz,
Descuebri li la cara e la fatz:
«Beto,» ditz Gui, «bem m'erat escapat,   1024
Em breu de temps seres be noirigatz.»

[XXVII]

«Daurel,» ditz Gui, «jamai no·us puec amar;
Mon enemic me voliat celar.»
«Senher,» dis el, «dretura m'o fes far,   1028
Que so senhor deu hom tostemps amar.»
So dit lo tracher: «Gardat qu'eu volrai far.»
Pren lo pels pes, dona ne a .i. pilar;
Amdos los ueilh li fes del cap volar   1032
E las servelas trastotas escampar.
«Beto,» dit Gui, «ben puec estar,
De vosta partz no·m cal jamai gardar.»
Tuh cil que i sso non o podo durar,   1036
Quobro lur caras e pendo·is a plorar;
E Guis s'en vai, es partitz de Monclar.
Dis l'us a l'altre: «Veiatz que vos en par;
Jhesu Crist senher, cum o podes durar?»   1040
E Daurel vai son efan ajustar,
En .i. bel pali l'a fait evolopar;
Se fo iratz no vos o sai comtar.
Tro a Peutieus no si vol estancar.   1044
Don' Esmengart au de son filh parlar,
Que Guis l'a mor, e pren gran dol a far.
Vec vos Daurel que venc al comensar,
Porta l'efan e va·l al pla pauzar,   1048
Tuh lo regardo e prendo·is a plorar.
Dona Emengart volia enblamar,   [94ᵛ]
Lo pros Daurel si la fai cofortar,
Trais la vas part e pres li merce clamar: 1052
«Domna,» dis el, «no·us cal desconortar
Qu'ieu l'en geri[r]ei, per los ueilh que vos gart,
Que mos filh era; ieu l'ai fah cambiar.
Mort es lo mieus, e fas lo vostre alachar.   1056

Prendet vos garda del castel de Monclar
C'ap vostre fil m'en irai oltra la mar;
Mon essien no·m veires retornar
Tro que·l pusca sos garnimens portar.» 1060
La franca dona lo vai .iii. ves baizar:
«Compaire senher, Dieus vos capdel e·us gar!
So aves fait que a[n]c hom mai non poc far,
C'om des so filh per so senhor salvar.» 1064
Lo dona vai so filoilh esgardar,
Conoc lo be, fai lo dol espasar.
Non vi tant gran dol per .i. filh de [j]oglar:
Apres lo duc va l'efan sostrerar, 1068
Per luy es mort, ben deu ondrat estar.
E·l pros Daurel torna s'en a Monclar,
Tostz e vias vai las naus adobar.
Pro i a mes a beure et [a] mangar. 1072
Met i sas armas per covinen estar,
Arpa i met e vihola per deportar,
.I. noirisa per l'efan noirigar,
Son palafre e son caval liar, 1076
Son escudier no i vol ges oblidar.
Sieu dos filhs se prendo a plorar,
D[r]esso lur velas e prendo·is ad anar,
E sa molher vai e la tor montar, [95ʳ] 1080
Aitant l'esgarda cum lo pot esgardar,
Pueisas si pres molt fort ad esmagar:
«Lassa! caitiva, que poirai aras far!
Mort es mos filh, no·l veirai recobrar, 1084
Mon pauc senhor aras ne vei anar
E mo marit que·m degra capdelar.»
Laissa·is cazer, que anc non poc levar
Tro que siei filhs la ve[n]ro ajudar, 1088
E mori se —que Domidieus ampar!—
Laisem Daurel et Betonet estar
E si parlem del senescalc n'Azemar.

[XXVIII]

Dona Emesgart apela so sirven; 1092
N'Azemar es, que es vengut corren,
E venc ploran, sos uuelh muellha soen.
«Domna,» ditz el, «molt ai mon cor dolen 1096
De Betonet que es mortz veramen.
Mort lo vosz a lo tracher mescreze*n.*»
«Amix,» dit ela, «non aias espaven
Qu'an es be vieus, se Dieus plas, veramen. 1100
Daurel l'en porta per mar alegramen;
De son pauc fil n'a fah cambiamen.
Monclar vos mete e vostre cauzimen,
Lai so li filh que estan maridamen. 1104
Vec vos aisi pro aur e pro argen
Et estables la tor e·l mandamen.
Pro lai metet sivada, seguel e formen [95ᵛ]
E carns e vis e neulas e pimen; 1108
Tro a .xv. ans lai metes fornimen
Quar ans de .xii. ans lai seres mai de cen.
Pro aias armas e altres garnimens,
Dia e nueh, amix, estais laïns 1112
E quie·us combat, tornatz vos belamen;
No seres [pres] per nulh home vi[v]en.
Ans de .xii. ans, per lo mieu esien,
Vendra Betos e Daurel issamen 1116
Ab cavalgadas e ab combatemen
Et ausira lo tracher mescrezen
E vos fara ric hom e manen.»
«Domna,» ditz el, «vostre comandamen 1120
Farai tostemps senes tot falhimen,
De vos servir ai be cor e talen;
Aicel castel capterai ben e gen
Mot ai mon cor alegre e jauzen 1124
De Betonet, car ieu lo sai viven.»

[XXIX]

En'Azemar, qu'es pros e leugier[s],
De clar formen empli tos los graniers,
E met n'i pro, a muh, a sestiers,   1128
Fen e civada als coredos destriers.
De bos bacos lai mes .iiii. meliers,
Pro de bo vi tant can lur n'a mestiers.
.XXX. arguiers lai mes e .xx. arbalestiers   1132
E de triat, .xl. cavaliers;
Gent[am]ent los homes e totas lurs molhers
Laïns noiriro austors, eparbiers,
E cas de cassa e corredors destriers;   [96ʳ] 1136
Jogon a taulas, ad escax, a diniers,
Dins lo castel meno grans alegriers.
Uei mai aguerra lo tracher lauzengiers.

[XXX]

[Q]uant lo fel Gui enten[det] la razo   1140
Que·l pros Daurel s'en anava ab Beto,
Vic de Monclar c'assi establitz fo,
Tira sa barba e rom som pelisso;
Donc sab el be qu'encaras n'aura tenso.   1144
Vai a la dona e met la a razo,
En .i. tor el l'a mes en preio;
.I. an la i tenc, c'anc res no lhi tenc pro.
Mandec sa gen: be .m. cavaliers so,   1148
Tro a Monclar non pres arestazo.
Gardec las tors e va lor d'enviro
Cilh de la vila no·l prezo .i. boto.
Lhi filh Daurel so molt e cortes e pro,   1152
Defendo se a guiza de baro,
Tuh esems crido e fant en aut .i. so:
«Mot prezam pauc lo fel tracher Guio
C'aucis lo duc e cujet far Beto.»   1156
En'Azemars comensec sa razo:
«Fel tracher Gui, ja non auras perdo,

Quar no t'en fuges en altra regio?
Vieus es mo senher; non auras garizo, 1160
Quar tu as mor to senhor a lairo.»
«Per Dieu!» ditz Gui, «mal m'en gabas, gloto.
Per cel senhor que fes lo cel e·l tro,
Totz vos prendrai sus en .i. cabiro!» [96ᵛ] 1164
Respon Bertrans que filh de Daurel fo:
«Mentitz n'aves en aquesta sazo,
Bens gardarem de vostra trasio.»
«Antona!» crido per gran alegrazo, 1168
E cant ve Guis res no li pot tener pro
Es s'en tornat ab corage felo.
Laissem Monclar e·l traïdor Guio,
Parlem de Daurel e de l'enfan Beto. 1172

[XXXI]

Vai s'en Daurel ab joi et ab [bau]dor
Per alta mar, per forsa e per vigor,
Mas ges no sap de sa gentil molher
Que·s laiset caszer de sus de l'[a]uta tor 1176
Si que mori sus el palais ausor.
Cant o sabra mot n'aura gran dolor.
Cant l'efas plora a lui non [a] sabor
E pren sa viola e fai .i. lais d'amor: 1180
«Ai!» so ditz el, «mon pauc gentil senhor,
Cum vos lonhat de vosta gran honor!
Fugem nos en ab mot gran dessonor.
Per vos ai dat lo miei filhet menor, 1184
Ieu vos e trah de mas de tra[ï]dor,
Filh es de duc e neps d'emperador
E fugem no·lh co siam raubador!
Vos no aves ni fraire ni seror 1188
Que ja vos venge de questa dissonor.»
Cant o hac dit no pot estar no plor,
Baga l'efan per gauc e per amor;
«Jhesu Crist senher, per la vostra dolsor, 1192
Vos nos menat a bon port salvador
E gardat nos de mal e [de] dolor!»

[XXXII]

[E]n Babilonia es Daurel aribat,   [97^r]
Ad .i. ric port, Dieus ne sia lauzat!   1196
Venc el palais on era l'amirat
E l'escudier porta l'efan el bras.
E l'amirat es de mangar levatz
E so .d. de cavaliers prezat,   1200
E Daurel venc, e a los gen saludatz:
«Dieus sal lo rey qu'es duc et amiratz,
E la regina e·ls cavaliers delatz.»
Cilh li resp[o]ndo: «Joglar, enan anatz;   1204
Bona sia l'ora que saïns es intrat!»
El va enant, a lor dels jocz mostratz,
Dels us e dels altres, qu'el ne sap pro asatz.
Pueis pres l'arpa, a .ii. laisses notatz   1208
Et ab la viola a los gen deportat;
Sauta e tomba, tuh s'en son alegratz
E·l rei mezis s'en tenc fort per pagatz.
So dis Daurel: «Senher, or m'escoltat: 1212
De lai de Fransa sai, soi a vos passatz,
Qu'e la cort Karlo es pels baros lauzat;
Tu iest lo melher rey que anc fos atrobatz.
E reis e comtes, tos los n'ai oblidatz   1216
Per vostr'amor ieu sai so aribat,
Ab vos serai aitan can ja vivatz.»
Lo rey sezia e es em pes levatz:
«Amicx,» dit el, «vostre nom me digat.»   1220
«Daurel ai nom, senher, se a vos platz.»
«Daurel,» dit el, «ab me vueilh remangatz
E dar vos ai una de mas cieutat;
Aur et argen aures vos pro assat.»   1224
«Senher,» dit el, «gran aver mi donat;
Ieu no vuelh tan, e teih m'en per pagat   [97^v]
Ab cest efan que noirir mi fasat;
El es mos filh, per mi er trop amat,   1228
Morta es ma [mo]lher e so ne fort iratz.»
Mentir si cuja, mas so es veritat.

So ditz lo rei: «A mi lo prezentat.»
Daurel lo·l baila et el lo pren viatz;　　　　　　　　1232
Ausa·lh lo pali, l'efas a·ls silhs levatz,
Geta .i. ris, e·l rei es ne pagatz:
«Efas,» ditz el, «ben iest bonaürat;
Anc mai no·m vis, cum s'e[s] alegrat!　　　　　　　1236
A gran honor vuelh que sias gardatz;
Domna regina, en garda l'agatz,
Fais lo noirir per l'amor que·m portat.»
«Senher,» dit ela, «e ma brassa·l pauzat;　　　　　1240
Per cel Senhor que totz naz a formatz,
Tam be sera noirit et alautat
Cum s'ie·l agues e mon ventre portat.»
Pren lo la dona e rescon lo [a] magat.　　　　　　　1244
Tan fo noirit tro ac .iii. ans passat,
Estec en crambas e si fo ben gardat,
Pueis ieis deforas e fo be remirat;
Tuh lo regardo car grans fo sa beutat:　　　　　　　1248
Los pels ac blons e gent afaisonat
E los ueilh vars cum a falcos mudatz,
Lo gola fresca cum roza en estat,
Blanc coma neus et ac genta la fatz.　　　　　　　　1252
So dit lo rei: «Cavaliers, escoltatz:
Anc aquest efas non fo de Daurel nat,
Ges no·l ressembla.» Daurel s'es d'el propiat:　　[98ʳ]
«Senher bos rei, pauc cre que mi amat　　　　　　　1256
Quar mon efan aisi·m desleialat.»
So dis lo rei: «Daurel, no·us irascat,
Non dic per mal, se m'ajutz caritat.»
[Q]uant ac .iiii. ans Beto fo fort prezatz,　　　　　1260
Vai s'en al rei et esetiet delatz
E pren sos gans et a los li rapatz.
Foron de drap entorn ab aur listrat,
Tol los al rei e jes no s'es trigat.　　　　　　　　　1264
A la regina si loz a prezentatz;
Ela los pren, a·lhi los uuelhs baizatz.
Lo rei s'en ri e dit: «Sai m'escoltatz:
Volgra·m costes .xiii. de mas cieutatz　　　　　　　1268
Qu'eu agues fil que fos de molher natz

C'aquest sembles, qu'el fora amiratz.
Miel li covengra que fos fil d'amirat
Que [de] joglar de paucas eretat!» 1272
[Q]uant ac Beto be .v. ans acabatz
Fon ben cregut e pros et essenhat;
Pueja cavals et a los abrivatz,
Fon bels parliers e gen enrazonatz, 1276
Joga a taulas, ad escax et a dat[z]
Et en la cort fo fort per tot amatz.
Laissem Daurel e Betonet em patz
E tornem sai a cels qu'avem laissatz. 1280

[XXXIII]

[L]o tracher Guis es anat ribairar
E son be .c. per lo comte garar.
Porto lur armas, no las volon laissar, [98ᵛ]
E .x. falcos per las gruas cassar. 1284
Una espia n'es venguda a Monclar
Que lor comta, et cilh van se adobar.
Vesto aulbercz, que son elme clar;
Guio bos brans per los grans colps donar. 1288
El prumier cap los guiza n'Azemar
E Bertran que fo fil del joglar.
Isson deforas rengat per batalhar;
.X. ne remado per lo castel garar. 1292
Ditz n'Azemars: «Senhor, vueilh vos pregar
En Brunas vals los anem sarcar,
Aqui los trobarem per los falcos gitar.»
Guis garda avant e vi los cavalgar, 1296
Laissa·ls falcos e cor si tost armar;
Crida als sieus: «Baro, al remenbrar
Que·us vos lai fairit los de Monclar.»
Ab las parulas hil se van adobar. 1300
Vec vos Bertran en .i. caval liar
E venc tantost cum pot esperonar.
En auta vos comenset a cridar:
«Fels tracher Gui, no·m podet escapar; 1304

La mort de mo fraire ara·us vuelh demandar,
De l'efantet que feris al pilar.»
Au o lo coms: sul caval va pujar
E venc vas lui lai on lo vic estar,   1308
Grans cops si fero pels escutz pessejar.
Bertran l'enpeih que·l cujet degolar
E·l coms Guis lui, que l'a fah darocar.
«Osta!» fai cel, «malvas filh de joglar,   1312
Ja mai ab com no·t vuelhas engagar!»
Sieu compaho li coron ajudar;   [99ʳ]
Grans critz guitero a las lansas baisar,
Aqui virat .i. gran tornei mesclar,   1316
Franger las astas e los escut brizar,
E las perpongas romper e·ls aubertz desmalhar.
Vec vos vengut lo cortes n'Azemar;
Baiset sa senha, laissa·l caval anar   1320
E fer Guio, mas no·l pot daroquar.
«Antona!» crida, «tot veires revelar
L'efant Beto que cujes mort laysar!»
Au o lo coms; cujet enrabiar   1324
E trais s'espeia, laissa·l caval anar,
Fer .i. donzel desus son elme clar,
Entro la[s] dens ne fes lo bran passar,
Mort l'en trebuca, que anc non poc levar.   1328
Fer demestz els, fes los esparpalhar:
«Aspramon!» crida, «vinet mi ajudar!
D'aicels fairit non veuret .i. tornar.»

[XXXIV]

Au o Bertrans, es s'en irascutz,   1332
Ponh lo destrier que va los sautz menutz,
E n'Azemar tenc se per cofondutz.
Contra Gui corro e son .xv. ab escutz,
Baisso lur astas e·ls pieutz esmolutz.   1336
Li tres le fero el ausbers qu'es menutz,
De tos los autes lo gandi son escutz;
Trasttut lo fero, mas el s'es ben tengutz,

Per els non a minja d'estrieup perdutz. 1340
El feri .i. que fo acosseugutz,
Demest los altres es mort cazut;
Vi o Bertrans e s'e[s] fort irascut,
Broca·l destrier e trais lo bran que lutz, 1344
Fer lo per l'e[l]me qu'es luzens et agutz [99ᵛ]
Que los dos caires el n'a jos abatutz,
De cada part fo lo chapeh tengutz.

[XXXV]

Vec vos vengut n'Azema lo leugier, 1348
Apres de lui son .iiii. cavalier;
Li .iii. lo fero el escut de cartier
Que·l gomfano li fan el cors mulhier,
E n'Azemar feri lhi son destier; 1352
Lo diestrier ca, lo com[s] pres a tumbier.
A tera cazet non fa per ablasmier,
De ca[da] part li van grans cops donier.
El se defen ab sa speia d'asier, 1356
Qui encausa, be lo fa trastumbier;
For lo respondo per los grans cops que fier.
Regardo sas mas no l'auzan toquier
Tro Bertrandet comenset a cridier: 1360
«Eia! baro, del tracher lauzengier
Cum es aiso no·l porrem daroquier?»
Van lo ferir cadaüns vol[on]tiers,
Que son escut li fan tantost falhier. 1364
Ab las palauras vec vos .i. cavalier,
Jaufre ac nom et vai ferir Requier,
Tant l'asta dura lo vai jos daroquier,
Per mieih las rennas va prenre lo destrier, 1368
Fer per la prieissa, comenset a cridier:
«Montatz, coms Gui, que be vos fa mestier!»
El salhi sus, pessa de l'espleitier;
Cel de Guio non podo plus durier, 1372
Fugen s'en torno dreit .i. cami plenier.
Ilh los encauso per las testas trenquier,

Soen los fero e los fan trabuquier,
.VII. n'an ausitz e .xx. ne fan menier. 1376
E lo fels Gui, cant ne pot escapier [100ʳ]
Tro Aspramon no·is vol pas rastanquier.
E·lh de Monclar s'en volo retornier,
Ab lor enca·ls que an fah de prumier. 1380
Aysels que an pres fan sobre Sainz jurer
Que de la guera lor vuelho aiudier
E que no sian ni fals ni lauzengier.

[XXXVI]

[L]o tracher Guis foc irat e dolens, 1384
Manda sas teras et aju[s]ta sas gens,
De cavaliers i ac .m. e .ccc.
E de triat i ac be .m. cirvens.
Tro a Monclar non pres arestamens, 1388
Asetjet los senes tot cauzimens,
Tendo lur traps enrivironamens,
Bastiso peireiras, trabuquest issamens;
Mas res que los fasso no lur te dampnamens. 1392
Pueis sobre Sainz a[n] fah los sagramens:
No s'en partran per nulh homes vivens
Tro que pendan aquelhs que so laïns!
De laïns cridon e dizon autamens: 1396
«A! traher Gui, malvas e mescrezens,
Tostz i seret prejus de tos fals sagramens!»
Dedins s'alegro e fan esbaudimens
E nueh e dia estan alegramens; 1400
An que mangar a .xii. [ans] perseguens,
Laïns an aigua molis e foreis e corens.
.XII. ans estero enclaus tuh de laïns,
Tro que Beto ac pres sos garnimens. 1404
Laissem Monclar e·ls asetiamens.
Qua[nt] ac Beto .vi. ans, foc bels e gens
La color fresca, los ueilh belh e rizens,
Ama·l lo rei e te lo caramens [100ᵛ] 1408
E la regina e sa filha issamens.

Fo la donzela de bels aculimens,
Ac nom Erimena e fo ben avinens.
Lo pros Daurel fo aras ben jauzens,   1412
L'efant apela e ditz li belamens:
«Bels filhs Beto, apendet d'esturmens,
D'arpa e de viola, seres ne plus jauzens.»
L'efas respon mot enseiadamens: 1416
«Bels senher paire, vostre comandamens,
Ve·us me aissi per far vostre talens.»

                        [XXXVII]

Qua[n]t ac .vii. ans Beto sap gen violar
E tocar citola e ricamen arpar   1420
E cansos dire, de se mezis trobar.
.I. jorn aven que Daurel fo en mar
En .i. nau per los dalfis pescar,
E Betonet vi los enfans jogar,   1424
Filh de baros qu'ero de ric afar.
El cor tantost son brizaut empenhar,
Cor al taulier e va s'i asetjar.
Cilh de la cort o van al rei comtar,   1428
Vi o lo rei e pren lo a gardar.
Ans que·n leves li detz —Dieus!— a gazanhar.
Que .x. enfans lai a fahs depolhar
De lor brizautz, que no lor vol laissar.   1432
Al col los leva e pren s'en ad anar,
E lo reis vai .i. donzel apelar:
«Amix,» ditz el, «gardat que·n volra far
D'aicels brizautz que·n vei al col portar.»   1436
«Senher,» ditz el, «ben la sabriei comtar.»
Beto ieis forras, comencetz a cridar
Permiei la vila et s'en pres ad anar:
«Qui vol brizaut a me venga parlar!»   [101ʳ]   1440
Als donzels vai los brizaut donar.
El palais torna, comencetz a gabar:
«Tozet,» dit el, «sabres ben tremolar;
Si mi crezeset altres n'ires talhar.»   1444

E lo donzel o va al rei comtar
Si cum a vist, que no·lh o vol celar.
E l'amiratz fai sa cort ajustar,
Qu'ades venga qui lui volra amar.   1448
Mai de .c.m. lai n'a fah ajustar
E la regina que motz fai a prezar.
So ditz lo rei: «Baro, que vos en par
D'aisel efan que vezet lai estar,   1452
De Betonet que ieu puec tant amar?
Tantas proesas ieu li vei comensar;
E .x. brizaut gazanhet al jogar
E cant los ac, dese los anec dar.   1456
Per cel senhor que tos nos fa parlar,
Ieu non creirai sia filh de joglar,
Que los cavals li vei fort abribar
E los ausbers vestir e despulhar   1460
E los escutz tener et abrasar.»
Ditz la regina: «Ie·usz o faria proar:
Ins en las crambas vos l'en mandat intrar
Que a ma filha an bels verses comtar.   1464
.C. mart d'argen lh[i] farai prezentar;
Si pren l'aver donc es filh de joglar,
Si no·l pren, anc re no·lh ac a far.»
Aicel cossel si van tuh ajustar   1468
E lo rei fa per l'efan enviar
Et el venc tost, pren se a ginoulhar.   [101ᵛ]
«Beto,» dit el, «ara·us vuelh fort pregar
Que ab ma filha vos anes deportar;   1472
De vostres laices vos li anes viholar;
Irada es, anas la·m apagar.»
«Senher,» ditz el, «aisso m'es bon a far.»
Vai s'en corren, pren sa vieula trempar.   1476
E la regina vai sa filha ensenhar:
«Filha,» dit ela, «ab vos volrai parlar.
.C. martz d'argen aissi vos vueilh laissar,
Que Betonetz vos venra deportar;   1480
Vos los li datz quantz s'en volra anar.»
Lo rei meszisses comensa a parlar:
«Baro,» ditz el, «anem los escoltar

En cal manieira si volra capdelar.»   1484
Entorn la cambra si van tuh amagar
Que auziran tot so que volran far.

[XXXVIII]

Sus a las cambras s'en es Beto intrat
En .i. brizaut que fo gentil cordatz,   1488
E la donzela es levada viat:
«Bo·m sap, amix, quar s'es saïns intrat.»
Ela es joves et es grans sa beutat,
Non a .x. ans enquara acabat.   1492
Ela fo agradabla, en sa ma te .iii. datz
Qu'ero d'aur fi et dedins tragitatz.
«Dona,» ditz el, «sai vos a eviat
Que·us mi trametz mos senher l'amiratz   1496
Et ieu mezis tenh m'en fort per pagat.
De bels verses sai, dona, vueilh que n'aujatz.»
E dit sos verses e fon ben escoltatz;
Lo rei l'auzi que s'era amagatz   1500
Entorn la cambra e·il reïna delatz,   [102ʳ]
Et ab lor so .c. cavaliers prezatz
Que tuh escolto cossi s'es deportatz.
Una gran pessa s'es laïns deportatz,   1504
Canta e vihola, es se fort alegratz.
«Dona,» dit el, «iriei m'en si a vos plat;
Totz jorn, ma dona, que·m volret mi mandatz.»
«Beto,» dit ela, «.i. petit m'escoltat.»   1508
.C. mart d'argen li a denan pauzatz:
«Amix,» ditz ela, «cest aver vueilh prengat,
Que compar ne·t palafres sojornat.
Mon prumier do en refut non agatz.»   1512
«Dona,» dit e[l], «.m. merces e .c. grat;
Que ieu ai, dona, aur et argen asat
Ab solamen que vos be mi volhatz.
Joglar venran, destrains e deprivatz,   1516
Ad els, ma dona, aquest aver donatz;
Lauzar vos an per estranhes regnatz

E vostre pret seran plus issausatz.
De vos, ma dona, me tenh for per pagatz,   1520
Que tot jour vos a mi pro donatz,
Que noiritz m'a mo senher l'amiratz.»
«Beto,» ditz ela, «per la fe que·m portatz
No vos n'anes que del miei non aiatz.»   1524
«Dona,» dit el, «per que m'en sermonatz?
Quantz ieu l'auria, seria ne enbargatz;
Mas solamen, car conosc que a vos platz,
De vostra ma prendrai aquels datz.»   1528
«Amix,» ditz ela, «ben pauc mi demandatz.
Tenet los doncz, per amor los portatz.»
Et el los pren, ela los li a donatz.
«Dona,» ditz el, «donatz mi comjatz.»   1532
«Beto,» dis ela, «en bon astre anatz;
Que Dieus done so que vos mai deziratz.»   [102ᵛ]
«Dona,» ditz el, «vos ab Dieus remanatz.»
L'efas ieis forras, a·ls donzels atrobatz,   1536
Van abergar los distriers sojornatz.
Quant el los vi no s'es pas atrigat,
Dreih a l'estable tantost s'en es anatz,
Pren lo caval del rei, es sus montatz   1540
Et ab los altres abeurar es anatz.
Lo rei ici de lai ond'era intratz
Et ac auzit Beto cossi fon deportatz,
Pueissas lo vi qu'es el caval montatz.   1544
«Baro,» ditz el, «e sai vos regardatz:
No m'es vejaire segon los mieus pesatz
Que aquest efas anc fos de Daurel natz.»
Tuh lhi respondo: «De nien en parlatz;   1548
Per cel senhor que tostz nosz a formatz
Fils es de duc, de ric o d'amiratz.»
«Baro,» dit el, «car no lo·m apelatz?»
Cilh lo·nlh apelo et el venc mot viatz.   1552
So ditz lo rei: «Beto, cum fos auzatz
Que mos destriers fos anc per vos tocatz?»
«Senher,» dis el, «uei no fo abeuratz,
Vostres escudiers es be malaüratz;   1556
Ieu[·l] menarai a l'aiga, si a vos platz.»

«Beto,» ditz el, «en garda lo agatz.»
«Senher,» dis el, «per mi er ben garatz.»
Partz se d'aqui, tuh dizo ad .i. clatz: 1560
«Aicel efas pessam que fos panatz.»
En aquel dia fo Beto esproatz;
D'aqui enan fo mil tans mai amatz.

[XXXIX]

Qua[n]t ac Beto .ix. ans foc del rei escudiers,   1564
Foc bels e gens e covinen parliers,
Joga a taulas, et ad excas, a diniers,
E va cassar ab cas et ab lebriers,   [103ʳ]
Ab los austors et ab los esparviers;   1568
Baissa las astas, abriva·n los destriers.
Ama·l lo rei, la regina a sobriers,
Sa genta filha que lo te motz en chiers;
Ama lo domnas, donzels et cavaliers.   1572
Et a las taulas servia als mangiers,
Denan lo rei estava prezentiers,
Servi li fort de so que·l fa mestiers;
Peussas los viola e canta volontiers.   1576
Vi o Daurel; ac ne grans alegriers.

[XL]

Quant ac .xi. ans el se sap gent escrimir,
Als cavaliers privadamen servir.
E·l pros Daurel de lui ac grant servir.   1580
Compra·ilh caval et armas per garnir,
Belas e paucas que las puesca sufrir,
Pueissas el fes .i. Sarazi venir
Que fo molt dels efantonet noirir: 1584
«Amix,» dis el, «aujatz que vos vuelh dir.»
E Betonet fes denan si venir.
Daurel comensa al Sarazi a dir:
«Aquest miei filh m'essenhat d'escrimir.»   1588

«Ben conosc aras que·l voles en riquir.»
L'efan ne mena, esenha·l d'escrimir
E so destrier de la tera salhir,
Ab son escut escelier e gandir   1592
Et en l'autruei de grans colpes ferrir,
Las dretas astas mamenar e brandir
E los distrier adresar e tenir,
Grans cops donar e dels altres gandir   1596
Et en tornei cum si deu mantenir.
.I. an lo tenc que re no ac que dir,
E sap d'escrima, de garnimens tenir.   [103ᵛ]

[XLI]

[Q]uant ac .xii. ans sap pro d'esernimens,   1600
Vi o Daurel, ac ne son cor jauzens;
Daurel l'apela, el venc viassamens:
«Bels filh,» dit el, «pren tostz tos garnimens,
Las bonas armas e los distriers correns;   1604
Irem lai forras ieu e vos solamens.»
«Ai! senher paire, vostres comandamens,
Si cum volretz, tot als vostres talens.»
Entrambidos van s'en en .i. bel prat verdens: 1608
«Bels filhs,» dit el, «armatz vos belamen.»
Et el s'adoba adzaut et covinen,
Qua[n]t fo armatz, el li dit en rien:
«Ai! senher paire, que vos ve a talen?»   1612
«Bels filhs,» dit el, «veirai vostr'ardimen;
Jondret ab mi, se Dieu plat, veramen.»
«Bels senher paire, ben parlat de nien!
Qu'ieu comtra vos dresses mon fer luzen,   1616
Non o faria per .c.m. marc d'argen.»
«A far vos er, per Dieu omnipoten!
De mi ferir non aiat cauzimen,
Qu'ieu vos ferriei a mon esforssamen.»   1620
Cascus se lonja .i. mezurat arpen,
Baisso las astas e fero·is duramen
Per los escut que·l fers intra dedins

Entro·ls aulbertz que de mort los defen. 1624
Daurel l'espenh molt vertudozamen
E l'efan lui, qu'a terra l'en dissen
E passa d'oltra e fai son torn mol gen.
Daurel s'en ri jos son elme luzen: 1628
«Beto,» dit el, «ben aia aital joven, [104ʳ]
Be·m par aras per mieu essien.
Ai! senher Dieus, grans grat vos en ren.»
L'efas dissen; plora mol greumen, 1632
Venc a Daurel e per sa ma lo pren:
«Ai! senher paire, mol fezes folamen.
Quar anc vas mi fezes essamen?
S'ie·us agues mort, ieu m'ausira issamen.» 1636
«Bels filhs,» dis el, «aras sai veramen
Que seret pros se vivet longamen.»
Las armas pauzo amboi cominalmen,
Van se ceze sus en l'erba verden. 1640

[XLII]

«Amix Beto,» dit Daurel lo joglar,
«Qui es vos filh? sabet m'o vos nomnar?»
«Senher, ieu vostre, e vulh o ben estar.»
«Non es, amix, per Dieu que·m fa parlar, 1644
Ans es mo senher, e devet o selar.
Grans et e bels, neh armas portar;
Duc et e coms, e vuelh vos o mostrar;
Neps es de Karlo que mol fai a prezar, 1648
Del melhor rei que hom pusca trobar,
Fils es de sa seror; ja no·l devet amar
Quar enaisi vos fai faiditz anar.
Lo duc tos paire el mi donec Monclar, 1652
.I. ric castel que esta sobre mar.
Us tracher coms que·is fa Gui apelar
Ausis vostre car paire quan fo ab lui cassar,
Pues compret vostre maire ab pro argen et aur. 1656
Vos noiria hom ins en irla de mar,
Cel tracher Guis vos i fes espiar,

Volc vos aucire, mas ie·us aniei panar;
E nulha guia no[·l]h pogui escapar   1660
Tro mon pauc filh per vos aniei donar;
Mos uelh vezens feri ne a .i. pilar   [104ᵛ]
Si que los uelh li fe del cap volar;
Quant l'ac delit, cujet vos mort laissar.   1664
Ieu, cant o vi, no pogui plus durar,
Fugi m'en sai, que vos volgui salvar.»
L'efas Beto se comensa a plorar:
«Senher,» dit el, «aisso cum poguet far!   1668
Cum vos poirai cestz fah gazardonar?»
«Mon car senher, ie·usz o sabrai comtar:
Em breu de temps nos ne volrem tornar,
Ausirem Gui que no·s pot escapar;   1672
T[r]astot Peitieus er al vostre mandar,
Bordels, Antona, tro al castel de Monclar.
Ieu ai .ii. filhs que·m fezetz vos laissar
E ma molher el castel de Monclar.   1676
Per vostre sen no·us volhatz capdelar,
Mas per lo mieu e no i poiretz pecar.
Celatz vos fortz tro·us ne volhat anar.»
«Bels senher paire, tot al vostre mandar.»   1680
Prendo lur armas e prendo·s [a] anar.
Sus el palais se prendo a violar,
Denan lo rei se van fort alegrar,
L'efas Beto si pres a ginolhar,   1684
Denan lo rei vai son esturmen pauzar.

[XLIII]

[Q]uant ac Beto .xiii. ans fo fort e prezatz
Et en la cort volgut e pels melhors onratz.
E·l rei Gormon ajustec son barnatz,   1688
Volo·is gran mal entre el e l'amiratz,
Guerra an aüda ben a .xx. ans passatz.
Ab gran poder es sobre lui anatz,
Ab be .xii.m. de cavaliers prezatz   [105ʳ]   1692
Ab .c.m. homes, que us non es restat.

En Babilonia es Gormons aribatz,
Per mieh la vila s'en es grans crit levatz.
E Betonet no s'es pas oblidatz, 1696
Dreh al drestier del rei s'en es anatz,
Met lhi·l fre e la boca e la cela el costat
E venc al rei; es denan lui anatz:
«Senher,» ditz el, «e vos car no montatz? 1700
Vostre caval es mol be esselat.»
«Beto,» dit el, «areires lo·m tornatz,
No i issirem, que no n'em adobatz;
Nos em petitz et ilh son trop assatz, 1704
Se i issirem seria gran foldatz.»
«Senher,» dit el, «aisi cum a vos platz.»
E torna areires et es se cossiratz
E menbra li del linatzge que'es natz; 1708
L'aubert del rei se gita als costatz,
E sinta l'espeiga e[s] se .iii. vetz senhatz,
E lassa l'elme qu'es ab aur listratz.
De plana tera es sul caval montatz, 1712
Dels adops del rei s'es ben aparelhatz
E pren l'escutz que es estreh belcatz
Ab .iiii. brocas d'[a]ur que i fo pauzatz,
E brandis l'asta e·l fers fo nielatz; 1716
Dels garnimens del rei s'es adobatz.
Broca·l destrier dels esperos daurat,
Tro al portal no s'es pas atrigat.
Ditz al portier: «Las portas alargatz 1720
Que lo rei ve e trastot sos barnat.»
El las li uebre; el ditz: «A Dieu siat!»
E lo rei es als fenestas montat [105ᵛ]
E vi Beto que fo molt abrivatz, 1724
Conoc lo be e s'en meravilhatz:
«Digas, regina, eforas esgaratz,
Vegat Beto cum s'es aparelhatz.
De mos adops be vei que s'es armatz, 1728
Lo mieus destriers cuh que c'era cambiat.»
«Senher,» ditz ela, «no sera se Dieu platz;
Fe que·m deves, a Dieus lo comandatz.
Be vos puesc dire que se el vieu asat 1732

De nos acore, er ben aparelhatz.
S'el es pres, be serai malevatz.»
De la gran ostz vos ne ve .ii. triatz
Que so vengutz entra prop dels valatz.   1736
Beto los vi et es se dels propchat,
Tuh lo esgardo dels murs e dels valatz.
En aut lur crida: «Baro, no·us ne fugatz,
L'us de vos dos ad huna part estatz,   1740
Ab lui jondrai, ab qual que vos volhatz;
Perdet destrier o aquest gazagatz.»
So li ditz l'us: «Companh, ab mi justatz.»
Cadaüs broca ab los espiest baissatz,   1744
Grans cops si fero els bos escutz listratz.
Be lo feri aicel desbatigat
Que entro l'auberc s'en es lo fer passatz;
Beto fer lui coma vasal proatz,   1748
L'escut li trauca a l'auberc l'a falssatz;
Vezen de tos s'es lo paias tumbatz.
So dit Beto: «Bon sap car et tumbat
Que ab joglar vos estes encontratz!»   1752
Vi o·l compainh, fon dolens et iratz
Et ac gran anta quar l'artre fon tumbatz;   [106ʳ]
Broca·l caval, venc vas lui abrivatz,
E Betonet no s'es pas oblidatz   1756
E brandis l'asta, e·l fers fo nielatz,
Gran cops si fero, ses totas pietatz,
Que lor escut i an trastotz briatz.
Be lo feri aicel desbatejatz   1760
E l'efas lui, que los arsos dauratz
En fa volier e trabuca·l els prat.
«Amix,» dis el, «a·n Gormon me digatz
Que fil de glojar vos a amdos tumbatz.»   1764
Lo reis o vi e totz l'altre barnatz,
Ab vos escria: «Cavaliers, escoltatz!
Per cel senhor que totz nosz a formatz
Se vieu .i. an el sera amiratz!»   1768
Del l'ost o viro si que s'en so triat
Mai de .iii.m., mas no·ls a esperat.
Abans s'en intra coma savis e menbrat

Ab .ii. destriers que·n mena esselat.   1772
Per mieh la vila s'en es gran brut levatz,
Coro en cambras; el s'es gen capdelat;
A .ii. donzels a los destrier donat
E mieh la plassa s'es l'efas desarmatz,   1776
Tuh lo rimiro quar grans fo sa beutatz.
Vec vos Daurel qu'es vengu viatz,
Que tenc .i. basto que fon gros e cairatz:
«Ai!» so dis el, «filh de joglar malvatz,   1780
Per cel senhor que totz nosz a formatz
Mala ieis senes los mieus mandatz!»
L'efas respon coma hom essenhatz:
«Ai! senher paire, per que vos corossatz?   1784
Molt n'ai gran gauh quar vos m'en castiatz.»   [106ᵛ]
Tuh li escrido: «Daurel, no·us irascatz,
Vegat l'efan cossi c'es razonatz.»
En pauca d'ora n'i ac mols ajustatz   1788
E lo reis venc e trastot sos barnat.

[XLIV]

[L]o reis i venc corren ad esdemes,
Aitan co·l poc portar sos palafres,
Venc a Daurel e pres lo pel cabes: 1792
«Per cel senhor que tot nosaltres fes,
Ins e ma carcer estares .xii. ans pres,
Que es escura, que re no lai veires;
No manjaretz lunha re de dos mes,   1796
Ni pa ni vi ni lunh altres conres
Se no·m dizes aquest efan qui es;
Qu'el non es vostres, se m'ajut Dieus ni fes!»
Respon Daurel que es pros e cortes: 1800
«Ai! senher rei, per Dieus, valham merces!
Fais ajustar vostra cort demanes,
E·ls chivalier e los melors borzes;
Pueisas dirai de l'efan de cui es.   1804
Non es mos fils, so sapiatz que vers es,
Non a el mon duc ni comte ni reis

Qui sia plus autz que·l sieu parentat es.»
E l'amiratz fa cornar .i. pages   1808
Que tost s'ajusto el palais majores.

[XLV]

A la cort veno tuh li mal e li bo
E·l pros Daurel poietz sus .i. peiro,
En auta votz comenset so sermo: 1812
«Ai! senhe reis e tuh vostre baro,
Entendet me, que nuh hom mot no i so.
Vezes l'efan ab lo var blizaudo:
Coms es e dux, ses tota mentizo   1816
Filhs fon del duc qu'apelava hom Buvo   [107ʳ]
De cel d'Anton, cui Jhesu Crist perdo!
Pus el [es] nes l'emperador Karlo,
Del melhor rei que sia ni anc fo.   1820
Carles lo rei det sa sor a Buvo
E lo duc Boves ac ne l'efan Beto,
E·l duc sos paire si pres a compaho
.I. comte sieu qu'apela hom Guio.   1824
Aquel l'ausis ab mol gran trasio
Pueis pres sa maire per forsa, no·il saup bo,
Don'Amenjartz ab la gentil faisso.
Ins en irlanda de mar noiri l'om a lairo.   1828
Volc lo auscire Guis ab lo cor felo,
Tant lai estet tro qu'espiatz i fo,
Ieu lo paniei; portiei l'en a maio,
Seguet me·l tracher per granda trasiho,   1832
Demandec lo·m; ieu dissi l'en de no.
Volia m'ardre, e mi e l'efan Beto,
E ieu, can vi non auria guerizo,
E luoc de lui diei li .i. mieu filho;   1836
Vezen de totz lo pres per lo talo,
Feri n'al mur et eservelet lo;
Ieu soi sos hom, fih lh'en cest gazardo.
Fugi m'en sai e vostra regio,   1840
Noirit l'aves e deu vos saber bo;

Tornar nos n'em, que ben es de sazo,
E vengar s'a del fel trachor Guio;
E qui·lh fes mal ja non aura perdo   1844
Que de proesa a ben comensazo.»

[XLVI]

[E] qua[n]t lo rei la paraula enten
Que·l neps de Karlo a noirit longamen,
Ven a Beto, entre sos bras lo pren,   1848
.C. ves lo baia e la regina icimen,
Tuh li baro li crido autamen:
«Rei, da·lh ta filha, que ben es d'avi[n]en.»   [107ᵛ]
Lo rei ac guah e dis li en rien: 1852
«Beto,» fai cel, «ma filha vos prezen.»
L'efas respon ab gran essenhamen:
«Senher,» dit el, «no la refut nien;
Si o vol mos paire que m'a datz garnimen   1856
Ieu la prendrai mol voluntieuramen.»
Daurel escria mol vertudozamen:
«Prendet la, senher, que ben n'es covinen,
Ab solamen que·us fassa .i. covinen —   1860
Per vostr'amor prendra batiamen —
Menar l'avetz a Peitieus veramen.»
E la reïna n'es intrada corren
Ins e las cambras, sa bela filha pren,   1864
Vezen de totz la tra a parlamen,
Pueis li demanda, si c'o viro .d.:
«Domna Erimena, voletz batiamen?
Beto o vol que a molher vos pren.»   1868
Domna Erimena li respon gentamen:
«O ieu, ma domna, a totz lo sieu talen.»
So dis Daurel: «Rei, da·lhi de ta gen,
Mai de tria milia homes que sian combaten   1872
E cadaüs que aia tot son bon garnimen,
Q[ue] d'uei en .xv. jorns nos n'irem veramen
Entrogas a Peitieus, que no i a tarzamen,
Dels enemix en penra vengamen;   1876

Pueissas penra la domna so sapias veramen,
Vos daret la·lh ab gran esbaudimen.»
Tuh li escrido que ben es avinen
E pueissa crido trastuh comunalmen: 1880
«Reis, jure la dese nostre vezen.»
So dit lo rei: «Beto, fais sagramen.»
«Senher,» dis el, «re no vos i conten;
Daurel mos paire jure prumeramen.» 1884
Lo rei mezis las bonas fes en pren,
Sobre .i. espieia amdoi fan sagramen,
E Daurel es a .i. cros d'argen.
Aqui mezis, que no i fan tarzamen, [108ʳ] 1888
Meto las naus e l'aparelhamen
E laïns meto de trop bels garnimen,
De tot aquo que a nau si coven;
E son dedins .m. e desobre .ccc. 1892
E l'efas pren ac[u]miadamen.
E met s'e mar Beto ab granda gen,
Dresso lor velas e det lur Dieus bo ven,
Tres mes complitz, meih de tempestamen 1896
S'en van per mar, pueis fan aribamen
Pres de Monclar alegre e jauzen.

[XLVII]

E Daurel garda e si a vist Monclar,
Aqui aribo, cuja laïns intrar; 1900
Entorn los viro assatiat estar,
Los trap tendutz, las cozinas fumar.
Vi o Daurel e pren l'o a mostrar:
«Senher,» dis el, «Dieus nos vol fort onrar; 1904
Vejaire m'es no·ns qual fort afanar,
Dels enemix aisi·ns podem vengar.
Vec vos lai Gui que no·ns pot escapar
Se pel mieu sen vos voletz capdelar. 1908
Fais vostres homes garnir et adobar.»
«Senher,» ditz el, «a totz al vostre mandar.»
Tuh se garnisso, c'us no se·n fan pregar.

E comensero del castel a gardar 1912
E pros Daurel vai lor l'escut mostrar;
Conogro·l be, viras los alegrar,
E l'us a l'autre comenset a parlar:
«So es mos senher que ve d'oltra la mar!» 1916
Dediens s'adobo per lai fors assautar,
Es*tan* menbrat cant auzirat cridar.
E Beto s'arma, viest .i. bon auberc clar
E la espeia jes no la vol laissar, 1920
E Daurel altre, ges non o vol tarzar; [108ᵛ]
Gran ac la barba, qu'om no·l poc albirar;
Ben a .vii. ans no la·is laisset ostar.
E·l pros Daurel los va tost ajustar 1924
E pueis tan gent si los vai castiar:
«Negus de vos no i an esperonar
Tro que nosaltres vos lai augatz cridar,
Pueissas vinetz, que degus no esper so·m par!» 1928
Una gran capa va Daurel afublar
E Betonet ne fai altra portar,
Prendo lor vieulas a guiza de joglar
E pros Daurel vai Beto essenar: 1932
«Senher,» dit el, «co·us sabret capdelar:
Ieu cantarai, vos devet escoltar.
Dirai tal re que·ilh poira enojar,
Mon essien el me volra tocar.» 1936
So dit Betonet: «Et ieu tost al vengar!»
Entro al trap no·is volo restancar,
E quant cilh vengro, Guis secia al manjar;
Guis lo escria: «Joglar, vinetz mangar.» 1940
So ditz Daurel: «Volem vos deportar.»
E Betonet pren .i. bel laise a notar
E·l pros Daurel comenset a cantar:
«Qui vol auzir canso, ieu lh'en dirai, so·m par, 1944
De tracio que no fai a celar
Del fel trachor Guio —cui Jhesus desampar!—
Qu'aucis lo duc quan fon ab lui cassar.»
E Guis tenc .i. coltel, va·l a Daurel lansar 1948
E pros Beto vai sa vieula gitar
E pres sa capa molt tost a despolhar

E trais la speia, va lhi .i. cop donar
Q[ue] lo bras destre fai a tera volhar.   1952
«Antona!» crida, molt altamen e clar,
Tuh es miei home, c'us no·is n'auzan tornar.»
Cil del castel quant auziro cridar,
Obron las portas, van si amb els mesclar.   [109ʳ]   1956
Vec vos pongen quels d'oltra la mar
Que re no i ac mas del desbaratar.
Aqui viratz tanta testa trencar
E tant baro caser e t[r]abucar,   1960
Tan chivalier morir e derocar,
Tant pe, tan poinh per mieh lo camp volar!
E Daurel vai los baros a[m]parar:
«Acels a pe, qu'om no·ls auza tocar,   1964
Que·l tracher Guis i fais forsat estar.»
Sos chivaliers laisa totz afolar;
Grans gaus n'an cilh que·n podo escapar,
Que anc negus no i atendec so·m par.   1968
L'efan Beto vai Gui fortz escapar,
Per mieh la gola fai .i. liam gitar.
E lhi fil de Daurel van lur senhor paire baiar
E pueissas van lur senhor *abrassar,*   1972
Aqui virat tan gran *gaia demenar.*
Lo pros Daurel comensa *demandar*:
«On es ma molher que ieu puec *tant* amar?»
Ilh li respondo: «No la podetz mostrar;   1976
Tant tost mori quan vos en vi anar.»
Daurel o au, non pot em pes estar,
Enblesmat ca, e van lo cofortar;
E Betonet vi Daurel engoissar,   1980
Ac ne tal dol comenset a plorar.
Trastut van Daurel cofortar,
Del dol que fa lo prendo a blasmar:
«Ab vostres fils vos deves alegrar.»   1984
Cominalmen .... ar
Tro al mati .... ar
Tuh vas *Peitieus eli* .... *ad* anar
E pros *Daurel* .... *Guio*   1988
Dret a la coa del bon caval liar.   [109ᵛ]

Entro a Peitieus, lo fan tras si cornar,
Cilh de la vila si fan los senhs sonar,
Tuh rev[e]stit van Beto amparar, 1992
E li borzes prendo·is Dieus a lauzar
Quar lor a dat lor senhor a cobrar.
Aqui virat tan gran gauh demenar,
Tant bon tapitz per las ruas gitar! 1996
Daus totas part los virat alegrar:
«Ai! senher Dieus, mol vos devem lauzar,
Que·ns aves fah nostre senhor cobrar!»
Don'Emengart au lo brutda levar, 2000
De l'aut palais comenset a garar
E vi Guio tot sanglen rosegar
E cor encontra pre novas demandar.
.I. donzel troba que be la saup comtar: 2004
«Domna,» dit el, «be·us..ve·us..alegrar;
Ve·us vostre filh qu'es *vengut* d'oltramar,
E·l tracher Guis *ac* .... menar.»
Au o la dona, no si vol estancar, 2008
So fih encontra, si lo vai tost baigar;
E·l pros Daurel si lo·ilh vai prenzentar
E fel Guio lhi van desse lieurar.
Dis o Daurel lhi: «Domna, fais cest tracher gardar.» 2012
So dit la dona: «Fais lo al vent levar.»
Daurel respon: «Farei lo cofesar
Qu'el ausis lo bon duc al vengar.»
E Betonet fa sa ost albergar; 2016
Ab molt gran gauh van el palais *m*ontar,
La nueh sojorna t*r*o *venc* ....
E pros Beto fa sa cort...........
E·l fel pescaire fa.................. 2020
So es Abram que·l..................

[XLVIII]

[C]ilh de Peitieus an lor senhor cobrat, [110ʳ]
Trastut essemp en an gran gauh menat;
Al bo mati son denan lui anat, 2024

Tant bel prezen li an aportatz;
Qui palafre, qui caval sojornatz,
Qui copas d'aur, qui ric palitz rodatz.
Aqui s'ajusto ab gran alegretatz   2028
Rendo·ilh las forsas de trastotz lo regnat,
Totas las vilas que ero del dugatz;
Coms es e dux e an lh'o autregat.
Ve·us lo borzes que tan l'a desziratz,   2032
Que·l dux sos paire l'avia tostemps onrat.
E n'Aicelina e sos frairel menbratz;
E n'Aicelina n'a Beton rasonat:
«Bel fils,» dis ela, «mol vos ai desiratz,   2036
Be sapiatz .c. vetz vos *ai* baizatz,
D[est]retan fui a tor et *a pecat*,
Mal m'en batet cel *traje* reneg*atz*
Que ieu vey lay estar encadenatz.   2040
De tal perilh ieu vos vey *escapat*
Lo mal que·m fero non ay pas *oblidat*:
Dat mi Abram que vos a espiatz.»
«Domna,» dis el, «be vos er autregatz.»   2044
Pueissas la pren e baia·l a privatz,
Be sap cum es, Daurel l'o a comtatz.
Enans qu'en parca el *lhi a mot d*onatz,
.I. ric castel ben *bo et asazat*,   2048
E·l fels pescaire.........*es vieus escorgatz*.
De totas partz *si foro ajustat*
E Betonet *si a Gui apelat*:
«Digas, fels coms, aujam la veritatz,   [110ᵛ]   2052
Cum fo del duc que aves afolatz?»
«Senher,» ditz el, «ja no vos er selatz;
Be lo ai mortz per granda foldat.»
E·l pros Daurel a Beto a pregat: 2056
«Coms debonaire, non aias pi[at]atz,
A mi donat; mo filh verrai vengatz
Qu'el m'ausis, ieu rendrai lh'en son grat.»
Respon Betos: «A vostra volontatz.»   2060
Vezen de totz el a Gui estacatz
Plan a la coa d'un destrier sojornatz,
Per mieh Peitieus l'a pertot rosegatz

E pueis lo fa gitar en .i. valatz.   2064
Aicest traïre i a pauc guazanhatz,
Que li voltor e li corp l'an mangatz.

[XLIX]

[T]uh li baro son en gran alegrier
Car an trobatz lur senhor dreturier.   2068
L'efas Betos pres Daurel apelier:
«Ai! senher paire, ...gran plenier,
Totas mas terras vos autrei per mandier.
Qui vos non amara ieu no·l volrai amier   2072
E qui vos ama ieu lo volrai amier.»
E n'Azemar que lh'ajudec molt volontier
Da·l Aspremon que mot fai a prezier.
E Bertran el a fah chivalier,   2076
Da·lh .ii. castels a trastot son mandier.
Del menor fraire el a fah escudier,
Quant sera tals......................
Aisi son...........................   2080
Pueissas trametz per sa gentil molher,   [111ʳ]
Ab ela vengro mai de .m. cavaliers,
So nom li laissa que no lo·lh vol cambier:
Domna Erimena si fai ben apelier.   2084
Lo coms la pres a Sant Alari el mostier,
Tostemp estero ab mot gran alegrier.

[L]

So es en mai quan li ram per la flor
E li boisso recobro lor odor;   2088
Lo coms Beto fo de granda valhor,
Venc a sa maire, baia la per amor:
«Domna,» dis el, «mot soi en gran tristor
Se ieu no·m vengue del fel emperador   2092
Que cosenti a don Gui lo traïdor,
Qu'aucis mon paire a dol et a tristor

E vos vendet a granda dissonor
Al felo traire que vos ac   2096
Que a Daurel ausis so filh *menor*.
Se no·m fugis al rei amparador
Que·m dec sa filha a la fresca color,
El m'agra mor, non agr'amparador.   2100
De Gui so venges, merce del cri*ator*,
Anc no fui filhs de Bovo·l *ponhador*
S'ieu ans d'u mes no·lh gasti sa honor;
El es mos oncles, Dieus l'en don *dissonor*!»   2104
«Fils,» dis la dona, «Dieus ti crega ta...
Car l'emperaire es de tan gran *ricor*,
Vostre parenh so sieis homes melhor,
Entre vos dos no·ns aia mala............   2108
.I. mesage prendetz ab destrier *corredor*,
Trametes lo a Karlo *l'emp*erador
Que·us fasa *dreit de* la gran dissonor,
Car el lieuret a   2112
Ce no fa non vol ....ador
Ans de .x. ans dresse son auriflor.   [111ᵛ]
Vos aves dret et rei sobre lor,
Ab vos iran .c. melia cavalgador,   2116
De l'amira vos venra gran socor.»
So dit lo coms: «Dieus fassa honor,
Que anc nulh hom non ac maire melhor.
Ieu vol vengar lo ric duc so senhor;   2120
Aisi o farai dona, que no i aura tras[t]or.»

[LI]

    Lo coms Beto si apela Bertran:
«Am[i]x,» dis el, «aliet vos adobar,
Et ab vos sian .ii. cavaliers valhan,   2124
L'us n'Azemart e l'autre Gauseran.
A l'emperaire vos n'anatz motz corran,
No·l saludetz ni·l fassatz bel semblan,
E digas li·m que ieu lo·n vau desfizan;   2128
Ne patz ni treva no lhi vau demandan

Car cosentic mon deszeretamantz;
.XV. saumiers cargatz d'aur e d'argen
Ac per ma maire, vendec la ab aitan.   2132
Ieu son ......er, merce Dieu veramen,
Ges no·l tenc per senhor ni per paran;
Tant cant ieu puesca portar mon garniman
Non aura patz a totz lo mieu vivan.   2136
Saludas mi lo palazi Roulan,
Per *a*mistat liei portat .i. mieu gan;
Mos parens es, no·m deu noser nian,
...................................Karlo a guiran   2140
....»
Ditz n'Azemar: «A vostre comandaman   [112ʳ]
Ja·l vostre dret non irem laissan.»
...bos destriers an celatz ab aitan   2144
......baro s'en van ardidaman,
Cadaüs a son riche garniman,
*A*lbercz e lan[c]es et espegas trencans.
...iii. jo[r]nieigas, ses totz reteneman   2148
...a Paris e l'ausor mandaman.

[LII]

...Azemar apelec lo portier:
«*A*mix,» ditz el, «laïns volem intrier,
*D*avas Peitieus em nos .iii. messagier.»   2152
*So·*lh respondo: «Per Dieu, motz volontier,
*M*as de lai foras remanran li distrier.»
E...ilh montero sus el palais plenier,
*Den*ant lo rei s'en van *tuh* ajustier   2156
E Gauserans a parlat *tot* prumier
Car el es vielhs e volo ....
E fon be savis per la *razo contier,*
Bos cavaliers per *las armas portier.*   2160
«Dieus sal et gartz Roulan et Olivier
E si saludi trastot los .xii. pier
De part de mi Beto, lo bon comte guerier.
No salut mia cel que a lo vis clier,   2164

Aiso es Carles cui Dieus don desturbier,
Car det sa sor per argen et per aur c*lier*.
En est palais vengro .xv. saumiers,
Al trachor Gui la donet per molher,   2168
Que Betonet cujet a mort lieurier;
En loc de lui feri ad .i. pelier
Ab .i. efan qu'era filh de joglier.
Pueis Dieu del cel cil n'a fahc [es]capier   [112ᵛ]   2172
La sua mort el vos vol demandier;
De Guis es vengues, vos no vol perdonier.
Ges no·us promet sodadas ni deniers
Mas, pel Senher que tot nos fa parlier,   2176
Ja no vieuret .i. mes trastot plenier
Qu'el vos fara irat e desturbier;
Tant *com* el puesca sos garnimens portier
Non................iiii. jorns repairier.»   2180
E l'emperaire pren l'en a regardier,
Pren s'en a rir .... *son* cap a crolier:
«Amix,» dis el, «mot as *corage* fier
Car tu aisi m'*es vengutz menasier*.   2184
Anc mai non...............................
Mas mon car....................... amier
....donier
....*sabra* jutgier
.................................*or chiva*lier   2188
....
....

TEXTUAL NOTES

76ᵛ begins with the last line of *La Passion Provençale* («Finita passionem [*sic*] Deu det vobis suam amorem. / AMEN.») On the following line, crossed out, there is a first title *So es lo romans de Beto e de Daurel*. The word order has been changed for reasons of euphonics or tradition (cf. «ni de Daurel ni de Beton» v. 120 of Cabrera's *Ensenhamen*). The correct title, unlike the deleted one, is perfectly centered and written in characters consistent with the text in size.

1 Indentation. In the right-hand margin, in ink matching that of the *Passion*, there is an abbreviation for *magister* or *maistre*.

2 *le* feminine is attested elsewhere (see *Girart* 9040 *eu le laisserai*, 9867; also C. Appel, *Provenzalische Chrestomathie*, 6th ed. (Leipzig, 1930) p. xiv.

5 MS *tray tran*.

6 *sazia*: it is common *Girart* practice to replace pretonic *e* by *a* (III, 498).

9 Meyer suggests emending this obviously faulty verse to *Non ac ne vila ne honor ne maizo*. One might also emend *Cel que no* [*n'ac*] *ne no n'a vila ne valor* for meter without disturbing MS reading. *Valor* is the equivalent here of *honor* in the sense of 'land ownership' or even 'region' or country (see K. J. Hollyman, *Le Développement du vocabulaire féodal en France pendant le haut moyen âge* [Genève, 1957], pp. 33-41).

10 MS *sol* superscript. Meyer corrects *Mas* [*que*] *sol*; Chab. suggests [*quant*].

MS *cal* could be a scribal error for OFr. *col* 'hillock,' but I prefer, for stylistic reasons, *ca*[*ste*]*l*, since a hillock does not match the demands of a tone-setting epic introduction.

12 *paube* (cf. *paubres* 80): for other examples of the reduction of *r* after plosive, see *aute* 30, *pivat* 549. The formula *mon paube hom* indicates clearly the vassalage of Guy to Bove. Although juridical formulas such as *hom de corps*, *homo proprius* (and in *Daurel*, *vostre hom* 85) usually designated a serf and *homme lige* a vassal, the differentiation remained incomplete (as Hollyman, *Vocabulaire féodal*, pp. 140-141, states: «Il est intéressant de noter d'ailleurs que ces tentatives de différenciation sont moins répandues, en ce qui concerne les serfs, dans le Midi que dans le Centre et le Nord; c'est que dans le Midi les différences de classe étaient moins accusées.»)

14 *seher*: the scribe, without discrimination, represents palatal *n* [ñ] with *g, h* or *nh* (cf. *seger* 16, *senher* 52; other exs. *passim*).

15-18 The general meaning of these verses, translated by J. Flach (*Origines*, II, 482 note) «je vous cède mon alleu, que les barons l'entendent / Et vous serez [à mon égal] seigneur de ma maison / Jurez-moi compagnie pour tous les jours de notre vie.», is clear, but the text is corrupt due to an obvious lacuna between 14 and 15.

[15] MS *Lo menague vos sol vi e au io baro* is interpreted by Meyer *Lo meu alue vos solvi et aujo [lolh] baro*. Chab. suggests retaining *menague* 'direction, government' and emending [*solh*], a solution less good than Meyer's *alue* (<Lat. *allodum*, attested as early as 899, according to Boutruche, *Seigneurie*, p. 349; a similar form *aloos* is attested in Prov. by Brunel, *Chartes*, p. 95, 1. 2). Chab.'s *menague* (= *menatge* < *-aticu*) would be a rare masculine form which parallels the common *mainada* 'ménage'.

The second hemistich poses greater problems, since the MS reading is patently unsatisfactory. There are at least three possible emendations worthy of consideration:

1) using an attested 3 plur. pres. ind. form (Anglade, *Grammaire*, p. 389) read *e auzon [mei] baro*.

2) read *aujan*, subjunctive or imp. form; *aujo* = *avio* in Toul. dialect (Grafström, *Etude*, p. 178).

3) working from a similar construction *veia o tos barnatz* 610, in which the collective plural noun takes a sing. form of the subjunctive used as the imp. (Anglade, *Grammaire*, p. 352 *veya*; *veiatz*) we can accept the MS *au* (Anglade, *Grammaire*, p. 289 *au*; *aujatz*), add the impersonal demonstrative pronoun [*o*] and emend *io* (or *jo*) to *lo,* reading *e au [o] lo baro*, or delete the *i*, adding [*mei*], and reading *e au o mei baro*. The essential difficulty is resolved by any of these emendations, but my choice, although quite arbitrary, does as little violence as possible to the text.

[16] ALT *ey gaun mi*: interpreted by Meyer *E seret [vos] en gaun seg[n]er*, which makes little sense here, nor does his suggested correction to *encar*. Chab. suggests *E seret enga[l] mi* (see *Chan. Crois. Alb.* 3494, 6481 *engal de* 'equal to') which is supported by the MS. The vocalization of *-l* to *-u* is very common in Prov. (Schultz-Gora, *Altprovenzalisches Elementarbuch* [Heidelberg, 1906], p. 62). Settegast's suggestion (*ZRPh*, XXIX (1905), 416-417 [note]) that *gaun* = *Gavan* (a Prov. placename) is gratuitous.

[17] MS *vivo ab...* (remainder of margin cut off): Chab. suggests *ab vos*; Meyer *que vivrom* (cf. *farom* 26). *Ab...* added by scribe in attempt to «clarify» text, obviously corrupted at this point, should be disregarded on basis of sense and meter.

[18] MS *mori* deleted before *prengui*; smudge appears over *venh*. Sense and meter favor the emendation [*no mi*].

[20] *maio* 'maison' (cf. 718) is common variant-form of *maizo* (Brunel, *Chartes*, p. 477, *passim*; form attested as early as 1120 in the Albigeois).

[23] Meyer emends [*ai*]*tal*.

[24] *gardaray* = 'to take charge of, to lead.' Meyer emends *guidaray*.

[25] *Pertot hom* (= *on*) 'everywhere, anywhere.' *lai on*: Kurt Lewent, «Old Provençal *lai, lai on* and *on*,» *Modern Language Notes*, LXXIX (1964), 296-301, describes these as local adverbs, the former having a demonstrative character, the latter a relative one. Both are also used with a temporal meaning («quand») or a figurative one («in case» or «if»).

[27] ALT *Fai* (see n. 256).

[28-29] The copyist erroneously interchanges the second hemistichs of these verses. MS *Juran si companhia lhi bauzo sus* (superscript) *el mento / Can si foron juratz juratz [sic] amdoy li compaho*. One could emend *lhi b.* to *si bauzo*, since sense is obviously «they kissed each other on the chin.»

37 *palaes*: Chab. refers to *paer* as «forme ordinaire de paire dans l'ancienne trad. limousine de l'*Ev. de St. Jean*.» However, this spelling is unique in *Daurel* and may be simply an error for *palais*, rather than a form of «peer.»

38 *corretz* (cf. *corren* 177): the *n* of Latin groups *-nd* and *-nt* generally remain in Prov. (cf. Anglade, *Grammaire*, p. 185); but as Schultz-Gora states (*Altprov. Elementarbuch*, p. 61): *n* «vorkonsonantisch ist es unmittelbar vor *s* stehend schon vulgärlateinisch geschwunden.» The graphy suggests the possibility that the Daurel scribe pronounced *-tz* as [s] or [z].

39 MS *K*. (see p. 134).

41 Meyer emends *trais l'a p.*, interpreting 3 sing. pret. of *traire* as past part.

43 MS *ue* of *Que* superscript over *eu* crossed out.

44 MS *sere*: Meyer emends *sere*[*t*]; one might also emend *sere*[*m*] (*m* dropped in anticipation of *manenh*).

45 *lei* (= *lai*): see Anglade, *Grammaire*, pp. 86-87, for exs. of confusion between diphthongs *ei* and *ai*, as well as *ai* > *au* and *ei* > *eu* in *Daurel*. Anglade cites this word *lei* as an example of confusion between diphthongs *ei* and *ai* «phonétiquement très voisines; *lei* pour *lai* (45, 90, 658), *gueiamen* pour *gaiamen* (79).»

48 MS *dona amix donara*.

50 *Etz anas*: *z* by-form used before vowel (see 41, 108, 816).

51 *verray* (= *venray*) fut. of *venir* is attested in Prov. (Appel, *Chrest.*, 46,5) as are other cases of assimilation of *-nr* > *rr* (*Girart*: 8126 *merrai*, 8254 *menrai*).

52 *comadamen* (cf. *comandamen* 201; n. 38).

53 MS *gran grau*: sense of *grat* 1513 supports Meyer's emendation, although *grah* 77 is equally justifiable.

54 *arculimen* (but *aculhimen* 193): cf. *arculhir* 116; Brunel *Chartes*, p. 452 *arculir*. An example of epenthetic *r* (Anglade, *Grammaire*, p. 205).

56-59 MS waterstained.

57 ALT *uelhas*: Meyer reads *uelhas*, explaining «*v* tombe devant *u* dans *uelhas* (<*voleas*) 57, *ulhas*, 82» (p. 1v). Neither *Girart* nor Appel (*Chrest.*) give exs. of such a form, and, according to Anglade (*Grammaire*, p. 146) «initial *v* se maintient.» Since scribe makes no distinction between *u* and *v*, either explanation is possible, but it appears more likely that initial *v* simply stands for the two letters *vu-* in actual pronunciation (*velhas* = *v*[*u*]*elhas*).

59 ALT *messange*.

63 Meyer emends *vol*[*rai*].

68 *dobero*: aphaeresis due to scribe. Meyer emends [*a*]*dobero*, as required by meter.

69 *so el*: Meyer emends *sus* (cf. 650). In view of MS *so*, one might also emend *sos* or *soz* (< *susum*) 'en haut,' instead of *sotz* (< *subtus*): cf. G. B. Pellegrini, *Appunti di grammatica storica del Provenzale* (Pisa, 1962), p. 268, ¶ 95.

70 Meyer emends *quan* [*lo*] *vi* on basis of syntax and meter.

73 MS *Menaray* (ALT *mendray*) *vos ay cũ companh a Paris cortegier*; the overlaid letter *a* (or *d*) is doubtful — but *menaray* is the more likely form (cf. 46). It appears as though the scribe has confused the simple future with the future of necessity ('avoir à') and has written both *menaray* and (*menar vos*) *ay*. Of the two futures, the latter is to be preferred in this context, in view of the previous verse *qu'eu an ab lui parlier*, and the fact that Bove is explaining to Guy why he must go along (*cum companh* has the sense

of «because you are my companion, I must take you to court in Paris»). The verse is in direct contrast to the simple futures in 45-46. One might also take *companh* as a vocative and drop *cum* (as Meyer does), thus emending both meter and syntax.

[78] Meyer reads *denant,* an alternate acceptable in this context.

[79] *gueiamen* doubtful reading (see n. 45).

[82] MS *ulhas* or *vlhas* (see n. 57).

[83] MS *li respon li r. q. ho s.* obvious errors.

[84] MS *motz* superscript over deletion.

[86] MS *ric riche.*

[88] MS first *so* superscript; *duc* superscript over *per.*

[93] *vayley*: what appears to be a *y* might be scribal error in anticipation of second *y*. However, Anglade (*Grammaire,* p. 159) cites the doublet *vaslet: vailet* as an example of *s* becoming *ï* before a consonant.

MS *Aremyer,* elsewhere *Azemar* (cf. 99), is an unattested variant of this name, doubtless invented by the scribe to satisfy the exigencies of this north-colored laisse. Emendation to *Azemier* serves to avoid confusion (see n. 100).

[95] MS *vestes la deberetz clier* doubtful reading. Meyer interprets *de bertz clier* (*bertz*: «peut-être le même que le français vair, sorte de fourrure.»); Chab. comments on the difficulty of this interpretation (*bertz* could hardly be < *uariu* 'variegated fur') and proposes correcting *bestz* (= 'vest'?). Neither explanation is satisfactory, since neither form is attested elsewhere.

Closer examination of the MS would probably guarantee *vestir* obscured by ink-stains from the page opposite. The rhyme word is certainly not *clier,* but *chier* with a stroke left off the *h* by the copyist (what appears to be an *l* is not written as usual).

Deberetz remains unattested, but is probably a variant form of the 2 plur. future *deuretz* by analogy with *temeretz.* (Note phonic affinity of labials -*b*- and -*m*-.)

[97] *lor me donatz* (= «Give them on my behalf»): a turn of phrase found elsewhere in *Daurel* (57 «Go to Aspremont for me»). See n. 748.

[98] *Ce* (= *se*): the copyist does not distinguish between *c* and *s.*

[100] *fier*: equivalent of Prov. *far* in this north-colored laisse.

MS *qui p.* emended by Meyer *que*; Chab. suggests *qu'i*, in my opinion the correct interpretation.

[101] MS *chivalier* deleted before *cavalgier*: OFr. *chivalier* (which occurs in 1803) is cited by R. Karch, *Die nord-französischen Elemente im Altprovenzalischen* (Heidelberg, 1901), p. 33, as an example of North-French influence on Provençal. The deletion indicates that the scribe first wrote the northern form (which he let stand in 1803), presumably under the influence of the -*ier* rhymes in this laisse.

[105] Meyer emends *a paregier,* adding syllable to *ric[he].* There is a better case for this emendation if one reads *apparegier* (= *aparelhar,* -*ejar* 'to prepare, to fit out'). However, the MS reading surpasses either conjecture (cf. *Girart,* p. 822, *pareisser*).

[106] *tradier*: scribal confusion between -*d*- and -*z*-; *ra* < *ar* metathesis (see p. 27). The northern form would be *targier* or *tardier* (as in 246), the Prov. *tardar.*

[107] MS *cŏphan.*

[110-111] The rhymes in these verses bear witness to the evident confusion of the scribe copying from a MS in which indentations were absent or faulty (e.g., XII, XXVIII, XL). Here, the scribe mistakenly begins to «correct»

rhymes from -*ir* to -*ier*, then realizes that he is copying a new laisse but fails to correct his «corrections.» There is a pause in the story after v. 109 — a night passes — and it would seem a logical place for a new paragraph. Neither *esclarier* nor *vister* is Prov. form (*esclairar, esclairir, esclarzir* 'to dawn'; *vestir* 'to don' or *vistar* 'to visit'), although *esclarzir* and *vestir* would have fit sense and meter perfectly.

On the basis of the rhyme alone, Meyer starts laisse IV at v. 112, emending *a vister* to *a juster*; Chab, rightly suggests correcting the rhymes and starting it at v. 110.

110 MS *can pres can pres.*

111 MS *le dui* (deleted) *duc Boves e G.* Meyer emends *a vister* to *a juster.*

117 *pre*: *re* < *er* metathesis (2003; cf. *ferca* 1407; in *Aigar* one finds *perparant* 264, *fremat* 453).

118 MS *elo* deleted after *sus.*

119 MS *Coms*: title of character confused (see also 149). Charlemagne is obviously addressing Duke Bove, not Count Guy.

120 MS *ab* (deleted) *ans queus vos layse tornier*: scribal confusion with following verse is evident. Meyer emends *ans qu'eu(s) vos lays(e) partir.* One might also read, as I choose to do, *que·ns vos layse[m]* which is supported by MS and by scribe's habit of dropping final *m* and *n*, a common trait in literary texts of Languedoc, Limousin, Agenais, Toulousain, Albigeois, according to Kurt Kutscha, *Das sogenannte n-mobile im alt-und neuprovenzalischen*, Romanistische Arbeiten, XXI (Halle, 1934), pp. 4, 79, 93. If subject were 1 sing., correct form would be *lais* (cf. 99, 359). The deletion indicates that the scribe first wrote *abans.*

126 Indentation (no capital).

129 *Avesques*: a North-French form; *arsebes*; a less learned form of *arcivesque* (see n. 151).

133 Meyer suggests correcting *Aminas mi ma seror; d.*; but Chab. disagrees, preferring *amenas mi ma sor*, based on 141 and 623 *de sa sor fai mercat.*

138 *Molra*: either a scribal error for pres. subj. *moira* (Pellegrini, *Appunti*, p. 252, ¶ 90) or dissimilation of intervocalic -*r*- of fut. *mora, morra* (cf. the discussion of $r > l$ by Knud Togeby, «Qu'est-ce que la dissimilation?» *RPh*, XVII [1964], 648 in his review of Rebecca R. Posner, *Consonantal Dissimilation in the Romance Languages*, Pub. Philol. Soc., XIX [Oxford, 1961] p. 105, 133 ff).

139 ALT *banier*: neither lesson is satisfactory, since neither Charles nor Oliver is customarily given the epithet 'Bavarian' or 'herald' (although the former is quite common in epic: Langlois, *Table*, p. 139, lists many exs. of *Bavier*, only one of which [in *Macaire*, 187] refers to Charles). The usual epithet for Charles in *Daurel* —*al vis clier*— was avoided because of the proximity of v. 141. Meyer suggests *lo ber* or *lo fier*, but Bavier, although unusual, is acceptable here and does no violence to the MS. *Banier*, on the other hand, does not fit the context at all.

141 *vi[s]*: cf. 156, 2165.

142 MS *abo m.*

143-144 The copyist erroneously interchanges the second hemistichs of these verses (blunder due to repetition of *fresca*). Read: *Ela fo fresca com roza de rozier / Sa color fresca fes la bel esgardier*. Unlike similar blunders in 28-29 and 150-151, syntax and meaning are too clear as MS stands to warrant editorial tampering.

[144] ALT *cum r.*

[145] MS *ape* deleted before *Boves* (cf. rhyme-word *apelier*). Meyer reads *Bobes.*

[146] MS letter deleted before *amic* (doubtful reading). One might easily interpret this lesson *del [D]anne Augier* (cf. *Fierabras; e lo Daynes Augier* 2913). F. Settegast, *ZRPh,* XXIX (1905), 413, suggests reading *Hermen* (= 'Armenier'), but Ogier le Danois is traditionally one of Charlemagne's peers and the father of Bove in *Daurel* as well as of Beuve in *Beuve de Hanstone.*

[148] MS *que eieu vos v.*

[149] MS *S dis lo coms*: it is obviously Bove who is answering the king (cf. 119).

[150-151] The copyist erroneously interchanges the second hemistichs of these verses (blunder due to repetition of *la·lh fay*) which as they stand in the MS — *Pren la lo rey .iii. ves la·lh fay bayzier / A l'arcivesques que K. la·lh fay donier* — mean roughly that «Ermenjart is kissed by the archbishop given to her by Charles.»

As emended in the text, the sense — «The king takes her [from Oliver]; Charles has her given (to him) / to the archbishop who has her kiss him [Bove] three times.» — is supported by v. 638 where Ermenjart is forced by Charles to kiss Guy three times to seal the marriage pact.

arcivesques: a French-influenced form (see Pellegrini, *Appunti,* ¶ 16); intervocalic $p > b$ in Prov. (cf. *arsebes* 129).

[153] MS *vist* (?) deleted after *los.*

[155] *destu[r]bier* (cf. *desturbier* 255). Speaking of the relationship between companionship and marriage, Flach (*Origines,* II, 477), using *Daurel* as an example, says: «le lien crée par l'un était de nature à nuire à l'autre.»

[160] ALT *s'asenha* (cf. *asenhal* 'banner') would permit the emendation *s'asenha [a] portier.* However, *senha* ('sign, mark, insignia') or *senhal* ('coat-of-arms, ornament, insignia') offer the proper sense of the verse: «and he takes the glove marked with [Charles'] insignia to carry it [as a sign of office]» or «He takes the glove bearing his [Charles'] insignia [symbolic of the office].» The former is preferable, since the *Daurel* author does not typically use infinitives as substantives.

[164] *quier* (= *car*).

[165] ALT *far n'an* (cf. n. 517).

[166] MS *fort* superscript over *fost* (?) deleted.

[171] Upper left-hand corner of 79^v is illegible.

[172] MS *Jhū: desamper = non ampar* 218.

[173] *Esmenjartz*: Kalbow (*Die germ. Personennamen,* p. 137) cites this and other exs. of *r > s* before cons.

[174] Indentation.

[180] MS *Guis* deleted before *g.*

[183] MS *Daries m. p. si cu* (?) *m.* What appears to be an *i* in *daries* may simply be an extra ligature.

[186] MS *oῑpoten*:

[196] General sense of this verse could be that the citizens fête Bove, Guy and their company with banquets and turn over the fortress to them. *viala* (as in Lat. *uīctuālia*) is clear enough: cf. *Jaufré* 4240 *vitala* 'vivres'; but *mandamen* poses a problem. Citing this verse as well as 1106 and 2148, Levy (*Suppl.,* V. 90-91) disagrees with Meyer's glossary ('gouvernement, juridiction'), suggesting that *ausor* is the usual epithet for *palais* in *Daurel.*

Miss Hackett suggests 'forteresse' with a question-mark (*Girart* 8364); similar meanings are found in Godefroy, V, p. 139 and C. H. Livingston's edition of Gautier le Leu (Cambridge, Mass., 1951), p. 366 (his line reference should be to VIII, 151, and not to VIII, 153). Many citations include such adjectives as *haut* and *maistre*, implying some sort of upper hall in a castle (but *not* a tower, nor a part necessarily used for defence).

203 Meyer reads *mulher*.

204-205 The meaning (*vis-à-vis* 203) of these verses is unclear and their syntax uncertain as they stand in the MS. Both syntax and sense would be served by inverting the first hemistichs, reading *Denan la dona ela pres a tombar / E Daurel vieula, gen si van deportar*. *tombar* seems to indicate that Beatrix did tumbling tricks in front of Ermenjart (although nowhere else in *Daurel* is there mention of her performing); however, one might interpret 203-204 «Now you see the jongleur's wife falling [on her knees to pay homage] before Lady [Ermenjart].»

si van deportar could refer to Daurel and his wife, to the duke and duchess or to everyone present (= 'on s'amuse'). Cf. also 169 *E Daurel vieula e mena alegrier* which lends support to suggested emendation.

206 ALT can L.

210 Meyer emends [*tot*] *en riba de mar*.

211 Meyer emends *que* [*sol*] *del port* and provides this explanation for *ondrat* (and *orratz* 413) in glossary: «honoré, qui est dans une situation considérable» (cf. *FEW*, IV, 464 *honorare;* OFr. *honoré* 'digne de respect').

214 Meyer emends (in his *errata*) *vieuras*. Chab. remarks that *vieurat* (= '*vivrez*') is a Gascon form (see p. 32).

222 MS *cal* (?) deleted after *loc* (which means 'somewhere' in this context).

227 *covider*: Meyer (p. xxxvii) explains the mixture of rhymes in laisse VIII (227 [misread *covidar*], 229, 230, 238-262) in these words: «Mais on n'a qu'à ramener tous les infinitifs [-*ier*] à la terminaison -*ar* pour que les rimes deviennent uniformes d'un bout à l'autre de la tirade.» One might, on the other hand, reverse Meyer's proposal and, starting a new laisse at 224 (where there is a definite break in the action and a change in scene), emend the rhymes in -*ar* to -*ier* after this point. Can we really know whether this laisse is composed of two «tirades» which have contaminated each other's rhyme, or one in which the scribe did not distinguish between -*ar* and -*ier* rhymes?

234 *colgas m'an vos*: Guy's brutal directness is typical of twelfth-century mores; see similar exs. cited by Jeanne Lods, «Quelques aspects de la vie quotidienne chez les conteurs du XIIᵉ siècle,» *CCM*, IV (1961), 35.

235 MS *G. lot.* Hollyman remarks (*Vocabulaire féodal*, p. 161) à propos of *Roland* (vv. 1230, 1251, 1337, 3456) that «*culvert* est étroitement associé à *glutun;* le gloton était également un pécheur et cela non seulement dans le sens indiqué par son nom, car il est en outre appelé *lechierre*.»

237 MS *sertas c.*

239 MS *desoudier* superscript over *dessouner* (deleted): a variant of the word entered by Levy as *desoptar* 'surprendre.' Cf. Tobler-Lomm., II, 1673 *desoter*. The scribe has written *desoudier* = 'take dupe by surprise,' a selection indicating hesitation before an unfamiliar or unclear form.

240 *trop lo podes amier* = 'you love him too much.'

241 MS *queus*; *lieiver*.

242 MS *.ii.* superscript over deleted numeral. *a mujer*: a variant-spelling unattested elsewhere in Prov. but MS is supported by *prendes* [*a*] *molher*

147; *Girart* 518 *la prent a muller li cons palaz,* 579 *aves pres a muillier.* Meyer reads *amuier,* justifiably emends *anuier* 'causer de l'ennui.'

[243] MS *que ieu lausiral e jes nõ pot escapapier: ausiral* has a hook in the final *l* which suggests scribe's attempt to change this letter into an *i* with accent stroke. For *nõ,* either *no·m* or *non* is satisfactory reading.

[256] MS *Fai so.*

[257] MS *desampaner*: cf. North-French *desemparer* 'leave a place' (Godefroy, IX, 330b). Meyes reads *descumpaner* 'fausser compagnie, abandonner' unattested in Raynouard. Prov., like OSp., had *am-* beside *em-parer* 'to protect'; *des-* 'to leave (unprotected), to abandon' < Lat. *anteparāre,* see Y. Malkiel, «Fuentes indígenas y exóticas de los substantivos y adjetivos verbales en *-e,*» *RLiR,* XXIV (1960), 213.

[262] MS *mosstier.*

[263] MS *desamplar* (?)

[268] ALT *La vosta mor; desebrar*: The copyist, influenced by *ausira* in the preceding verse, misinterprets the word division of *nost'amor* (ALT *vost'amor*) and the meaning of the rhyme-word *desebrar* or *desevrar* ('séparer, priver' < Lat. *sēperāre,* see Y. Malkiel, *RLiR,* XXIV [1960], 239-242) which he evidently took to be a compound of *obrar* 'mettre en oeuvre.' The sense intended by the author is not «He will bring about your death,» a repetition of v. 268, but rather «He will destroy [annul, separate, deprive us of] our love.» *Desevrar* is related to *dessoivrement,* a medieval form of divorce or annulment (see Gautier, *La Chevalerie,* p. 360).

[270-271] «He only said it to test whether any man could deceive you.»

[272] MS *que* deleted before *quieu; amar* superscript over *fizar* deleted (introduced in anticipation of 273).

[274] MS *que jo neis*: there are at least two solutions for this obscurity: 1) emend *Que [Guis] neis l.* «For Guy himself killed him when they went hunting together!» 2) Retain MS reading, interpreting *io* as interjection (Anglade, *Grammaire,* p. 370 *oye! yey! oy!,* exs. which might fit the sense required here) and read *Que — io! neis l.,* a construction unattested elsewhere in *Daurel.* In my opinion, the former is preferably simpler and clearer.

[275] Indentation.

[275-281] Cf. *Jourdain de Blaivie*:

> Un fil il orent, plus bel ne convint iestre,
> Plus de mil home en loent Deu et servent.
> Il le tramistrent Renier le fil Gontelme,
> Cil le leva des sains fons et de l'aigue.
> Jordains ot non et tuit ainsiz l'apellent,
> Plus crut l'anfant teuls dolors et teuls guerre, ...(26)

[278] *bateie* (and *batie* 279) OFr. = Prov. *batejar,* (cf. Godefroy, I, 576 *baptoier* (variant-spellings *batier, bateier*) e.g., *La le tienge [l'enfant] en funz e bateit.*

[281] One might also emend *[tray] gran afan* on basis of *tray gran pasio* 5.

[284] MS *recobaratz.*

[285] *guah*: metathesis of *gauh* 823, 866. Levy (*Suppl.* IV, 86) notes this form in *Daurel* and a similar one *gauch* (*Passion* 1751; also *guah* 1752) and remarks: «Ist die Forme haltbar?»

[286] ALT *norritz* (cf. *norriger* 96; *noirir* 1584). There is no accent over the first *i.*

[287] Meyer emends *.i. [tal] desturbamen* on basis of meter. *Ardena*: see p. 40.

[290] *pros* is feminine form of *prodis,* invariable in masc. and fem. (*tantas pros daimas* 496; *Girart* 7718 *proz*).

[294] Though not unaware of other possible interpretations of this rather obscure verse, I suggest keeping it and reading: «They hunt him everywhere, and especially in the mast [oak and beech acorn] fields,» on the basis of the following evidence.

los refers to *.i. singlar;* the *s* can be explained in several ways: (1) abbreviation of *singlar* erroneously interpreted by scribe (cf. 370); explanation not supported by meter, unless one wished to read these verses as alexandrines. (2) *lo·s* = *se lo* is most suitable for this verse, but does not help in 370. (3) Scribal error for *lo;* hard to accept because of repetition in 370.

cas: (1) could = 'dogs' permitting one to read *Pertot* [*asalh*] *los cas* «he [attacks] dogs everywhere.» (2) = 'broken, weak' (cf. Levy *Suppl.* I, 223) which does not fit context. (3) = 3 sing. pres. ind. of *cassar* (cf. Lommatzsch, *Leben,* I, 20a, 8 *catz* and II, 4, 54 *chas,* both 1 sing.)

dabant: (1) = 3 sing. Prov. form of Godefroy, II, p. 424 *davancier, davancir* «mettre en avant, prévenir» with sense here of putting out bundles (cf. Godefroy, IV, p. 287 *glane* «botte poignée») of food or gleanings either as bait or to keep boar away from inhabited places. (2) = *davant* 'devant' (Mistral, *Trésor,* I, 702 attests forms *dabant* in Béarnais, *dabans* in Languedocien, meaning 'avant, plutôt', here *dabant* = 'avant tout.'

l'aglan: Meyer reads *la glan* in text, but suggests «p-ê. *l'aglan* = 'gland'.» *Glan* generally being masc. in both OFr. and Prov., the reading *l'aglan* seems preferable and is supported by the following example from Raynouard III, 473: *En lo boscatge porcx gardan / A la pastura del aglan* (*Brev. d'Amor*) and by the well-known affinity of boars for mast.

The remaining difficulty, the absence of a preposition meaning 'in' might be solved by emending *Pertot lo·s cas, dabant tot* [*e*]· *l aglan.*

[300] *mon* (= *mout*) is a common nasalized variant of *molt.*

[304] MS *guiren:* The scribe has clumsily corrected a *d* into an *e. Guiren* = 'garant, protecteur' (cf. *Chan. Crois. Alb.* 3121, 3209, 3449).

[307] *Puesca:* cf. *FEW* IX, p. 231 *posse* 'être en état de faire qch., ayant la force, l'autorité nécessaire.' As long as Gui has strength, Bove need fear nothing while he lives, for Guy is his sworn companion and will protect him.

[314-329] Change of hand: these lines are written in a style very formal compared with the cursive style used elsewhere. Ligatures are very pronounced, *r* and *z* are virtually identical, capitals are ornate and, most important, the text is quite obscure at several points.

[314] *causea:* = OFr. *cauchie, chaussie* 'chemin.'

[315] MS *causural* (cf. 243). Meyer reads *venaro* here (and *raro* in 317 and 324; *creiras* in 328) mistakenly in my opinion, since there is little evidence to support the change of *z* to *r* in these cases. (The only examples cited by Anglade, *Grammaire,* p. 158, are from Meyer's edition of *Daurel:* «*venaro* pour *venaso, raro* pour *razo, creras* pour *crezas*; des changements de ce genre ont été signalés, mais aux XIVe-XVe siècles, en Languedoc, en Roussillon, en Limousin.»)

e = *en* (cf. Lommatzsch, *Leben* II, 17,7; 21, 41). *Venazo* = *venazon* 'la chasse' (Levy *Suppl.* VIII, 624). The verse can be rendered «For he will kill the duke while he is at the hunt.»

[316] MS *el blalens de Beto: blalens* or *plalens* makes no known sense whatsoever, and were one to emend it to *balet* «gallery» one would still have to reject *Beto* in this context. It is inconceivable that Guy, no lover of babies,

would upon his arrival go into Beton's room, gallery or nursery. Why not assume that the second scribe has confused *Beto* with *Buvo*? This emendation is supported by *Bo[v]es* in 317. The emendation to *palais* is, of course, arbitrary, and one might prefer *balet*, although this word, not found otherwise in *Daurel*, is rather rare in Prov.

317 ALT *raro*: Meyer remarks in his note to this verse «—*Raro*, ou *p.-ê. razo*, l'*r* ressemble à un *z* dans *tracio* (v. 314), *intret* (v. 316), *conquero* (v. 321), *cramba* (v. 323), *creras* (v. 328), *vostre* (v. 329); pour *venaro* (v. 315) l'*r* n'est pas douteuse.»

318 *casarem*: Meyer emends *casarom* to match *farom* 26. Chab.'s suggestion *casa hom* makes little sense here, where a 1 plur. future is needed. One could emend on basis of 319, *Bel companh, .i. singlar casarem [nos]* leaving out *senher*, which is mere padding.

319 Meyer suggests *lo conquerrom* (cf. 318, 321).

320 *mot mi sat bo* (=*saber bo* 'sembler bon' a common locution whose original meaning 'to taste good' shines through), elsewhere *sap bo* 334; *saup bo* 1826. Meyer renders this locution 'être avantageux à quelqu'un' in four passages of *Flamenca* (p. 395); cf. *Daurel* 334.

321 Meyer suggests *non er tan fort* (cf. 342).

322 MS *aportatar*

323 *cramba* (see p. 27).

324 ALT *raro* (cf. n. 315).

328 *crezas*: Meyer reads *creras*, although this is as close to a distinct *z* as one will find in the second scribe's passage, which ends here. *Crezas* is a pres. subj. used as imperative (cf. Anglade, *Grammaire*, p. 296) or rather a prohibitive in a negative context.

330 MS *crezes* doubtful reading, partly effaced, *r* superscript. Meyer reads *creires*, but a subjunctive form is required here (cf. 328, 329) and *crezes* is either pres. ind. or imp. subj. (cf. Anglade, *Grammaire*, p. 296) while *creiretz* is attested only as 2 plur. future (Appel, *Chrest.* 7, 305).

332 MS *sermo*.

332–333 «you are speaking foolishness. We shall quarrel over it.»

336 Indentation.

339 *venados*: The reduction of *r* before *s* is quite common in the Prov. epic (see *desties* 340 *saumies* 568; *Aigar* 808 *guerries*; *Roland à S.* 1235 *saumies*).

340 *els* = *en los*

345 MS *ploro*.

346 MS *montar* superscript over *mond*-(?) deleted.

353 *enansar* = 'réussir' (*Jaufré* 5380) or 'faire avancer l'entreprise' (Levy *Suppl.* II, p. 415).

354 Levy's entry for *enansar* (*Suppl.* II, p. 415) questions Meyer's reading *a l'aporta[t]*: «schreibe *a la porta*?»

363 *alagar* (cf. *alargar* 1720).

365 MS *port*: scribe has neglected final stroke of *c*.

366 MS *sans a m*.

368 MS *adesviar* or *adesniar*: although one might read *adesviar* (as a transitive verb *a + desviar*) in the sense of 'detour into,' the context supports the emendation to *adesar* 'approach, attain' which is found as a hunting term in Godefroy I, p. 99; e.g., *Brut*, vv. 819-822 Ivor Arnold ed.:

> Li reis, ço dient, ad fait vié
> Qu'il n'i ait bersé ne chacié

Ne adesee veneisun
En la forest, se par lui nun.

The verse appears to mean simply that *Ardena*, a very thick forest, is unsuitable for hunting; therefore, Bove and Guy must catch the boar before he enters it, and being on horseback must leave their unmounted hunters behind to accomplish this. Meyer's emendation *adesmar* 'estimer' has little to recommend it in this context, since the *i* seems assured by the MS, but is nevertheless a possibility.

370 *los e.* (see n. 294).

379 *l'espaular*: either an infinitive used as noun or southern form of Godefroy's *espaulier* 'partie de l'armure qui protège l'épaule' (*Lexique*, p. 205).

380 MS *lie*

381 Meyer's reading *eversar* 'renverser' supported by Godefroy III, 674; e.g., *Beuve* I 4570 *et abatu et deseur enversé*.

383 *el* = *en lo.*

384 MS *deiginolhos*; *apla* deleted before *a parlar.*

390 MS *be* superscript.

397 ALT *compahs*: The *y* may be an imperfectly-formed *h*; MS *cū mo f.*

401 *e vostes spieut e vos*: scribe has written final *s* on *voste* instead of beginning *e* of *espieut* (cf. 461) and has repeated *e vos* from the beginning of the verse, which clearly means «Place the boar's teeth in my side and plant your pike in the boar» (see 443-444). *Spieu* is found as a variant of *espieu* in *Roland à S.* (186, 801) and Grafström (*Etude*, p. 86, ¶21) cites several exs. of lack of prosthetic *e* after vowel in *Boecis, Sainte Foy*, Toul. and Alb. dialects.

    voste: Anglade, *Grammaire*, p. 196, remarks: «*R* peut disparaître dans le groupe consonne (surtout *s*) + *tr*;» citing the following essentially unstressed words from *Daurel*: *noste, voste* and *ente* (=*entre* 438); this reduction is found in Modern Prov. *noste, voste.*

403 Meyer reads *tornat*, not supported by context. I prefer Chab.'s suggestion *torvat* = 'troublé' (*Flamenca* 4027 *destorbar*; Levy *Suppl.* II, 170), although one might also emend *trobat* (error due to scribal metathesis) «You will not be called a liar nor found out.»

405-409 See pp. 106-107.

417 MS *vulh* superscript. Sense of verse is «Of all his possessions, you shall have half.»

418 Cf. Albéric *Alexandre* 61 «Tal regart fay cum leu qui est preys.»

423 MS *sel el.* Sense: «If he falls into my hands, neither city nor fortress can save him.»

425 MS *el no es elcabatz.* There are two distinct possibilities for the interpretation of the second hemistich: (1) *nŏ* = *non* «I have killed you; he is not yet dispatched.» (2) *nŏ* = *nom*; *el* = *e l* «I have killed you, and the lineage is finished.» (cf. Godefroy V, 522a for *non* 'lignage.'

428 MS *f. e vos.* Vv. 426-428 are cited by J.D.M. Ford («*To bite the dust and Symbolic Lay Communion*,» *PMLA*, XX [1905], 197-240) in his list of Old French and Provençal exs. of communion by means of grass or foliage in the absence of clergy; G. L. Hamilton («The Sources of the Symbolic Lay Communion,» *Romanic Review*, IV [1913], 221-240) supplements Ford with numerous exs. drawn from folklore and history. R. K. Bowman, *The Connections of the Geste des Loherains with other French Epics and Medieval Genres*, Diss. Columbia Univ. (New York, 1940), p. 56, mistakenly cites *Daurel* as a case of communion with three blades of grass; Sister

212   DAUREL ET BETON

M. Gildea, *Expressions of Religious Thought and Feeling in the Chansons de Geste*, Diss. Catholic Univ. (Washington, 1943), pp. 245 ff, does not include *Daurel* among her numerous examples. Kenneth Urwin («La Mort de Vivien et la genèse des chansons de geste,» *Romania*, LXXVIII [1957], 392-404) discusses the liturgical history of the lay sacrament and concludes that the institution existed as late as the twelfth century.

⁴³¹ Cf. *Jaufré* 9046 *Aver trag lo cor a pessas d'intz lo ventre* translated by Brunel «Le cœur déchiré en pièces dans le corps.»

⁴³⁴ MS *ni ne m.* Bove advises Guy to eat some of his heart. See pp. 106-107.

⁴³⁵⁻⁴³⁹ Bove's prayer is not among the eighty-three enumerated by E.-R. Labande, «Le 'Credo' épique: à propos des prières dans les chansons de geste,» *Recueil de travaux offert à M. Clovis Brunel* (Paris, 1955), II, 62-80, who includes *Daurel* in list of works which don't offer any examples.

⁴³⁷ Read *S.M.D., ie·us prec, si·us platz.*

⁴⁴³ Meyer reads *aficat* (*Girart* 2670 [*fichar*]), and starts laisse XIV at this point, distinguishing between rhymes in -*atz* and -*at* (p. xlvii): «Quoique *at* et *atz* soient bien distincts, néanmoins on remarque un petit nombre de finales en *at* égarées parmi celles en *atz*, vv. 590, 608, 955, 980, 1243, 1251, 1263, 1270, 1550.» and emending to -*at*[*z*] 394, 402, 403, 409, 411, 412, 442 and to -*at*(*z*) 445, 446, 449, 450, 452, 455, 456, 461, 475.

⁴⁴⁵ MS *menit p.* Meyer emends *pertuzat*(*z*) (cf. *FEW* VIII, 221a *percutere*: OFr. *percuter* 'transpercer' Prov. *percutir* 'frapper, heurter').

⁴⁴⁶ MS *cle* deleted before *cel.*

⁴⁴⁸ MS *Ehi c.* (cf. 472). Rhyme word in -*an* testifies to corruption of this verse. Meyer emends *esclasat* «pressé, qui se hâte (comme celui que est appelé par le tocsin)» which Chab. finds «peu acceptable» suggesting *esglaiat* 'fear' (Levy *Suppl.* III, 227). Levy cites this verse and 856 *esclesat* under the entry *esclat, esglat* 'bruit, fracas' (*Suppl.* III, 169) and not under *esclatar* 'erglänzen.' *Esclasan* could conceivably be a scribal error for *esclaman* (cf. Wartburg, *FEW* III, 274 Modern Prov. (*s'*) *esclama* 's'écrier'). *FEW* II, p. 746 **classum* cites OProv. *aclassar* 'faire du bruit' as a 12th c. form.

⁴⁵¹ MS *meiradis*(?): Scribe tried to rewrite the last three letters of this word; what remains looks like *meiradis,* which makes no known sense.

⁴⁵⁴ «I had nothing to gain from it.»

⁴⁶³ MS *espeiatatz* (see n. 464).

⁴⁶⁴ MS *quel duc al mort.* Vv. 463-464 are obscure, but can be solved in the following manner: emend to *espleiatz* 'agir' on basis of *espleitar* 852 (cf. *Girart* 9281 *espleites* 'profiter de l'occasion,' Wartburg, *FEW* III, 310b *explicare*: OProv. *esplegar* 's'occuper de, réussir, employer'; N.B. *esplicar* 'expliquer' is not attested before 14th c.), read, as Meyer does *Quil duc as mort* [*trop*] *as fah gran pecat,* or accept, as I prefer to do, the MS *Que·l =* 'Que [tu] as tué le duc.'

The passage can be rendered: «'Traitor,' said one of them, 'you have behaved badly. You have killed the duke; you have committed a great sin, of which we will all be accused.'» One might prefer a comma after 463.

⁴⁶⁹ «I wouldn't think of it, not for anything in God's gift.» (cf. 606).

⁴⁷⁵ MS *gauh* written over by *gaia* (?). Meyer suggests *mas de fors a p.* which is the reading one would expect here.

⁴⁷⁶ Indentation.

⁴⁸⁵ MS *en ar glot.*

[491] Laisse XV and XVI are considered by Meyer as one laisse (in *-ar*), in spite of indentation at 511 (see note). It is quite true that all the *-ier* rhymes can easily be emended to *-ar*, and that mixed laisses of this type are common in the Prov. epic (Meyer cites *Aigar* and *Chan. Crois. Alb.*, pp. xli ff), but I choose to respect the scribe's indentations. Thus, the concordance between my text and Meyer's is as follows:

M. XIII & XIV = K. XIII vv. 394-475
M. XV = K. XIV 476-490
M. XVI = K. XV & XVI 491-533

[493] ALT *destirier*: either spelling is acceptable, (see Godefroy II, p. 687 *detirer;* e.g., *Lors commenca fort a plorer / E ses chevels a detirier; Beuve* I 3647, 6719, 4872 *descirer, deskira*) but MS seems clearly to read *c*.

[499] *decosta ce estier*: *ce* = *se*; *estier* = *estar* 'se tenir debout, demeurer' (cf. *Girart* 4108 for *estar* inf. used as substantive). Sense of this verse is «She saw Guy, who was standing next to her.»

[500] *ssospirier*: The double *s* is undoubtedly a scribal trait, more common in the later medieval centuries.

[506] MS *-ssar* of *menassar* deleted; *-sier* superscript.

[510] MS *cor vos*.

[511] Indentation. Meyer remarks: «Le ms. indique à tort, par une capitale, une nouvelle tirade.» Verse may be rendered «Beware of appearances in this matter.»

[515] «She tears out pieces of her delicate flesh.» (Levy *Suppl*. VI, 546 cites as example of *prim* «delicat» verse 2489 from *Flamenca*: *Lo cuer ac blanc e prim e tenre*.)

[517] *lan* obscure: One may interpret *l'an* = 'on' (13th c. northern form attributable to scribe) «One would have heard more than 10,000 cry out.» or as 'l'ont' in which case one would render the verse «More than 10,000 heard her cry out: 'Oh! my lord the duke...'» on the condition of emending the conditional *auzirat* to the past participle *auzit*.

My choice of the former rests on the MS and on similar lines in *Jourdain* (135-143), in which the citizens *plorent por lor seignor... «He! Girart sire, com mar i fustez vouz...»*

[522] *Geta·iss* (cf. n. 500; n. 50).

[523] MS *e tan r*.

[530] *sostrar* = *sosterar* or *sostrerar*

[532] MS *pres de l.*: The *de* cannot be construed logically here, and the meter favors its elimination. *Arma* (cf. n. 565).

[534] *sostreratz* (cf. 530, 1068): Schultz-Gora (*Altprov. Elementarbuch*, ¶63) remarks: «Recht selten ist die Assimilation bei getrennten Konsonanten: *circulum* > *celcle* neben *cercle* (see *Daurel* 675 *colssel*, 1511 MS *plalafres*; n. 1754 *artre*).

[537] MS *snehors*.

[539] MS *A. non .xv. somiers*. (See n. 339 for *somiers*).

[548] *co sai* (cf. *cossi* 587).

[556] MS *ne* superscript over *las*.

[560-561] «If it were (possible) through grieving, know this for true, we have grieved so much for him (already) that he would have been brought back to life.»

[562] *Parlar* is obviously faulty rhyme as is *cassar* 599 in same laisse. Both are grammatically correct and can possibly be explained as vestiges of an older assonanced poem.

[565] *mermatz* (= 'diminished') Anglade, *Grammaire*, p. 186, remarks: «Devant *m n* peut passer à *r* par dissimilation» (e.g., *animum* > *arma*, **minimare* > *mermar*).

[566] *logadiers* (= *soudadiers*) is a manifest cognate of 'loyer' < *locare*. For the importance of large sums of money in hiring mercenaries and keeping vassals faithful to the medieval lord, see Flach, *Origines*, II, p. 502; Ernest Neumann, *Der Söldner (soudoyer) in Mittelalter, nach den französischen (und provenzalischen) Heldenepen* (Diss. Marburg, 1905).

[568] *ve·us vo·nh* 'voyez-vous-en' (grammatically the equivalent of 'vous en voyez-vous').

[569] *fis esmeratz* 'highly refined' (= OFr. *fins esmerez*).

[570-572] Although Guy, as the sworn companion of Bove, is legal heir to half of his estate, he must first pay homage to the overlord in order to enter into full possession of the fief. Guy, who has been receiving the *rentes* from all the land between Bordeaux and Agen (cf. 197-201), can afford to offer the king a very handsome sum of money.

[577] MS *quel t.*

[579] MS *ei* superscript over *n* of *dinat*.

[580] ALT *cant a·n* 'Quant il en a' (*a·n* = *a en* unattested elsewhere in *Daurel*, where usual form would be *n'a*); Meyer reads *cant au* «Quant il entend» which seems preferable in this context, although one might prefer to interpret *cant an* «since they have» or «now that they have.»

[584] MS *at* (?) deleted before *ac; ab* superscript.

[593] MS *.x. gras* (= *degra* 'degré').

[594] MS *ua* (?) deleted after *los*.

[606] MS *cieitatz*.

[607] MS *R.e.* [*dis la dona* (superscript) *so que eieu d.*

[612] MS *nom magatz*.

[615] MS *t* of *contendre* superscript.

[630] MS *do* (?) deleted before *aiatz*. Meyer suggests correcting *tracher no sia mos enfans apelatz*.

[631] ALT *temais*, unlikely, since (*se*) *tener per pagatz* is such a common expression in *Daurel* (cf. 897, 1015, 1211). I suggest *tenia* = *tenga, tenha;* the pres. subjunctive is exactly parallel to *sia* in 630.

[633] *postats*: Meyer emends *Mai val* [*us*] *coms que no fa po*[*e*]*statz*. It is not quite clear what the rank of a *poestat* (< *potestate*) was, but the relationship inferred here between a count and *poestat* was certainly that of «haut baron» and «vassal roturier» (see Flach, *Origines*, II, p. 511). «Roturier» would be the normal meaning for Poitou, where the domain of the free-holder («l'homme de poeste») could be vast (K. Baldinger, «Le Champ onomasiologique du roturier,» *RLiR*, XXVI [1962], 329-331). In *Jaufré* (9727) and *Chan. Crois. Alb.* (8236) he is a 'puissant personnage, seigneur,' Wartburg, *FEW*, IX, 254, cites ex. of *poestat* = 'gouverneur d'une ville' in thirteenth century Provence.

[636] Read *si·us platz*.

[638] MS *ple* deleted before *pel*.

[641] *Parga* = 3 sing. pres. subj. *parcer* 'pardonner,' but the sense of the verse should be «may lightening strike you before you return home!»

[644] Indentation.

[646] MS *Fort l.*: [*a*] needed for syntax and meter. Meyer emends *fors* [*de*].

651 *Dauretz lo joglar bo*: according to Chab. *Dauretz* is a Gascon form. The rhyme and syntax suggest that the redactor, faced with the northern French *jogleor*, had to rearrange the Prov. word order to come up with a rhyme in *-o*.

653 ALT *pahor*: the *h* is doubtful.

657 MS *Eetro*.

658 *lei = lai*.

663 Note absence of relative here and in 687. One could emend *tro [que] sia* on basis of 657, but this would not be supported by meter.

671 MS *lom mausis*.

673 *durada* 'délai' (Chab.).

680 MS *a* superscript after *vos; ques* (deleted) *queus*.

682 MS *fai* (deleted) *aves*.

683 *cosseh* (cf. 15, note).

686 Indentation. Unsatisfactory rhyme-word and *le* in next verse indicate northern influence.

687 Verse appears to mean, «Guy will comfort him until he returns to his senses (?)», but context requires something on the order of: «Charles needs no comforting, and his good sense will not return to him.»

688 MS *Per* is abbreviated here for first time in text.

690 Hypermetric: read *E·l venc. Pon* = 'point'.

698 *malapres* = 'malapris, grossier.' Meyer reads mistakenly *mal l'a pres*.

700 MS *v* of *voles* is doubtful and appears to have been made over into *foles*.

701 MS Verse begins with deletion superscript over deletion, both undecipherable. Sense appears to be: «I'll have (the child) taken care of on the strand (bank) in the sea.» (See Levy *Petit*, p. 210 *gra, gras* «coupure par laquelle la mer communique avec un étang du littoral.») *Gras* is a cognate of **grava* = «grève» (*FEW* IV, 254). The rhyme calls for *gres* 'terrain graveleux').

705 MS *lha* deleted after *ma*.

706 ALT *lo tieu*.

709 MS *lorx* (?).

715 *Irla* (=*isla* 1657, *irlanda* 1828). Anglade, *Grammaire*, p. 158, remarks: «Il peut aussi se produire une différenciation de *s* en *r*: on a ainsi *almorna* et *almosna; isnel* et *irnel...*»

716 MS *naisilinetata*: first *ta* deleted.

721 MS *lo leo* or *l'olco*: This verse and 722 are obscure. The context certainly cannot admit a lion, and *l'olco*, which Chab. suggests = «barques»?) remains unattested. The context calls for some sort of structure or dwelling place with good walls (cf. 722 *am bel mur*). The lesson in the MS is presumably a scribal error: *lo lco* for *lo loc* by metathesis. The emendation *lo loc* (= 'dwelling') offers the most satisfactory solution, and is supported by Wartburg, *FEW*, V, 386b *localis*: OProv. *logal* «lieu, terrain, demeure (cf. 10, which one might emend on basis of this entry to *hun [lo]cal*); FEW V, 391-2 *locus*: OProv. *loc, loic* «hameau, localité, gîte, maison de campagne». Levy (*Suppl.* IV, 416) gives three examples of *loc* «ortschaft» one of which bears on the context here: in a verse from B. de Born, *Gisortz, aut luoc et aut paes, luoc* refers to Gisors, an almost impregnable fortress.

722 *viro* (= *virol* 'tower'). The sense of this verse is inconsistent with 718-719, unless the poet is describing an old abandoned fortress of the type used to defend the coast against the Moors. It is quite probable that such a

building would have strong walls, a gate and towers, but would be lacking in the amenities to which a child of Beton's class would be accustomed.

[725] *bauza*: here and in 729, a variant-spelling of *baizar*; the usual meaning of *bauzar* 'tromper, trahir' is not suitable in this context.

[726] MS the fourth letter of *envolopa* is smudged.

[728] *Aprot* (= 'ensuite'). Gautier (*La Chevalerie*, p. 104) renders these verses «Sur les yeux et le visage de l'enfant les baisers pleuvent; et on lui chante déjà des berceuses. Pas n'est besoin de parler des prières.»

[736] MS This metrically deficient verse inserted between lines by scribe, probably to fill an obvious lacuna after 735 (737 begins in the middle of a dialogue between Guy and Ermenjart).

[740] MS *fais lo* (?): the *o* appears to have been corrected from an *e*.

[742] MS *.G. ranbe.*

[744] MS *bĕ.*

[748] *trobe* = *trobei* (Chab.); the *me* appears to be a dative: «I found Beton dead at my side,» but I find no other examples of this syntax in *Daurel*, except for the imperative *vay me* 57 and *lor me* 97 constructions.

[754] *finavatz*: cited by Levy (*Suppl.* III, 493) as example of figurative use of *finar* 'finir, payer, régler un compte.' Chab. translates: «Vous me payiez d'un plus grand mensonge» and rejects Meyer's interpretation of *finar* = *fenher* 'feindre.'

[755] MS *ques no*. «Because I know it well and even better than you would wish me to know it.»

[762] MS *a donatz* superscript.

[763] MS *s. ilhi pels. ishi* is a variant form of *issir* found in *Passion* (p. 142) and *Chan. Crois. Alb.* (2049).

[764] MS *mon* = *m'en*, although one might prefer to read *no·m* (interpreting *mon* as scribal error) thus inverting the meaning of the verse completely («I beg you not to kill me» instead of «I beg you to do me in»).

[767] MS *cant* superscript over -*tz* (?) deleted.

[770] MS *r* of *cornadors* superscript over ink blot.

[771] *vai*, the sing. imperative form (cf. 57, 66) is used with a plural here as in 610. However, *vai* may be interpreted as simply an interjection («eh bien») in this context, with the true imperative being the rhymeword *cornatz*.

[778] MS *.i.* superscript after *fo.*

[783] MS *l'efan le b.* metathesis (cf. 807).

[784] MS deletion after *risia.*

[790] MS *ia* of *piatatz* smudged.

[793] MS *das* superscript over *agar.*

[797] Sense of this verse and the following one is «Alas! [If] you should point him out to the traitor, sir, he would kill him.» One might emend (as does Meyer) the *ay* to *si*, in order to provide the causal «if,» but the *ay* is quite acceptable in this context (cf. 880, 884).

[798] MS *l* deleted before *vas.* Meyer emends *auzir[i]a*, although *auzira* is already a conditional (< Lat. plup. ind.).

[801] *aribatz* = 'sauvé.'

[804] *estais*, which Meyer interprets as a reflexive, is 2 plur. imperative.

[809] «You will be the better for it, as long as you live.»

[812] MS *ses ag a.*

[816] *Daz* (= *davas* 2152 'de, du côté de') cf. *daus* 1997.

[820] MS *Ebrartz* (deleted) *Ebrartz.*

[820-821] MS The rhyme-words have been cut off in binding.

828 *Ostat!*: cf. *Passion* 2324 «assez! ne parlez pas ainsi.»

834 MS *f* in *far* appears to have been corrected from *p*. The meaning of the second hemistich is far from clear. Meyer reads *de faren re magar*, «corrompu (?)» which makes little sense. *Agarar* 'regarder' is to be preferred in this context to *amagar* 'cacher' (see *FEW* XVI, 497 *magan* (got.) where *magar* is attested as variant of *amagar* 'plier, envelopper'). I suggest interpreting this verse «It is to my advantage to do this right away,» although one could also read «It behooves me not to do this at all» putting this verse in the mouth of Daurel, as suggested by Chab. who may be correct in seeing this line as «la réunion du premier hémistiche d'un vers et du second d'un autre.» If we accept this explanation, Daurel would be saying this as an aside.

835 MS *seres* deleted before *siatz*.

836 *trobe* (cf. 748).

842 MS *coshe* deleted before *coselh*.

844 ALT *jones*.

845 MS *aribar* superscript over *clamar* deleted.

853 The reflexive can be either proclitic or enclitic here.

865 MS *bontatz*: the *z* is doubtful.

874 ALT *foro g.* (cf. 898).

876 ALT *velhatz*: the *e* is doubtful.

878 MS *sanc no*: cited by Levy (*Suppl.* VII, 460) as from of verb *sancnar, sagn-, saun-* «bluten» (e.g., *Fierabras* 1962 *car trop avia sancnat*). Meyer emends *qu'a son caval ne sancno*, thus clarifying the meaning of this verse in respect to *tant* in 877. *Sancno*, evidently a 3 plur. form, is troublesome, unless one considers the spurs as the logical subject of this verb.

879 MS *et* (deleted) *et el. Acabat* (= «put an end to») is not very satisfactory here. According to Chab. «*apagat* vaudrait mieux pour le sens et serait plus près de la leçon du ms.» (than *appelat* proposed by Meyer). *Apagar* = 'appease, placate' (cf. 1474).

881 MS *avia* (?) deleted before *aga*.

882 MS *r. triac.*

887 MS *que nuna.*

888 MS *loilh lha.*

889 MS *ella tenec.*

900 Indentation: capital letter lacking.

903 MS *et e van.*

904 MS deletion before *pel.*

905 *fa forsa* = «se soucier de, faire cas.»

907 MS *tremo la nau.*

913 MS *per cel del cle* (?): Doubtful reading. One would expect, as in 2172, *Dieu del cel*; however, by emending the minor scribal error to *cel*, the MS reading is rendered quite acceptable «by Him of heaven.»

914 *mardiers*: scribal hesitation between *murdriers* (Levy, *Suppl.*, V, p. 348 *murtrier* 'murderer'), and *mardriers* (= 'martin hunter' according to Gustaf Wüster, *Die Tiere in der altfranzösischen Literatur* [Diss. Göttingen, 1916], p. 81), although context supports *maroniers* (Meyer's emendation) or *mariniers* = 'sailors,' suggested by Chab., who adds «en tout cas, la forme *maroniers* n'étant pas sûre, il ne paraît pas juste de reprocher ce gallicisme au copiste du ms., comme M. M[eyer] l'a fait dans l'introduction, p. xlix.» The verse may be an echo of *Amis* 2625; *les felons maronniers* take Amis across only on payment of one of his men; in a similar situation in *Jourdain* 3140, we find *Et maronniers qui la mer ont guiee.*

919 *A[d]eis* = 'forthwith' (Meyer accepts MS *eis,* translating in glossary 'même').

921 *aüdas* 'épines' is according to Chab. «un adjectif *(aigües)* se rapportant à *espinas,* représenté par *en.*»

922 This verse, in spite of its metrical and syntactical faults, clearly means that the hundred *aüdas* «caused blood and milk to mix and spurt out.»

925 MS *nosu* deleted before *nous.*

929 MS *nõ avem.* Sense of this verse and those following seems to be «Let's go home, night has fallen and we have nothing to eat; we will go to Monclar in the morning. The child should still be where I can find him.»

933 MS *gar* of *colgar* superscript over *quier* deleted.

935 For *obs* with preposition and infinitive, see Appel's edition of Bernart de Ventadorn, p. 223; also Godefroy, VIII, 112a. Both exs. call for *de* after *obs (ues* in northern French). I find no examples of this word governing a direct infinitive.

940 MS *vuleil p.*

941 MS *lo* deleted before *senher.*

943 MS *c. Guis dels: Guis* is repeated by scribe from previous verse and is rejected as obvious error as well as on basis of meter.

951 *veltitz* = *voltitz* 'voûté'; *voltas talhatz* = «tours à arêtes vives.»

952 MS deletion before *cayrat.*

955 ALT *efariat:* could be related to *esferar* «s'effaroucher (?)» (cf. Levy *Suppl.* III, 216), but both exs. given by Levy are doubtful. *Esariat* is a variant spelling of *eisarrat* «embarrassé, en peine» (Wartburg, *FEW,* III, 292b *exerrare).*

956 MS *vos* (?) deleted before *vas.*

958 MS *arsat* superscript over *as arsat* deleted.

959 MS *r* of *parlar* superscript.

961 Sense of this verse and 962: «No matter what harsh treatment you may see done to me, don't you promise my dear lord to him.» *vegat* = *veiat* pres. subjunctive.

93ʳ Crude illustration in right-hand margin, showing the three towers and walled enclosure of Monclar, with a stick figure looking out one of the windows of the center tower.

965 MS *nuich:* one stroke of *u* missing (cf. *nueh* 1007).

969 MS *el lhan.* «Daurel goes forth and they shut the gate after him.»

987 ALT *vuelh:* One may interpret this graphy either as a case of development of *v* before *o,* or as simply a doubling of the *u* (see n. 57).

994 ALT *e on son e.* Meyer reads *e cason e.*

997 ALT *oi eu.*

1000 MS *Biatris* superscript over *Bosautris* (?). *e vos autres* introduced in anticipation of next verse and lack of rhyme-word attest to scribal error in second hemistich. In view of what follows, one would expect *aujatz* as a rhyme-word, but one can only guess at what the original was, although the meaning of the passage is clear.

1002 ALT *queus.* Sense of this and following verse: «Lady, what do you hide from us? Because here you see that we are ready to do your bidding, even before you speak.»

1006 MS *v. frayre e mos filh: frayre* makes no sense in this context, since the meaning of the verse is clearly, «your lord and my own son were both born the same night.» The emendation to *senher* is supported by the context and by vv. 962, 977, 1013 in which Beton is accorded this title.

Propiatz seems to be a confusion of two forms: *propi, propri* «proche parent» (*FEW* IX, 454 *propius*) and *propriat*, a 14th century form meaning «qui appartient à» (*FEW* IX, 457b *proprius*).

1011 MS *en nostre*.

1013 See pp. 121-122; the heroism of Beatrix is echoed by that of Erembourc in *Jourdain* who proposes much the same solution to her husband in these words:

> Por no seignor delivronz nostre fil,
> Onques Fromons ne sa gens ne le vit
> Et d'un aé et d'un samblant sont il (489).

94^r Crude illustration depicting Beatrix in tower looking upon scene of her son's death (or perhaps upon the departure of Daurel in 95^r?).

1019 ALT *lhiu* (Meyer emends *lhui*). *n'oqu'a* = OFr. *n'onques à* or *nonques à*.

1030 ALT *que·n* makes equally good sense here.

1039 MS *ene par*.

1041 MS *Daulel* deleted before *Daurel*.

1056 MS *e* (superscript) *fas e lo*.

1066 *fai lo dol espasar* = «fait éclater sa douleur» (Chab.).

1067 MS *degolar* makes no sense in this context, although Chab. proposes keeping it, interpreting «'je ne vis jamais persone témoigner tant de douleur pour un fils,' c'est-à-dire pour son propre fils.» However, it seems clear that the class-conscious author is referring to the paradox of public mourning for such an insignificant person as a *jongleur*'s child.

1068 MS *sot* (?) deleted before *sostrerar*.

1073 MS *-nen* superscript over deletion.

1079 MS *an adnar* Meyer emends *ad annar*. One might also propose *a nadar* 'they set sail' emendation requiring deletion of only one letter (*n*), but I base my emendation of this scribal error on *ad anar* 1433.

1082 *esmagar* = «se désoler» (Chab.); < *ex magan* (Pellegrini, *Appunti*, p. 210, ¶65).

1087 MS *ac* deleted before *anc*.

1089 MS *Domi* [*due* (deleted) *dieus*.

1091 MS *de* deleted before *nazemar*.

1092 MS Modern hand has rewritten *ona* of *Dona*.

1093-1094 MS After 1092 the following verses are introduced: (1093) *Nna* (deleted) *vai me a nazemar que a my venga parlier* (1094) *Nazemar es que es* [*pros e leugier* (deleted).

However, while the first of these lines has been allowed to stand in the MS, the second has been crudely «corrected»: its first *es* is put in superscript, whereas *pros e leugier* (deleted) is replaced in superscript by *vengut corren*. Verse 1093 is an obvious error (cf. 1126) and has been omitted in the edited text. 1094, which by its corrections bears witness to the scribe's attempt to mitigate his error, does not necessarily represent the original form of the verse, but is quite acceptable as it stands in the MS.

1098 MS *en* of *mescrezen* effaced; what appears to be a *z* in *vosz* may simply be an expunged *c*.

1106 *mandamen*: see 196 (note).

1107 *sivada* = 'avoine' (cf. Godefroy VII, 432b *sivade*).

1109 *.xv. ans*: a numerical error (cf. 1110, 1115 *.xii. ans*) unless fifteen years' supply was needed for a seige of twelve years.

1113 *quie·us* (= *qui vos*): A questionable form. Anglade remarks (*Grammaire*, p. 71) «dans les textes de la Provence on trouve *siei* pour *si*. On trouve aussi *quiei* pour *qui*, et *complieis* pour *complis* (Chab.),» but cites no specific examples of *quie*. One can certainly not read *qu'ie·us* in this context.

1114 ALT *vieu* (for *vi[v]en*) unsuitable here because of rhyme (cf. 1125).

1120 MS Modern hand has rewritten *omn* of *Domna*.

1122 MS Modern hand has changed *u* of *uos* to *v*.

1126 *leugier[s]*: scribe generally respects case system in epithets and proper names, yet of all the rhyme-words in this *-iers* laisse, only the first is lacking an *s*.

1129 MS *ci* of *civada* rewritten by modern hand.

1134 *gent[am]ent* = 'convenablement'. This emendation serves to link verse with verbs *noiriro* 1135 and *jogan* 1137. One might also emend *tan gen,* ending the verse with a period, or accept the MS, reading *G'entent* «I mean,» although this would be a very serious gallicism, unsupported by other exs.

1135 MS *austors* superscript over *ausos* deleted.

1140 Indentation: capital letter lacking.

1142 MS Ink blot obscures first word which appears to be *vic*.

1147 ALT *lai t*.

1151 MS *prozo .i.* (cf. *Passion* 940 *Ne tos no·us preze .v. botos* glossed as «locution qui sert à désigner un objet de peu de valeur.»).

1152 MS *e pro e cortes*.

1176 MS *que l*.

1179 MS *non sap bor*: Levy (*Suppl.* VII, 407) cites many exs. of *aver sabor* «gefallen, den Anschein von etwas haben,» (e.g., *Flamenca* 4063 *N'o m'a sabor mos bos sabers*»). However, were it not for the rhyme, one could emend *non sap bo* with much less violence to the text. Either meaning fits quite well in this context.

1183 MS *fugen*.

1185 *e*: an unusual graphy for *ai*, «trait gascon qu'on aurait dû conserver» according to Chab. (Meyer emends *ai*).

1187 *no·lh* = *nos* li (Chab.). Meyer emends *nos*.

1189 *de questa*: «autre trait dialectal effacé à tort» according to Chab. (Meyer emends *d'aquesta*).

1195 Indentation: capital letter missing.

1203 MS *Elsi c*. One might also interpret this as an error for *E lhi* (one stroke missing from *h*).

1206 MS *va ennat*.

1208 Meyer emends *pres l[a] arpa*; Chab. prefers *[a] pres l'arpa,* since other verbs of this passage are in past indefinite. I can find no other exs. of *laisses* in the masc. (cf. 1473 *laices*).

1209 MS *vioula* deleted before *viola*.

1214-1215 The sense of this passage is, inverting the lines and eliminating *tu iest* in 1215, «From over there in France, I have come to you, the best king that ever was, since you are praised by the barons in Charles' court.» As the verses stand in the MS, the syntax is awkward and rather confusing. This suggested reading serves to clarify the text and eliminate the extra syllables in 1215 without changing the meaning as Meyer does by eliminating *rey* and placing a period after 1214.

1219 MS *sezia te*. The *t* is in error here for the imperfect. Meyer reads *sezia, el es*.

97^v Small crude illustration in right-hand margin depicting a tower with pennant flying.

1230 MS c. [*mas* (deleted) *mas lo es* [*fort* (deleted) *v*.

1231 MS *lor rei.*

1235 MS *ben* superscript after *beu* deleted.

1236 *s' = si* (cf. 1343). Meyer emends *si* [*t'es*] (cf. 812).

1238 *agatz = aiatz* imperative (cf. 628).

1241 MS *que tost naz.*

1243 MS *c. siel laguet.*

1244 MS first *lo* superscript; *lo magat* or *lo anagat*. It seems likely that *e rescon* = 'en cachette' and that the scribe meant to write *lo magatz, lo an* [*m*]*agat*, or, more likely, *lo a magat* 'she hid him', (see note on *amagar* 834).

However, one might accept *rescon* as the verb and read *an agat* = «*en aguets*» (cf. Godefroy, I, *Complément,* VIII, 51) or interpret *agat* as the past part. of *aver.*

1245 MS *n. tra.*

1247 MS *gardat* deleted before *remirat.*

1249 MS *bon* deleted before *blons.*

1252 MS the *z* of *fatz* is doubtful.

1260 Indentation: capital letter missing, but small letter is present in margin.

1261 MS *eseties.*

1266 MS *alli los uuelhes.*

1270 MS *semlbes* (?) deleted before *sembles.*

1273 Indentation: capital letter missing, small letter in margin.

1275 MS *puejas.*

1278 MS *frort per.*

1281 Indentation: capital letter missing, small letter in margin.

1283 MS deletion before *uolon.*

1287 MS *e* (?) deleted before *que. Son elme clar* is obviously in error, and seems to anticipate 1326 on facing folio.

1288 *Guio* is obscure. It could possibly mean 'arrange' here. Although this is not the usual meaning of *guiar,* but is attested to in northern French *guier* (Godefroy IV, 382a-b). One might also emend, as Chab. suggests, [*A*]*gujo·ls brans* «They sharpen their swords» the loss of the *a* being explained by aphaeresis (cf. [*A*]*dobero* 68).

1292 MS *pel lo*: one might eliminate *lo* and read *pel castel. Remado*: «forme gasconne» (Chab.).

1294 MS *los* smudged out (?) before *los* superscript. Suggested emendation: *los* [*en*] *anem* or [*nos*] *los anem* (on basis of meter). *Sarcar* = 'chercher' (cf. *Passion* 211 *sercar*).

1295 MS *trobarem* written over.

1297 MS *laissalc.*

1298 MS *al remenbrar* superscript over *al cavalgar* deleted.

1299 MS *Queus vos lai los fairit de M.*: obscure. Levy cites *fairit* (*Suppl.* III, 388) questioning Meyer's explanation in glossary: «*fairitz* (pour *frairitz*) 1299, 1331, originairement pauvre, faible, ici vaurien, scélérat.» «Ein frairit ist m. W. sonst nicht belegt.» remarks Levy, but offers no other solution.

I propose interpreting *fairit* as a variant form of *ferir* (cf. 1306) which can mean as a reflexive verb «se jeter, se précipiter avec ardeur, aborder» and reading «that you throw yourselves with ardor [upon] those of Monclar.»

[1300] MS *para* deleted before *parulas*. *Hil* = *il* nom. plur. or possibly a scribal error for *Cilh* (cf. 1286 *cilh van se adobar*).

[1301] MS *c. lirar*.

[1302] MS deletion before *venc*.

[1318] *las perpongas*: usually masc. in Provençal (*perpunt*).

[1321-22] Written in later hand by a third scribe.

[1324] MS *Ca uo lo coms; enrabirar* (?).

[1331] Guy has been taking a large toll of his opponents. He rallies his followers with his battle cry «Aspramon!» and exhorts them in the following manner: «of those (that I have) struck down, not one will you see return to battle.» (*fairit* = 'blessé, frappé' cf. 1299).

[1339] MS *trastuit* or *trasttut* (with accent over second stroke of *u*).

[1344] MS deletion before *lutz*.

[1359] *Regardo sas mas* is obscure in this context, which calls for *Regardo vas* [*lui*], *mas no l'auzan toquier*.

[1362] MS *nol porrem* superscript over deletion.

[1363] MS *ferit c.*

[1368] MS *an prenre*. *Prenre* is a Picard form.

[1371] MS *del despleitier*: scribal error for *espleitar* (cf. 463, 852); *desplegar* = 'dire, annoncer' makes no sense in this context.

[1374] MS *Lil*.

[1381] MS *S*: this abbreviation, which appears here and in 1393, is common in medieval French manuscripts, and is expanded to *Sainz* (cf. *Girart* 274, 7748, 7909, which M. Hackett renders «reliques des saints»; cf. also Godefroy X, 611c).

[1384] Indentation: capital letter missing, small letter in margin.

MS *e* superscript after *irat*.

[1386] Verse cited by Neumann, *Der Söldner im Mittelalter* (Marburg, 1905), p. 25, as example of rounding off of number of soldiers.

[1392] MS *q̃ los fosso*. *Dampnamen* (Cited by Levy *Suppl.* II, 3) = «dommage, perte.» Sense of line is «But no matter what they do it doesn't hurt those of Monclar.»

[1396] MS *crodon*.

[1402] *aiga molis* «mill water» (a derivative of *molin d'aiga* «Wassermühl» according to Levy *Suppl.* V, 299) may be related to Catalan *aiguamoix* or *aiguamoll*: «l'indred on l'aigua s'enxarca es conegut per aiguamoll» (= 'large puddle, evaporation pool') says A. Griera, «L'Aiguamoll,» in *Etymologica* (Tübingen, 1958), p. 315. Levy cites only one ex. of verb *foreisir* (fälschlich *forsiessir* «herausgehen») *que de ma boca forsisca* (*Suppl.* III, 541). Although one might easily emend to *freis* by eliminating only one letter (*o*), it seems preferable to accept the MS as it stands.

[1407] MS *c. ferca*.

[1411] MS *avieneis*.

[1430] *gazanhar* = «faire du butin» (Levy *Suppl.* IV, 96). *Dieus* is superfluous here and could be eliminated on basis of meter and sense.

[1431] MS *en* of *enfans* superscript.

[1437] MS *ben ba s. Ba* is a Gascon form = *o*, according to Chab.

[101r] Crude illustration in lower right-hand margin showing Beton (?) standing in front of a large crenellated *donjon*.

[1443] *tremolar* (= «trembler, frémir» here, according to Levy *Suppl.* VIII, 429) appears to be a gaming term. These verses can be rendered rather freely: «You'll really know how to shake (the dice when you grow up);

take my word for it, you'll fleece many others.» But it is not clear who is saying these lines.

1449 MS *lan na.*

1456 MS *t* of *cant* superscript.

1460 MS *uarbers* (?): hole in MS before this word.

1464 MS *dels v.*

1466 MS *donc er es.*

1469 MS deletion before *fa per.*

1470 MS *tatost* deleted before *tost.*

1476 *trempar* (metathesis of *temprar*) cited by Levy *Suppl.* VIII, 123 «stimmen, abstimmen (ein Instrument)» e.g., *Sapchas arpar / E ben temprar* (G. de Calanson). *Vieula* (elsewhere *viola*) is a northern form.

1486 MS *auziram.*

1490 MS *sanis i.*

1490 bis MS *Ela es* ... (effaced by scribe). Line started in error, rubbed out, rewritten *Ela es* and abandoned by scribe.

1491 ALT *jones.*

1497 MS *tenih;* Meyer reads *teinh,* an attested variant of *tenc.* However, *tenh* is the more common variant.

1502 MS *pregratz.*

1505 MS the *z* of *alegratz* is doubtful.

1511 MS *plalafres.*

1518 MS *r* of *regnatz* superscript.

1520 MS *teni* (cf. 1497); Meyer reads *tein.*

1551 MS *car* superscript.

1554 MS *n* of *anc* superscript.

1558 MS *g. lagat lo agatz.*

1564 The *escudiers* was considered a *chevalier* in training and his «éducation du corps» was already well underway by the age of nine. What appears to be an exaggeration of Beton's precociousness is in reality a true-to-life portrait of the activities of a noble boy of that age (Gautier, *La Chevalerie,* p. 172 ff.).

1578 MS *escrimir* written over.

1580 MS *El poros.*

1585 Misplaced verse: apparently addressed to the Saracen; therefore, belongs after 1587.

1589 The Saracen appears to be speaking to Daurel. This verse, like 1585, is misplaced.

1592 *escelier* (= northern French *escheler* 'donner l'assaut'). Meyer emends to *esculhir.*

1595 MS *e venir.*

1600 Indentation: capital letter missing. *esernimens* is cited by Levy (*Suppl.* II, 334) as meaning «sagesse, jugement» along with one other ex. from Raim. Vidal. Cf. *issernitz* 'intelligent' in *Castia-Gilos,* 35 (Appel, *Chrest.,* p. 27).

1608 ALT *ban s'en.*

1620 *ferriei:* the *r* of the future stem has been lost, doubtless by dissimilation.

1623 MS *fer es i.* One might also emend *que·l fer es intra[t],* but the rest of the passage is in the present tense.

1627 MS *e fetz* (?)

1628 MS *ri [for* (deleted) *jos.*

1632 MS *dit cen p.*

1635 MS *vas* written over *vi* (?) by modern hand (16th century or later).

[1638] MS *u* of *viuet* superscript over ink blot.

[1642] MS *De qui*: the *De* appears to have been deleted by scribe and rewritten superscript by later hand.

[1646] *neh*: Gascon form (cf. *dreh* 1697).

[1653] MS *esta* superscript.

[1664] MS *vos* or *bos*: Here, as in 1665, the scribe writes his initial *v* with a long stem. Two examples of *valatz* (1736, 1738) clearly demonstrate both types of *v*, one of which resembles a *b* and the other the usual *u*.

[1677] *capdelar* in the reflexive = «se comporter, se conduire; se garder» (cf. 1908). Sense of this verse and the following: «Don't guide your actions by your understanding of the matter, but you cannot go wrong by following mine.»

[1678] MS *e* superscript before *no*.

[1686] Indentation: capital letter missing. It was not unusual for a boy to reach maturity at the age of thirteen, although the average age was closer to fifteen, according to Gautier (*La Chevalerie*, p. 242).

[1690] MS *Querra ann a*.

[105r] Crude illustration in lower right-hand corner depicting Beton on horseback unhorsing an opponent with his lance.

[1694] MS *Em b*.

[1707] MS *cossiraratz*.

[1712] MS *e* of *tera* superscript.

[1716] MS *nielcatz* (cf. 1757).

[1727] MS *to* of *beto* superscript.

[1730] The incomplete sense of 1730-1733 seems to indicate a lacuna before this verse in which the king expresses the fear that Beton is too young to wear his armor and will be killed.

[1732-1733] These verses can be improved and clarified by interchanging the second hemistichs and reading «I can tell you that he will be well equipped to help us, if he lives long enough.» The suggested emendation of *es* 1732 to *se* is supported by 1768 *se vieu .i. an* and by the parallel construction in 1734.

[1734] MS *malevetz*.

[1751-1752] *tumbat; joglar*: play on words. A rare example of battlefield humor in *Daurel*, similar in its ridicule of weakness, but not nearly so grim and unsympathetic as the examples from *Raoul* and *Guillaume* analyzed by Ronald N. Walpole, «Humor and People in Twelfth-Century France,» *RPh*, XI (1958), 216-217.

[1753] MS *compaiñ*.

[1754] *artre*: assimilation of the rare type *circulo* > *celcel* (Pellegrini, *Appunti*, p. 149, ¶ 33, cites no exs. of *l* > *r*).

[1759] MS *e. iai t*.

[1787] MS *es* deleted before *ces*.

[1790] Indentation: capital letter missing.

[1810] *li mal e li bo*: the sense of this cliché is doubtless simply «they all came.»

[1820] MS *molhor r*.

[1824] MS *que pela h*.

[1827] MS *faissa*.

[1828] *irlanda* (see n. 715).

[1846] Indentation: capital letter missing.

[1852] *guah* (cf. 285).

1853 MS *prezen* (deleted) *prezen*.

1870 MS *na* of *domna* superscript.

1883 ALT *no nos*.

108r Crude illustration in lower right-hand margin showing Daurel and Beton in ship with sail set and pennant flying.

1892 *E son de .x.m.*: Meyer corrects *dedins .m.*, justifiable in view of *tria milia homes* 1872 and *.x. gras* 593. Chab. suggests omitting *de*: «Le copiste avait commencé d'écrire *detz* en toutes lettres, et s'est repris sans effacer *de*. Le sens paraît être: 'Ils sont dix mille et 300 par-dessus,' c'est-à-dire, 10,300 en tout.»

1907 ALT *no·us*.

1909 MS deletion or ink spot after *gar-*.

1917 MS *las forsas sautar*: I have adapted Chab.'s suggested emendation.

1918 This misplaced verse (blunder cf. 1955) indicates a possible lacuna of several lines at this point. According to Chab. *auzirat* is a Gascon future rather than a conditional.

1919 MS *Boto; mest* (?) *.i.*

1932 MS *via beto.*

1938 MS deletion between *En* and *tro.*

1942 MS *Botonet.*

1946 Meyer omits this verse in his edition. Therefore, his numbering in relation to mine is plus one from this point.

1953 MS *el clar.*

1954 MS *cus* (deleted) *cus.*

1956 MS *vai si.*

1960 MS *et e tabucar.*

1961 MS *cihvalier.*

1964-1965 *qu'om* 1964 induces one to accept these verses as direct discourse: «Let no man dare to touch those on foot, since they were forced into service by the traitor Guy.» However, the usual introductory *ditz* is missing from the previous line.

1969 *escapar*: rhyme-word introduced in error from 1967. One might emend *estacar* (as suggested by Chab.) or *encaussar* (cf. 370, 1374), but it is probable that the original had something quite different, such as *vai Gui fortz a liar;* therefore any emendation is sheer guesswork.

109r From this point on, due to waterstains and worm holes, MS deteriorates increasingly folio by folio. Where readings are only partially legible but can be interpreted with a fair amount of accuracy, no notation is made. If a word is totally illegible on photocopy, but reading is obvious because of requirements of rhyme and syntax, I have supplied it in italics.

Undoubtedly, many of the gaps which have been left incomplete in this edition will be made legible by ultraviolet or chemical examination of the MS.

1996 *rua*: cited by Karch, *Die nordfran. Elemente im Altprov.*, p. 54, as northern form.

1997 *Daus* = *davas* (cf. 2152).

2000 *brutda* = 'bruit' (cf. *Chan. Crois. Alb.* 5831 *brutla;* P. Cardenal, Lavaud ed., p. 757 *bruda*).

2003 *pre* (see 117).

2013 MS *lo* superscript; *venc l.*

2022 Indentation: capital letter missing.

2023 MS *trastut* partially effaced.

[2031] MS *conis es.*
[2034] MS *e* written over.
[2038-2043] Written in a different hand by a fourth scribe.
[2039] ALT *trade* (?) *r.*
[2040] MS *estar estar.*
[2049] MS *vieues* (?)
[2059] MS *rendran.*
[2060] MS *betos betos.*
[2061] MS deletion before *totz.*
[2065] MS *guazazniatz.*
[2067] Indentation: capital letter missing.
[2068] ALT *senher.*
[2083] MS *no liolh* (?); ALT *no vo·lh.*
[2087] See pp. 83-85 (esp. note 38).
[2088] MS *basso* deleted before *biosso.*
[2096] MS *Cl* (?) *felo;* Meyer reads *ad oissor,* which seems doubtful here.
[2098] MS *Se mon.*
[2103] MS *.du. mes.*
[2104] MS *Et es;* wormhole.
[2108] MS *nõ s aia.*
[2115] *rei* < *rĕge* (Pellegrini, *Appunti,* p. 137, ¶ 26). Sense = «right and rule.»
[2122] Indentation: capital letter missing.
[2128] ALT *lou vau.*
[2133-2141] MS badly damaged by wormholes.
[2144-2158] Left margin faded.
[112v] This is the last folio in the «Didot» MS, and is very badly deteriorated due to fading, moisture and wormholes. It becomes increasingly illegible after the middle of the page.
[2189] The folio continues for 10 more lines, of which only a few last letters are legible. The last two indicate a new laisse in -*ar.*

LIST OF WORKS CITED

Aigar et Maurin. See Brossmer, A.

Alexandre. See Armstrong, E. C.

Amis et Amiles. See Hofmann, K.

ANGLADE, JOSEPH. *Grammaire de l'ancien provençal ou ancienne langue d'oc.* Paris; Klincksieck, 1921.

Apollonius. See Oroz, R. and Marden, C.

APPEL, C., ed. *Bernart von Ventadorn: seine Lieder,* Halle, 1915.

———, *Provenzalische Chrestomathie.* 6th ed. Leipzig, 1930.

ARMSTRONG, E. C. et al., eds. *The Medieval French Roman d'Alexandre.* Elliot Monographs Nos. 36-42. 7 vols. Princeton: Princeton University Press, 1937-55.

Aye d'Avignon. APF, Vol. 6. See Guessard, M.

BALDINGER, KURT, «Le Champ onomasiologique du roturier.» *RLiR,* XXVI (1962), 329-331.

———. «La langue des documents en ancien gascon.» *RLiR,* XXVI (1962), 331-362.

BÉDIER, JOSEPH, ed. and trans. *La Chanson de Roland.* Paris: L'Edition d'Art H. Piazza [1937].

———. *La Chanson de Roland commentée.* Paris: L'Edition d'Art H. Piazza, 1927.

———. *Les Légendes épiques.* 3rd ed. 4 vols. Paris: H. Champion, 1926-29.

BELL, ALEXANDER, ed. *Le Lai d'Haveloc and Gaimar's Haveloc Episode,* Manchester: Manchester Univ. Press, 1925.

BENDER, KARL. «Les Métamorphoses de la royauté de Charlemagne dans les premières épopées franco-italiennes.» *Cultura Neolatina,* XXI (1961), 164-174.

Beues of Hamtoun. See Kölbing, E.

BEZZOLA, RETO R. *Les Origines et la formation de la littérature courtoise en occident* (500-1200). Biblio. de l'Ecole des Hautes Etudes, fasc. 286, 313, 2 vols. Paris: H. Champion, 1958-60.

———. «A propos de la valeur littéraire des chansons féodales.» *Technique,* pp. 183-195.

BISHOP, WALTER H., ed. «A Critical Edition of *Jourdain de Blaivies* with Introduction, Notes and Glossary.» Diss. Univ. of North Carolina, 1962.

BLOCH, MARC. *La Société féodale.* L'Evolution de l'Humanité, 34-34 bis. 2 vols. Paris: Albin Michel, 1949.

Boecis. See Lavaud, R.

Boeve de Haumtone. See Stimming, A.

Boutière, Jean. «Les 3ᵉ personnes du singulier en *a* des parfaits de 1ʳᵉ conjugaison dans les 'Biographies' des troubadours.» *RLiR*, XXVIII (1964), 1-11.

Boutruche, Robert. Vol. I: *Le Premier âge des liens d'homme à homme. Seigneurie et féodalité.* Paris: Aubier, 1959.

Bowman, Russell Keith. *The Connections of the Geste des Loherains with other French Epics and Medieval Genres.* Diss. Columbia Univ. New York, 1940.

Brossmer, Alfred, ed. «*Aigar et Maurin.* Bruchstücke einer Chanson de Geste.» *Romanische Forschungen*, XIV (1902), 1-102.

Brun, A. *Recherches historiques sur l'introduction du français dans les provinces du midi.* Paris: H. Champion, 1923.

Brunel, Clovis. *Bibliographie des manuscrits littéraires en ancien provençal.* Paris: E. Droz, 1935.

――――. *Les plus anciennes chartes en langue provençal.* Paris: Auguste Picard, 1926.

――――. *Supplément.* Paris, 1952.

――――, ed. *Jaufré: roman arthurien du XIIIᵉ siècle en vers provençaux.* SATF. 2 vols. Paris, 1942.

Bueve de Hantone. See Stimming, A.

Burger, André. «La Question rolandienne: faits et hypothèses.» *CCM*, IV (1961), 268-291.

Calin, William C. *The Old French Epic of Revolt: Raoul de Cambrai, Renaud de Montauban, Gormond et Isembard.* Geneva: E. Droz; Paris: Minard, 1962.

Calmette, Joseph. *Le Monde féodal.* New ed. rev. by Charles Higounet. Paris: Presses Univ. de France, 1951.

Chabaneau, Camille. [Review of *Daurel et Beton*]. *RLR*, XX (1881), 246-60.

Chanson de la Croisade contre les Albigeois. See Meyer, P.

Chanson de Guillaume. See McMillan, D.

Chanson de Roland. See Bédier, J.

Chaytor, H. J. *The Provençal Chanson de Geste.* The Taylorian Lecture 1946. London: Oxford Univ. Press, 1946.

――――. *From Script to Print: an Introduction to Medieval Literature.* Cambridge, Eng.: Cambridge Univ. Press, 1945.

Cluzel, Irénée. «A propos de l'Ensenhamen du troubadour catalan Guiraut de Cabrera,» *Boletín de la Real Ac. de buenas letras de Barcelona*, XXVI (1954-56), 87-93.

Comfort, W. W. «The Character Types in the Old French *Chansons de Geste*.» *PMLA*, XXI (1906), 179-434.

――――. «The Literary rôle of the Saracens in the French Epic.» *PMLA*, LV (1940), 628-659.

Coppin, Joseph. *Amour et mariage dans la littérature française au Nord du moyen âge.* Paris: D'Argences, 1961.

Daurel et Beton. See Meyer, P.

Delbouille, Maurice. «Dans un atelier de copistes.» *CCM*, III (1960), 14-22.

――――. «Les Chansons de geste et le livre.» *Technique*, pp. 295-407.

Dessau, Adalbert. «L'idée de la trahison au moyen âge et son rôle dans la motivation de quelques chansons de geste.» *CCM*, III (1960), 23-26.

DOBELMANN, S. *La langue de Cahors des origines à la fin du XVIe siècle.* Biblio. Méridionale, 1e Série, 24. Toulouse, Paris, 1944.

Doon de Mayence. APF, Vol. 2. See Guessard, M.

Eledus et Serene. See Reinhard, J.

EMERY, RICHARD W. «The Use of the Surname in the Study of Medieval Economic History.» *Medievalia et Humanistica,* VII (1952), 43-50.

FARAL, EDMOND. *Les Jongleurs en France au moyen-âge.* Biblio. de l'Ecole des Hautes Études, fasc. 187. Paris: H. Champion, 1910.

FAVREAU, ROBERT. «Les écoles et la culture à Saint-Hilaire-le-grand de Poitiers des origines au début du XIIe siècle.» *CCM,* III (1960), 473-478.

FLACH, JACQUES. *Les Origines de l'ancienne France.* 3 vols. Paris, 1893.

Flamenca. See Meyer, P.

Floriant et Florete, See Williams, H.

FLUTRE, LOUIS-FERNAND. *Table des noms propres avec toutes leurs variantes figurant dans les romans du moyen âge écrits en français ou en provençal et actuellement publiés ou analysés.* Pub. du Centre d'Etudes Supérieures de Civ. Médiévale, 2. Poitiers, 1962.

FORD, J. D. M. «To Bite the Dust and Symbolic Lay Communion.» *PMLA,* XX (1905), 197-230.

FÖRSTEMANN, ERNST. *Altdeutsches namenbuch.* Vol. I: *Personnennamen.* 2nd ed. Bonn, 1900.

FRAPPIER, JEAN. «Les destriers et leurs épithètes.» *Technique,* pp. 85-104.

———. «Reflexions sur les rapports des chansons de geste et de l'histoire.» *ZRPh,* LXXIII (1957), 1-19.

FUNDENBURG, GEORGE BAER. *Feudal France in the French Epic.* Diss. Columbia Univ. Princeton: University Press, 1918.

GANSHOF, F. L. *Feudalism.* Trans. by Philip Grierson. Harper Torchbook. 2nd English ed. New York: Harper & Brothers, 1961.

GAUTIER, LÉON. *La Chevalerie.* Paris, 1884.

———. *Les Epopées françaises.* 2nd ed. rev. 3 vols. Paris, 1878-92.

GAVEL, H. «A propos de la *Chanson de Sainte Foy.*» *Annales du Midi,* 56-60 (1944-48), 210-230.

GILDEA, SISTER MARIANNA. *Expressions of Religious Thought and Feeling in the Chansons de Geste.* Diss. Catholic University. Washington, D. C., 1943.

Girart de Roussillon [*Girart*]. See Hackett, W. M.

Girart de Vienne. See Yeandle, F.

GOSSEN, CARL THEODOR. «Die Einheit der französischen Schriftsprache im 15. un 16. Jahrhundert.» *ZRPh,* LXXIII (1957), 427-459.

———. «De l'histoire des langues écrites du domaine d'oïl.» *RLiR,* XXVI (1962), 271-284.

GRAFSTRÖM, AKE. *Etude sur la graphie des plus anciennes chartes languedociennes avec un essai d'interprétation phonétique.* Diss. Uppsala. Uppsala: Almquist, 1958.

GREEN, HERMAN J. «Fromont, a Traitor in the *Chansons de Geste.*» *Modern Language Notes,* LVI (1941) 329-37.

GRIERA, A. «L'Aiguamoll.» *Etymologica: Walther von Wartburg zum siebzigsten Geburtstag.* Tubingen, Max Niemeyer, 1958, pp. 313-319.

GUESSARD, M. F., gen. ed. *Les Anciens poètes de la France.* Vols. II-VI. Paris, 1859-1861.

Gui de Nanteuil. APF, Vol. 6. See Guessard, M.

Guillaume. See McMillan, D.

HACKETT, W. MARY, ed. *Girart de Roussillon: chanson de geste.* SATF. 3 vols. Paris: Picard, 1953.

HAMILTON, GEORGE L. «The Sources of the Symbolic Lay Communion.» *Romanic Review,* IV (1913), 221-240.

Haveloc. See Bell, A.

Historia Apollonii. See Oroz, R.

HOEPFFNER, ERNEST, ed. *La Chanson de Sainte Foy.* Pub. de la Faculté des Lettres de l'Univ. de Strasbourg, fasc. 32. 2 vols. Paris: Les Belles Lettres, 1926.

HOFMANN, KONRAD, ed. *Amis et Amiles und Jourdains de Blaivies.* 2nd ed. rev. Erlangen, 1882.

HOLLYMAN, K. J. *Le Développement du vocabulaire féodal en France pendant le haut moyen âge.* Société de Pub. Romanes et Françaises, LVIII. Genève: E. Droz, 1957.

HOLMES, URBAN T., JR. *A History of Old French Literature from the Origins to 1300.* New rev. ed. New York: Russell and Russell, Inc., 1962.

Huon de Bordeaux. See Ruelle, P.

JACKSON, W. T. H. *The Literature of the Middle Ages.* New York: Columbia University Press, 1960.

Jaufré. See Brunel, C.

JEANROY, ALFRED. *La Poésie lyrique de troubadours.* 2 vols. Toulouse: Privat; Paris: Didier, 1934.

JODOGNE, OMER. «Sur l'originalité de *Raoul de Cambrai.*» *Technique,* pp. 37-56.

JONES, GEORGE FENWICK. *The Ethos of the Song of Roland.* Baltimore: Johns Hopkins Press, 1963.

Jourdain de Blaye. See Hofmann, K.; Bishop, W.

KALBOW, WERNER. *Die germanischen Personnennamen des altfranzösischen Heldenepos.* Halle: Max Niemeyer, 1913.

KARCH, ROBERT. *Die nordfranzösischen Elemente im Altprovenzalischen.* Diss. Heidelberg. Darmstadt, 1901.

KER, W. P. *Epic and Romance: Essays on Medieval Literature.* New York: Dover Publications Inc., 1957 [1908].

KÖLBING, EUGEN, ed. *The Romance of Sir Beues of Hamtoun.* EETS Extra Series, XLVI, XLVIII, LXV. London, 1885-94.

KOLL, HANS-GEORG. «Pour une étude des rapports entre langue et pensée dans la poésie des troubadours occitans.» *RLiR,* XXVIII (1964), 29-33.

KRALIK, DIETRICH VON. *Die Sigfridtrilogie im Nibelungenlied und in der Thidrekessaga.* Halle: Max Niemeyer, 1941.

KUTSCHA, KURT. *Das sogenannte N-mobile im alt-und neuprovenzalischen.* Romanistische Arbeiten, XXI. Halle: Max Niemeyer, 1934.

LABANDE, E. R. «Le 'Credo' épique: à propos des prières dans les chansons de geste.» *Recueil de Travaux offert à M. Clovis Brunel.* Paris: Société de l'école des Chartes, 1955, II, 62-80.

LANGLOIS, ERNEST. *Table des noms propres de toute nature compris dans les chansons de geste imprimées.* Paris: Emile Bouillon, 1904.

LAVAUD, RENÉ AND MACHICOT, GEORGE, eds. *Poème sur Boèce (fragment): le plus ancien texte littéraire occitan réédité, traduit et commenté.* Toulouse: Institut d'Etudes Occitanes, 1950.

LEACH, McEDWARD, ed. *Amis and Amiloun.* EETS Orig. Series, 203. London: Oxford Univ. Press, 1937.

LeGENTIL, P. «A propos de l'origine des chansons de geste: le problème de l'auteur.» *Coloquios de Roncesvalles.* Zaragoza, 1956, pp. 113-121.

LEGENTIL, P. «*Girard de Roussillon*: sens et structure du poème.» *Romania,* LXXVIII (1957), 328-89, 463-510.

———. «Ogier le Danois, héros épique.» *Romania,* LXXVIII (1957), 199-233.

———. «Réflexions sur la création littéraire au moyen âge.» *Chanson de geste und hofischer Roman* (Heidelberger Kolloquium, 30 jan. 1961). Studia romanica, 4. Heidelberg: Winter, 1963, pp. 9-20.

LEJEUNE, RITA. *Recherches sur le thème: les chansons de geste et l'histoire.* Biblio. de la Faculté de Philosophie et Lettres de l'Univer. de Liège, fasc. CVIII. Liège, 1948.

———. «Technique formulaire et chansons de geste.» *Moyen Age,* LX (1954), 311-334.

LEVY, EMIL AND KARL APPEL. *Provenzalisches Supplement Wörterbuch: Berichtigungen und Ergänzungen zu Raynouards Lexique Roman.* 8 vols. Leipzig, 1894-1924.

———. *Petit dictionnaire provençal-français.* Sammlung Romanischer Elementar-und Handbücher, III, 2. Heidelberg; Winter 1909. [Repr. 1963].

LÉVY, PAUL. *Les Noms des Israélites en France.* Paris: Presses Univ. de France, 1960.

LEVY, RAPHAEL. «Chronologie approximative de la littérature française du moyen âge.» Beihefte 98 zur *ZRPh.* Halle. 1957.

———. «The Determination of Chronology in Old French Literature.» *Romanistisches Jahrbuch,* X (1959), 39-52.

LEWENT, KURT. «Old Provençal *lai, lai on* and *on.*» *Modern Language Notes,* LXXIX (1964), 296-308.

LEWIS, EWART. «Personality in the *Chansons de Geste.*» *Philological Quarterly,* XV (1936), 273-285.

Libro de Apolonio. See Marden, C., Oroz, R.

LIVINGSTON, CHARLES H. *Le Jongleur Gautier le Leu: étude sur les fabliaux.* Harvard Studies in Romance Languages, XXIV. Cambridge, Mass.: Harvard Univ. Press, 1951.

LODS, JEANNE. «Quelques aspects de la vie quotidienne chez les conteurs du XIIᵉ siècle.» *CCM,* IV, 1 (1961), 23-45.

———. «Le thème de l'enfance dans l'épopée française.» *CCM,* III (1960), 58-62.

LOMMATZSCH, ERHARD, ed. *Leben und Lieder der provenzalischen Troubadours.* 2 vols., Berlin: Akademia-Verlag, 1957-59.

LOPEZ, ROBERT SABATINO. «Concerning Surnames and Places of Origins.» *Medievalia et Humanistica,* VIII (1954), 6-16.

LOT, FERDINAND. *Etudes sur les légendes épiques françaises.* Paris: H. Champion, 1958.

LOUIS, RENÉ. *De l'histoire à la légende.* Vol. II: *Girart, Comte de Vienne dans les chansons de geste: Girart de Vienne, Girart de Fraite, Girart de Roussillon.* Auxerre: Imprimerie Moderne, 1947.

———. «Qu'est-ce que l'épopée vivante?» *La Table Ronde,* No. 132 (Dec. 1958), 9-17.

MALKIEL, YAKOV. «Fuentes indígenas y exóticas de los sustantivos y adjetivos verbales en -*e*.» *RLiR,* pt. 1, XXIII (1959), 80-111; pt. 2, XXIV (1960), 201-253.

MARDEN, C. CARROLL, ed. *Libro de Apolonio.* Elliot Monographs, 6. Baltimore: Johns Hopkins Press, 1917.

MATARASSO, P. *Recherches historiques et littéraires sur «Raoul de Cambrai.»* Paris: Nizet, 1962.

McGUIRE, THOMAS A. *The Conception of the Knight in the Old French Epics of the Southern Cycle...* Diss. Univ. of Mich. East Lansing, Mich.: The Campus Press, Inc., 1939.

McMILLAN, DUNCAN, ed. *La Chanson de Guillaume*, SATF. 2 vols. Paris: Picard, 1949-50.

————. «A propos de traditions orales (résumé).» *CCM*, III (1960), 67-71.

MELLER, WALTER CLIFFORD. *A Knight's Life in the Days of Chivalry.* New York: Greenberg, Publisher, Inc., 1924.

MENÉNDEZ PIDAL, RAMÓN. *La Chanson de Roland et la tradition épique des francs*, 2nd ed. rev. by René Louis and trans. from Span. by Irénée-Marcel Cluzel. Paris: Picard, 1960.

————. *Poesía juglaresca y orígenes de las literaturas románicas.* 6th ed. rev. and enl. Madrid: Instituto de Estudios Políticos, 1957.

MEYER, PAUL, ed. *La Chanson de la croisade contre les Albigeois commencée par Guillaume de Tudèle et continuée par un poète anonyme.* 2 vols. Paris, 1875.

————, ed. *Daurel et Beton: chanson de geste provençale.* SATF. Paris: Firmin Didot, 1880.

————, ed. *Le Roman de Flamenca.* 2nd ed. Vol. I [Vol. II announced but never published]. Paris, 1901.

————. «L'influence des troubadours,» *Romania*, V (1876), 257-268.

———— and LONGNON, A., eds. *Raoul de Cambrai.* SATF. Paris, 1882.

————. [Rebuttal to Chabaneau's review of *Daurel et Beton*]. *Romania*, XI (1882), 161-162.

MILÀ Y FONTANALS, MANUEL. *De la poesía heroico-popular castellana* [Vol. I of *Obras.*] ed. Martín de Riquer. Barcelona, 1959. [Reedition of works orig. pub. 1874.]

MONTEVERDI, ANGELO. «La laisse épique.» *Technique*, pp. 127-140.

MORGAN, JR., RALEIGH, «Old French *jogleor* and Kindred Terms.» *RPh*, VII (1954), 279-325.

NÈGRE, E. «Traits caractéristiques de l'Albigeois.» *RLiR*, XXVIII (1964), 91-94.

NELLI, RENÉ. *L'Erotique des troubadours.* Biblio. Méridionale, 2ᵉ Série, XXXVIII. Toulouse: Edouard Privat, 1963.

————. «Sur l'amour provençal.» *Cahiers du Sud*, No. 347 (1958), 1-37.

NEUMANN, ERNST. *Der Söldner (soudoyer) im Mittelalter, nach den französischen (und provenzalischen) Heldenepen.* Diss. Marburg. Marburg, 1905.

NICHOLS, STEPHEN G., JR. *Formulaic Diction and Thematic Composition in the Chanson de Roland.* Studies Romance Lang. and Lit., 36. Chapel Hill: University of North Carolina Press, 1961.

NYROP, CRISTOFORO. *Storia dell'epopea francese nel medio evo.* Trans. by Egidio Gorra. Torino, 1888.

Ogier de Danemarche. See Paris, Raimbert de.

OROZ, RODOLFO, ed. and trans. *Historia de Apolonio de Tiro* [*Historia Apollonii*]. Bilingual ed. Santiago de Chile [1954].

Orson de Beauvais. See Paris, G.

PAINTER, SIDNEY. «Castellans of the Plain of Poitou in the Eleventh and Twelfth Centuries.» *Speculum*, XXXI (1956), 243-257.

PAINTER, SIDNEY. *French Chivalry*. Great Seal Books. Ithaca: Cornell Univ. Press, 1957 [1940].

PARIS, GASTON. *Histoire poétique de Charlemagne*. New ed. rev. and enl. by Paul Meyer. Paris: Emile Bouillon, 1905.

————. *Mélanges de littérature française du moyen âge*. ed. by Mario Roques. Paris: H. Champion, 1912.

————, ed. *Orson de Beauvais: chanson de geste du XIIe siècle*. SATF. Paris: Firmin Didot, 1899.

PARIS, RAIMBERT DE. *La Chevalerie Ogier de Danemarche: poème du XIIe siècle*. Paris, 1842.

Parise la Duchesse. APF, Vol. 4. See Guessard, M.

Passion provençale. See Shepard, W.

PELLEGRINI, G. B. *Appunti di grammatica storica del Provenzale*. New rev. ed. Univ. degli Studi di Pisa. Pisa: Libreria Goliardica, 1962.

PETIT-DUTAILLIS, CHARLES. *The Feudal Monarchy in France and England from the Tenth to the Thirteenth Century*. trans. E. D. Hunt. Harper Torchbook. New York, Evanston: Harper and Row, 1964 [1936].

PLATH, KARL. *Der Typ des Verräters in den älteren Chansons de Geste*. Diss. Halle: Carl Nieft, 1934.

RAJNA, PIO. *Le Origini dell'epopea francese*. Firenze: Sansoni, 1884 [repr. 1956].

Raoul de Cambrai. See Meyer, P.

RAYNAUD DE LAGE, G. «Les Romans antiques et la représentation de l'Antiquité.» *Moyen Age*, LXVII (1961), 274-292.

REINHARD, JOHN R., ed. *Le Roman d'Eledus et Serene*. Austin: Univ. of Texas Press, 1923.

RICHARD, ALFRED. *Histoire des Comtes de Poitou* (778-1204). 2 vols. Paris, 1903.

RICHTHOFEN, ERICH VON. *Estudios épicos medievales con algunos trabajos inéditos*. Trans. from Germ. by José Pérez Riesco. Biblioteca Románica hispánica. Madrid: Editorial Gredos, 1954.

RIEDEL, F. CARL. *Crime and Punishment in the Old French Romances*. Studies in English and Comparative Literature, 135. New York: Columbia Univ. Press, 1938.

RIQUER, MARTÍN DE. *Les Chansons de geste françaises*. 2nd ed. rev. trans. by I. Cluzel. Paris: Nizet, 1957.

————. «Epopée jongleresque à écouter et épopée romanesque à lire.» *Technique*, pp. 75-82.

ROBSON, C. A. «Aux Origines de la poésie épique romane: art narratif et mnémotechnie (pt. 1).» *Moyen Age*, LXVIII, (1961), 41-84.

Roland à Saragosse. See Roques, M.

RONJAT, JULES. *Grammaire istorique des parlers provençaux modernes*. 4 vols. Montpellier: Société des Langues Romanes, 1930-41.

ROQUES, MARIO, ed. *Roland à Saragosse: poème épique méridional du XIVe siècle*. CFMA, 83. Paris: H. Champion, 1956.

ROUQUETTE, JEAN. *La Littérature d'oc*. Que Sais-je?, 1039. Paris: Presses Univ. de France, 1963.

ROUSSE, MICHEL. «Niniane en Petite-Bretagne.» *Bull. Biblio. de la Société Internationale Arthurienne*, No. 16 (1964), 107-120.

RUELLE, PIERRE, ed. *Huon de Bordeaux*, Univ. Libre de Bruxelles: Travaux de la Faculté de Phil. et Lettres, XX. Bruxelles/Paris: Presses Univ. de France, 1960.

Rychner, Jean. *La Chanson de geste: essai sur l'art épique des jongleurs.* Société de pub. Romanes et Francaises, LIII. Genève: E. Droz, 1955.

————. «La Chanson de geste, épopée vivante.» *La Table Ronde,* No. 132 (Dec. 1958), 152-167.

Sainte Foi. See Thomas, A.; Hoepffner, E.

Scharten, T. «La Posizione linguistica de 'Poitou.'» *Studj Romanzi,* XXIX (1942), 5-130.

Schober, Willy. *Die Geographie der altfranzösischen Chansons de Geste.* Vol. I. Diss. Marburg. Marburg, 1902.

Schultz-Gora, O. *Altprovenzalisches Elementarbuch.* 2nd ed. Heidelberg: Winter, 1911.

Segre, Cesare. «Il *Boeci,* i poemetti agiografici e le origini della forma epica.» *Atti della Accademia delle Scienze di Torino,* LXXXIX, ii (1954-55), 242-292.

Semrau, Franz. *Würfel und Würfelspiel im alten Frankreich.* Diss. Albertus-univ. zu Königsberg. Halle: E. Karras, 1909.

Settegast, Franz. «Armenisches im *Daurel et Beton.*» *ZRPh,* XXIX (1905), 413-417.

Shepard, William P., ed. *La Passion provençale du manuscrit Didot: mystère du XIV* siècle. SATF. Paris: H. Champion, 1927.

Siciliano, Italo. *Les Origines des chansons de geste: théories et discussions.* Trans. from Ital. by P. Antonetti, Paris: Picard, 1951.

Skidmore, Mark. *The Moral Traits of Christian and Saracen as Portrayed by the Chansons de Geste.* Diss. Columbia Univ. Colorado College Pub., gen. series, 203; Studies Series, 20. [Colo. Springs, 1935.]

Smeets, J. R. «*Alexis* et la *Bible* de Herman de Valenciennes: le problème de l'origine de la laisse.» *CCM,* VI (1963), 315-325.

Smith, H. A. «La Femme dans les chansons de geste (pt. 2)» *Colorado College Studies,* X (1903), 24-40.

Stimming, Albert, ed. *Der anglonormannische Boeve de Haumtone.* Biblio. Normannica, VII. Halle; Max Niemeyer, 1899.

————, ed. *Der festländische Bueve de Hantone:* I, II, III. Gesellschaft fur Romanische Literatur, Bde. 25, 30, 34, 42. Dresden, 1914-20.

Stowell, W. A. «Personal Relationships in Medieval France.» *PMLA,* XXVIII (1913), 388-416.

Thomas, Antoine, ed. *La Chanson de Sainte Foi d'Agen: Poème provençal du XI* siècle. CFMA, 45. Paris: H. Champion, 1925.

La Technique littéraire des chansons de geste (Actes du Colloque de Liège, Sept. 1957). Univ. de Liège: Biblio. de la Faculté de Phil. et Lettres, fasc. CL. Paris: Les Belles Lettres, 1959.

Thompson, Stith. *Motif-Index of Folk Literature.* Rev. enl. ed. 5 vols. Bloomington, Ind.: Indiana Univ. Press, 1957.

Tiemann, Hermann. «Die Datierungen der altfranzösischen Literatur (Kritische Anmerkungen der Chronologie von R. Lévy).» *Romanistisches Jahrbuch,* VIII (1957), 110-131.

Togeby, Knut. «Qu'est-ce que la dissimilation?» *RPh,* XVII (1964), 642-667.

Urwin, Kenneth. «La Mort de Vivien et la genèse des chansons de geste.» *Romania,* LXXVIII (1957), 392-404.

Walpole, Ronald N. «Humor and People in Twelfth-Century France.» *RPh,* XI (1958), 210-225.

————. [Review of Menéndez Pidal, *La Chanson de Roland et la tradition épique des francs*]. *Speculum,* XXXVIII (1963), 373-382.

WALSHE, M. O'C. *Medieval German Literature: A Survey*. Cambridge, Mass.: Harvard Univ. Press, 1962.

WHITNEY, MARIAN P. «Queen of Mediaeval Virtues: *Largesse*.» *Vassar Mediaeval Studies*. C. F. Fiske, ed. New Haven: Yale Univ. Press, 1923, pp. 183-215.

WILLIAMS, HARRY F., ed. *Floriant et Florete*. Ann Arbor: Univ. of Michigan Press, 1947.

WILMOTTE, MAURICE. *L'Epopée francaise: origine et élaboration*. Paris: Boivin [1939].

WÜSTER, GUSTAF. *Die Tiere in der altfranzösischen Literatur*. Diss. Göttingen. Göttingen; E. Hofer, 1916.

YEANDLE, FREDERIC G., ed. *Girart de Vienne*. New York: Columbia Univ. Press, 1930.

ZENKER, RUDOLF. *Boeve — Amlethus: das altfranzösische Epos von Boeve de Hamtone und der Ursprung der Hamletsage*. Literarhistorische Forschungen, XXXII. Berlin: Emil Felber, 1905.

ZUMTHOR, PAUL. *Histoire littéraire de la France médiévale* (VIᵉ—XIVᵉ siècles). Paris: Presses Univ. de France, 1954.

————. *Langue et techniques poétiques à l'époque romane (XIᵉ—XIIIᵉ siècles)*. Biblio. Française et Romane, Faculté des Lettres de Strasbourg, Série C, No. 4. Paris: Klincksieck, 1963.

ABBREVIATIONS

APF = Les Anciens Poètes de la France
CCM = *Cahiers de Civilisation Médiévales*
CFMA = Classiques Français du Moyen Âge
EETS = Early English Text Society
FEW = *Französisches Etymologisches Wörterbuch*
RLR = *Revue des Langues Romanes*
RLiR = *Revue de Linguistique Romane*
RPh = *Romance Philology*
SATF = Société des Anciens Textes Français
Technique = *La Technique littéraire des chansons de geste* (q.v.)
ZRPh = *Zeitschrift für romanische Philologie*